Syntax-Phonology Interface

This book centers on theoretical issues of phonology-syntax interface based on tone sandhi in Chinese dialects. It uses patterns in tone sandhi to study how speech should be divided into domains of various sizes or levels.

Tone sandhi refers to tonal changes that occur to a sequence of adjacent syllables or words. The size of this sequence (or the domain) is determined by various factors, in particular the syntactic structure of the words and the original tones of the words. Chinese dialects offer a rich body of data on tone sandhi and are hence great evidence for examining the phonology-syntax interface and for examining the resulting levels of domains (the prosodic hierarchy).

Syntax-Phonology Interface: Argumentation from Tone Sandhi in Chinese Dialects is an extremely valuable text for graduate students and scholars in the fields of linguistics and Chinese.

Hongming Zhang is a leading expert on tone sandhi, and this book is the culmination of a lifetime of research.

Routledge Studies in Chinese Linguistics
Series editor: Hongming Zhang

Titles in the series:

Clause-Based Chinese Grammar Theory and Analyses *(forthcoming)*
Fuyi Xing

Cognition-Based Studies on Chinese Grammar *(forthcoming)*
Yulin Yuan, translated by Guoxiang Wu

Dimensions of Variation in Written Chinese *(forthcoming)*
Zheng-Sheng Zhang

Lexical Ontological Semantics *(forthcoming)*
Yulin Yuan, translated by Guoxiang Wu

Mandarin Chinese Words and Parts of Speech
Corpus-Based Foundational Studies *(forthcoming)*
Huang Chu-Ren, Keh-Jiann Chen and Shu-Kai Hsieh

Partition and Quantity
Numeral Classifiers, Measurement, and Partitive
Constructions in Mandarin Chinese *(forthcoming)*
Jing Jin

Syntax-Phonology Interface
Argumentation from Tone Sandhi in Chinese Dialects
Hongming Zhang

Syntax-Phonology Interface
Argumentation from Tone Sandhi in Chinese Dialects

Hongming Zhang

LONDON AND NEW YORK

First published 2017
by Routledge
2 Park Square, Milton Park, Abingdon, Oxon OX14 4RN

and by Routledge
711 Third Avenue, New York, NY 10017

Routledge is an imprint of the Taylor & Francis Group, an informa business

© 2017 Hongming Zhang

The right of Hongming Zhang to be identified as author of this work has been asserted by him in accordance with sections 77 and 78 of the Copyright, Designs and Patents Act 1988.

All rights reserved. No part of this book may be reprinted or reproduced or utilised in any form or by any electronic, mechanical, or other means, now known or hereafter invented, including photocopying and recording, or in any information storage or retrieval system, without permission in writing from the publishers.

Trademark notice: Product or corporate names may be trademarks or registered trademarks, and are used only for identification and explanation without intent to infringe.

British Library Cataloguing in Publication Data
A catalogue record for this book is available from the British Library

Library of Congress Cataloging in Publication Data
A catalogue record for this book has been requested

ISBN: 978-1-138-93481-8 (hbk)
ISBN: 978-1-317-38901-9 (ebk)

Typeset in Times New Roman
by Apex CoVantage, LLC

To Lilly and Louise

"All models are wrong, but some are useful."
—George Box (1919–2013)

Contents

	Abbreviations	viii
	Acknowledgments	xi
	Introduction	1
1	Theoretical issues of syntax-phonology interface	4
2	Functional relations in tone sandhi	19
3	The c-command condition in phonology	59
4	Some issues in Mandarin interface studies	105
5	Function words and rhythmic effect	135
6	Theoretical discussions	181
7	Concluding remarks	212
	Bibliography	215
	Author index	228
	Language index	230
	Subject index	231

Abbreviations

#	tonal boundary/phonological process blocked
$	citation tone form is kept in tone sandhi
( )	to indicate prosodic structure
*	ungrammatical form/metrical grid slot
[]	to indicate syntactic structure
=	application of a rule
3T	third tone
3TS	Mandarin third tone sandhi
A	argument
AC	Association Convention
AP	adjective phrase
ARG	argument
ASP	aspect
AvP	adverb phrase
BM	base melody
BT	base tone
C/COM/Comp	complementizer
CG	clitic group
Cl/Cla	classifier
CLR	column lowering rule
CP	complementizer phrase
CT	citation tone
CTS	clitic tone sandhi
CTS-L	left-branching clitic tone sandhi
CTS-R	right-branching clitic tone sandhi
DIR	directional
DM	duple meter/direct mapping
DP	determiner phrase
DRA	direct reference approach
DT	default tone
E	even tone
FFR	Foot Formation Rule
Ft	foot
FW	function word

Abbreviations ix

GB	Government and Binding
H	high tone
HR	high register
IC	immediate constituent
Infl	inflection
INT	interrogative
IP	inflectional phrase
Iph	intonational phrase
IRA	Indirect Reference Approach
L	low tone
LCC	Lexical Category Condition
LF	logical form
LR	low register
LS	locative structure
LTS	lexical tone sandhi
M	modifier/middle tone/undergoing metricalization
M~NM	metricalization is optional
MaP	major prosodic category
MH	modifier-head
MHa	adverbial MH
MHb	adnominal MH
MiP	minor prosodic category
MOD	mood
MP	Minimalist Program
MR	reduplicated measure word
MRU	minimal rhythmic unit
n	neutral tone
NHS	non-head stress
NM	number-measure/not undergoing metricalization
NoStr	no straddling
NP	noun phrase
O	oblique tone
OT	Optimality Theory
P	preposition
PF	phonetic form
PP	preposition phrase
PPh	phonological phrase
Pr	predicate
PrP	predication phrase
PSA	Prosodically Syntax-Sensitive Approach
PTS	phrasal tone sandhi/post-lexical tone sandhi
PU	phonological utterance
PW/PWd	prosodic word/phonological word
q	glottal stop
QP	quantifier phrase
QR	quantifier raising

x   *Abbreviations*

RED	reduplicated
S/S	sentence/main stress
s	stresslessness/strong
SCR	Stress Clash Rule
SEC	Stress Equalization Convention
SLH	Strict Layer Hypothesis
SP	subject-predicate
SPE	*The Sound Pattern of English*
Spec	specifier
SRR	Stress Reduction Rule
T	citation tone
T'	sandhi tone
TBU	tone bearing unit
TD	tone deletion
TDF	tonal domain formation
TE	time expression
TG/tg	tone group
Top	topic
TS	tone sandhi
TSA	tone sandhi type A
TSB	tone sandhi type B
TSD	tone sandhi domain
TS-G	tone sandhi in broad used form
TSR	tone sandhi rule
TS-Z	tone sandhi in narrow used form
T-t	left-prominent type tone sandhi
t-T	right-prominent type tone sandhi
Utt	utterance
V	verb
VD	verb plus directional complement
VO	verb-object
VP	verb phrase
VPr	verb-pronoun
VR	verb-resultative
w	weak
WFR	word final rise
XP	maximal projection of X (a lexical head)
ɩ	intonational phrase
μ	mora
Σ	foot
σ	syllable
ʋ	utterance
φ	phonological phrase
φ'	maximal prosodic phrase
ω	prosodic word
ω'	maximal prosodic word

Acknowledgments

I would like to express my deep gratitude to Matthew Y. Chen, my mentor and life friend who guided me, counseled me, and in all other ways helped me through the years of my academic pursuit at the University of California-San Diego. It is owing to him that I turned myself from a layman into a linguist; during the process of which, what he gave me is invaluable as well as immeasurable. It is most impressive that he has always encouraged me to argue with him in search of the truth. I also want to thank the late Sige-Yuki Kuroda who broadened my view with his expertise in syntactic theories and semantic knowledge. I am very grateful to Andrea Hartill for her encouragement and patience, which made the publication of this book possible, and Robert Kidd who helped me make fewer mistakes in English writing. I also benefited greatly from my advisees (Yu-lin Chiu, Huimin Dong, Fengmei Du, Xiaojuan Jin, Runlan Ke, Tae Eun Kim, Wenjing Li, Hai Liu, Lu Lu, Yangtian Luo, Xiang Lü, Shuxiang Ma, Zhe Ma, Youyong Qian, Peng Qin, Lin Shi, Chenqing Song, Xi Song, Henghua Su, Rui Wang, Tianlin Wang, Yanwen Wu, Fang Yan, Han Yan, Hong Yan, Yuxia Yin, Shuxiang You, Hui Yu, Na Yuchi, and Shengping Zhan) from both the University of Wisconsin-Madison and Nankai University, who took the seminar classes, including *Chinese Prosodic Studies*, with me these past years. I feel grateful to Thomas Hun-tak Lee, Danqing Liu, and Jianhua Hu who have persistently encouraged and pushed me all these years during my writing of this book. I want to thank Wei-Tien Dylan Tsai for his help with the analysis of some syntactic data. I also want to thank those scholars and students with whom I exchanged views at various conferences, symposiums, workshops, and lectures both at home and abroad. I wish to give special thanks to Youyong Qian, too, who lent me assistance with the compilation of the notational conventions, the author index, the subject index, and the language index of the book. Above all, I want to thank my wife, Lilly, and my daughter, Louise, who supported and encouraged me in writing this book, in spite of all the times it took me away from them. It was a long and difficult journey for them.

Finally, I would like to express my gratitude to the Graduate School of the University of Wisconsin-Madison for its support in the form of the 2003–2006/2008–2010/2013–2014 research grants, *Vilas Associate Award* (awarded by UW-Madison, 2003–2005), *CCK Research Grant* (awarded by "Chiang Ching-Kuo Foundation for International Scholarly Exchange," 1997–1999 and 2005–2006), and the

Chang Jiang Scholar Grant (2009–2015) granted by the Ministry of Education of People's Republic of China and Nankai University. Their support was crucial in making the completion of this book possible.

It is my wish that this book will receive attention from scholars who also work on this topic from a cross-linguistic perspective. I by no means want to replace their role in this area of study. On the contrary, my views, methods, and discoveries are intended to be complementary to that of theirs.

Last but not least, I beg forgiveness from all those who have been working with me over the course of the years and whose names I have failed to mention.

Introduction

The aim of this book centers on the interface between phonology and syntax, and especially on how phonology is sensitive to syntactic or prosodic structure at the phrasal level. This topic has long been noticed but is yet unsolved. About a half century ago, discussions by Chomsky, Halle, and Lukoff (1956) and Chomsky and Halle (1968) about the cyclic mode and the domain of rule application already touched upon the impact of morphosyntax on phonology. However, the study of post-lexical rules sensitive to syntactic or prosodic structure still contains many outstanding issues, although quite a few influential theories and approaches have been proposed.

In this book, I am going to probe deep into the nature of the syntax-phonology interface across Chinese dialects and try to answer such questions as how the phonological components are organized, which specific syntactic properties affect the application of phonological rules, and how these syntactic properties should be incorporated into phonology. The complex mapping from syntax to phonology is not determined in just one way, but determined by several different conditions, including functional relations, c/m-command domains, the edge condition, IC cuts, and so on. In this book, I will discuss one by one, in detail, how these different conditions affect phonology using tone sandhi (hereafter TS) data from various Chinese dialects. Based on this discussion, I will inquire further into the organization of prosodic hierarchies, the properties of prosodic structure, and the relationships between different rules at the post-lexical level. Then, having given a general evaluation of several leading theories and assumptions, I will present the model that shows that the process of syntactic accessibility to phonology is a process during which the prosodic structure is coded by syntactic information. In other words, syntactic conditions are effective within prosodic domains. The model that I propose for the mapping between syntax and phonology is called the prosodic-syntax model, as seen in (1a), with the prosodic structure of which can be profiled as given in (1b).

2 *Introduction*

(1) a. Mapping between syntax and phonology

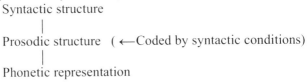

b. Syntax-based prosodic hierarchy

        PPh (←Syntactic condition A, a, ...)
         |
        CG   (←Syntactic condition B, b, ...)
         |
        ω   (←Syntactic condition C, c, ...)[1]

And the trisected model proposed in this book for the organization of prosodic hierarchies is as seen in (2).

(2) The organization of prosodic hierarchy[2]

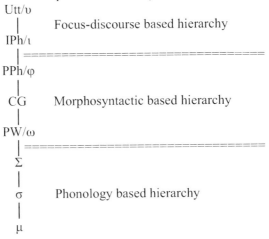

With the results obtained from the discussion in this book, I hope to improve the understanding of prosodic phonology in general with respect to certain points, such as the accessibility of grammatical information to phonology, the prosodic hierarchy, the strict layer hypothesis, and Optimality Theory, and to propose, from the perspective of Chinese prosodic phonology, some new hypotheses and assumptions for a universal explanation of the organization of prosodic components.

This book consists of seven chapters. Chapter 1 introduces some theoretical issues carried in the recent literature concerning the nature of interface between phonology and syntax, and it discusses the definition of prosodic structure and issues such as what is a prosodic unit, how a specific unit is defined, how to build up the prosodic hierarchy in Chinese, and so on.

Chapter 2 discusses how phonology is sensitive to the functional distinction between arguments and adjuncts. For example, in an adjunct-head structure in English, the stress of compounds falls on the head rather than on the adjunct, while in argument-head structures, it falls on the argument instead of on the head. With a clear understanding of the distinction between arguments and adjuncts, I will analyze how TS is sensitive to functional relations and how functional categories, such as adjunct, argument, and head, play their roles in prosodic phonology with detailed analyses of some Chinese dialects such as Southern Min (Xiamen), Northern Min (Fuzhou), and Wu (Shanghai, Chongming, Huinan, Xinzhuang, Wenzhou, etc.).

In Chapter 3, a detailed analysis is made of the important role played by the c-command notion in determining TS domains, TS types, and the modes of TS rule application in Chinese dialects. Generally speaking, TS reacts in many ways to the c-command condition. Specifically, c-command determines what domain a tone will spread to, as in the Danyang case; whether the TS rule is applied or blocked, as in the Ruicheng case; and what kind of rule application mode will be chosen, as in the Pingyao case. Chapter 3 ends with a discussion of the condition for the association domain and c-command within functional relations in Shanghai.

Chapter 4 is a case study of Mandarin, which is a representative of standard Chinese. Reflecting on the problems in previous studies of Mandarin prosody, particularly in studies on foot and prosodic word, I reanalyzed some phenomena of Chinese prosodic study and clarify the interface relations of various types between syntax and phonology. Through the discussion on the domain issues from the Optimality Theory (OT) perspective, this chapter also clears up some concepts related to prosodic hierarchy.

In Chapter 5, I discuss some peculiar cases, such as the TS of function words (FW) and the rhythmic phenomenon in the quadrisyllabic TS of Chinese dialects. In many languages, the phonological behavior of FW is different from that of lexical words and phrases. What I try to do in this chapter is to show that the TS of FW is not so simple. Taking Chinese dialects for example, in some dialects, the different TS behaviors between FW and lexical words or phrases are represented by the different formations of tonal domains, but in others, they are embodied by either different types of TS rules or different modes of TS rule application. The other problem that I discuss in this chapter is the rhythmic effect on quadrisyllabic TS, a fairly popular phenomenon in Chinese dialects, with the purpose of finding some possible accounts for some exceptional TS cases.

Chapter 6 includes some theoretical discussions, presents some new hypotheses and assumptions for the mapping relationship between syntax and phonology for the organization of prosodic hierarchy, suggests the possible way to revise the strict layer hypothesis, and analyzes the problems in the OT. Chapter 7 summarizes the conclusions reached in this book.

1 Theoretical issues of syntax-phonology interface

1.1 Introduction

This study assumes the general organization of phonology within the grammar that has been developed in phrasal phonology, prosodic phonology, or post-lexical phonology, which is understood as a property of the interface between syntax and phonology (Selkirk 1984, 1986, 1996, 2000, 2009; Kaisse 1985, 1987, 1990; Nespor & Vogel 1986, 2007; Hayes 1989, 1990; and others). The interface between syntax and phonology is one of the major issues of generative phonology. As the cornerstone of generative phonology, the *Sound Pattern of English* (SPE) already notices the mismatch between syntax and phonology, as seen in (1).

(1) a. [This is [the cat that caught [the rat that stole [the cheese]]]]
    b. This is the cat % that caught the rat % that stole the cheese.

If the sentence in (1a) is read as (1b), broken into three parts with % indicating the pauses, (1b) obviously disaccords with the syntactic structure of (1a). SPE handled this case with the application of the readjustment rule. However, the real study on interface systematically began in the 1980s within the framework of Government and Binding (GB). According to the GB model, syntax is the input for both phonetic form (PF) and logical form (LF), as seen in (2) (Chomsky 1986a, 1986b; Baker 1988; Haegeman 1991).

(2)

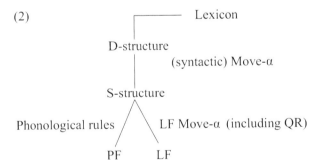

The model in (2) is also called the T-model. Roughly speaking, a representation at each of these levels (except for lexicon and PF) is a phrase marker that expresses a relationship of constituency. LF is the system's link with meaning, and here predication relationships, the scope of quantifiers, operators of various kinds, and the basic thematic relations among items are explicitly represented. PF is the system's link with acoustic form, and it is the level of interface between the language ability and the perceptual and motor abilities.

The 1990s saw some new development in generative grammar, the most important of which is the Minimalist Program (Chomsky 1993, 1995, 1999, 2001), simplified as MP. The model of grammar in the MP framework is given in (3).

(3)

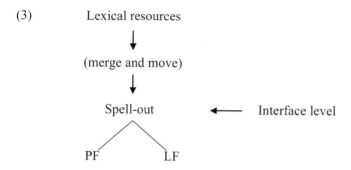

It can be seen from a comparison between (2) and (3) that the major difference between MP and GB lies in the fact that MP's syntactic process contains neither D-structure nor S-structure, and the operational process after spell-out splits into two directions, i.e., PF and LF. The syntactic process is derived from the lexicon through syntactic operation while PF and LF interact with the articulatory perceptual system and semantic-conceptual system of cognition, respectively, after spell-out. According to MP, both the articulatory perceptual system and semantic-conceptual system of cognition have some constraints to generate sentences. Therefore, syntax is the mechanism to connect phonology and semantics in a grammatical system, which operates based on economic principle. Spell-out is the node for syntax to get to PF and LF, the level of interface. Having gone through spell-out, the sentence structure will come close to the form used in real communication. That is why Chomsky (1995, 1999) considers that what is required of PF is simple because all it need do is turn the combination of the stem and morphological mark or the combination of phonological and semantic features into phonetic values. Therefore, Chomsky has not really touched the topic of the actual operational process of PF.

However, although in the models given in (2) and (3), the phonological shapes and groupings of items are directly represented, many linguists consider that the relationship between the syntactic structure and the phonological form is not a direct one, but a much more complicated one as depicted in (4).

(4)

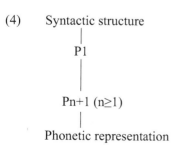

6 *Theoretical issues of syntax-phonology interface*

At the least, there are three questions directly related to (4), and they are a) how the phonological components are organized, b) which specific syntactic properties affect the application of phonological rules, and c) how these syntactic properties should be incorporated into phonology. These questions involve many issues such as the relationships between lexical and post-lexical rules, the organization of prosodic hierarchies, the properties of prosodic structure, syntactic representations, and phonological shapes. The following is a brief introduction to some theoretical issues that are concerned problems studied in this book.

1.2 Interface issues in lexical/post-lexical phonology

According to the framework of lexical phonology, the phonology is divided into two components: the lexical phonology and post-lexical phonology (Kiparsky 1982a, 1985; Kaisse 1985, 1987, 1990; Mohanan 1986; Pulleyblank 1986; and others). This division is motivated by the different ways in which phonological rules apply in each component. Mohanan (1986) summarizes two fundamental principles governing this distinction as follows in (5).

(5) a.   A rule application requiring morphological information must take place in the lexicon.
     b.   Rule application across words (= output of the lexicon) must take place post-lexically.

The second point involves the order of rule application, i.e., lexical rules apply pre-syntactically and post-lexical rules apply post-syntactically. One particular consequence of this is that if a rule applies both lexically and post-lexically, its lexical application is guaranteed to precede its post-lexical application. As for the distinction of rule application between lexical and post-lexical levels, Pulleyblank (1986) has provided us with a more detailed discussion, according to which there are as many as seven distinctive features between lexical and post-lexical rules, which are given in (6) and (7), respectively.

(6) Lexical rules

    a.   may refer to word-internal structure;
    b.   may not apply across words;
    c.   may be cyclic;
    d.   if cyclic, subject to strict cycle;
    e.   structure-preserving;
    f.   may have lexical exceptions;
    g.   must precede all post-lexical rule applications.

(7) Post-lexical rules

    a.   cannot refer to word-internal structure;
    b.   may apply across words;
    c.   may not be cyclic;

d. non-cyclic, hence across the board;
e. need not be structure-preserving;
f. cannot have lexical exceptions;
g. must follow all lexical rule applications.

In sum, lexical phonology hypothesizes that phonological rules are assigned either to a lexical level or to a post-lexical level.

1.3 Kaisse's model

Kaisse's model is cast within the framework of lexical phonology. However, being different from lexical phonology, which centers on the word level, her model (Kaisse 1985, 1987, 1990) mainly encompasses both word level and phrase level, and she still treats the rules of the phrasal phonology within a lexical phonology model. According to Kaisse, the post-lexical phonology is divided into two levels. One is called the P1 rules, consisting of the rules that are sensitive to sentence structure, specifically to the structural relationship between words in sentences. These rules have the properties of the lexical rules that are shown in (6). The second level is called the P2 rules, containing the rules that apply across the board and have the properties of the post-lexical rules in (7). The model proposed by Kaisse (1985) is given in (8).

(8) Kaisse's model

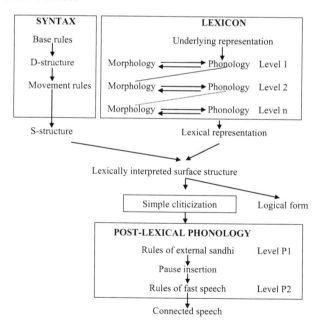

According to Kaisse, rules such as Auxiliary Reduction in English should be assigned to the level of "simple cliticizations," while rules such as High Vowel Devoicing in Japanese and Flapping in English are treated as P2 rules. As for the rules of external sandhi, they are P1 rules. In Kaisse's view, there is a direct interface between the labeled bracketing that emerges from the syntactic component and P1 rules.

In regard to the parameterization of a phonological phrase construction rule, Kaisse (1985) claims that phonological rules are directly sensitive to syntactic relations, i.e., c-command relations. Kaisse (1985) gives the definition of domain c-command as follows in (9).

(9) Domain c-command
In the structure $[X^{max} \ldots \alpha \ldots]$, X^{max} is defined as the domain of α.
Then α c-commands any β in its domain.

Based on (9), Kaisse suggests that the domain of a sandhi rule application is a c-command domain seen as follows in (10).

(10) C-command relation
For a rule to apply to a sequence of two words α and β
(i) α must domain-c-command β or
(ii) β must domain-c-command α.

According to the principles in (10), Kaisse has reanalyzed the Kimatuumbi vowel shortening, French liaison, Mandarin TS, and Ewe TS and formulated for these languages some distinct rules characterized in the aforementioned way. The major idea of this approach is that the domain, to which phonological rules are applied, is directly defined by syntactic relations, but not by way of any prosodic level.

1.4 Selkirk's model

Kaisse's model in (8) is one of the two most influential models of syntax-phonology interface study. The other one is proposed by Selkirk (1984, 1986, 1995, 2006, 2009). Before we take a closer look at Kaisse's model, we should learn about the model proposed by Selkirk and make a comparison between these two models so as to have a better understanding of the interface issues. The early version of Selkirk's (1986) model of the syntax-phonology interface is quoted as follows in (11).

(11) Selkirk's model

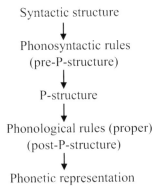

Theoretical issues of syntax-phonology interface 9

Not a few of those in syntax-phonology interface study consider that the models proposed by Kaisse and Selkirk are two counterposed theories. The former is generally called the Direct Reference Approach, which argues for a more direct syntax-phonology interface, while the latter is named the Indirect Reference Approach, which claims that phonology can only get access to syntax indirectly (Hyman, Katamba, & Walusimbi 1987).

However, if we carefully compare these two theories, we will see that Kaisse and Selkirk share something in common regarding the organization of the phonological components. In Kaisse's model, she supposes that there are two different sets of post-lexical rules: the external sandhi rules at the P1 level and the fast speech rules at the P2 level. The former apply before the pause insertion and are sensitive to the syntactic or morph-lexical environment in which their phonological terms appear. And the latter apply after the pause insertion and are dependent only on speech rate, syllabification, and the features of the focus, as well as of the determinant. In other words, the P1 rules depend on grammatical notions of adjacency, while the P2 rules rely on phonological notions of adjacency, such as absence of pause between segments.

As can be seen in the model in (11), Selkirk also maintains that there are two different sets of post-lexical rules, namely phonosyntactic rules and proper phonological rules, respectively. According to Selkirk, there is a level, which she calls P-structure, between these two different sets of rules. Hence the phonosyntactic rules are also addressed pre-P-structure rules, while the properly phonological rules are also called the post-P-structure rules. Roughly speaking, Selkirk's pre-P-structure rules correspond to Kaisse's P1 rules and Selkirk's post-P-structure rules correspond to Kaisse's P2 rules. The real difference between Kaisse and Selkirk lies in the fact that Kaisse attaches importance to the properties of the P1 rules as well as to the problem of what the domain of rule application at the P1 level is. However, Selkirk lays stress on the organization of prosodic structures (including both the P1 and P2 levels), the property of prosodic hierarchy, the conditions for the rule application in prosodic domain, and the problem of how to set the domain parameter. The properties of the P1 rules are proposed by Kaisse (1990) as given in (12). As for the conditions for prosodic structure and rule application of Selkirk, I will discuss them later in Sections 1.6 and 1.7 of this chapter.

(12) The properties of P1 rules

    a. sensitive primarily to syntactic information, syntactically local in a domain whose size is not variable, insensitive to intonational phrasing

    b. possibly requiring syntactic or lexical information beyond category-neutral, X-bar statements

    c. possibly cyclic

    d. neutralizing (structure-preserving)

    e. ingredient (categorical)

    f. style sensitive, rate insensitive

    g. possibly having lexical exceptions

    h. having a lexicalizable output

10 *Theoretical issues of syntax-phonology interface*

    i.   possibly showing strict cycle effects
    j.   pause sensitive only if creating linked structures
    k. having an output available to rules of versification
    l.   ordered before all P2 rules

1.5 The metrical approach

The metrical approach was originally developed as a theory of stress (Liberman & Prince 1977; Hayes 1981), although it has extended its domain to include syllable theory, the tonal phenomenon of downstep, vowel harmony, and various other types of harmony. However, in this book, the metrical approach is applied mainly as a theory of stress.

In Halle and Vergnaud (1987), the stress system of a language is determined by a set of parameters, such as left/right headness and boundness. To be specific, its purpose is to insert constituent boundaries at certain points, such as at the left or right edge of a syllable. Halle and Vergnaud further consider that the stress assignment may be sensitive both to phonological entities, such as the syllable and the rime segment, and to syntactic entities, such as word and phrase boundaries. Included in their proposal are more important assumptions as seen in (13) (Halle & Vergnaud 1987).

(13) a.   Stress equalization convention

         When two or more constituents are conjoined into a single higher-level constituent, the asterisk columns of the heads of the constituents are equalized by adding asterisks to the lesser column(s).

     b.   Stress erasure convention

         The input to the rules of cyclic strata information about stress generated on previous passes through the cyclic rules is carried over only if the affixed constituent is itself a domain for the cyclic stress rules. If the affixed constituent is not a domain for the cyclic stress rules, information about stresses assigned on previous passes is erased.

     c.   Clash deletion

$$* \longrightarrow \emptyset \ / \ \underline{\quad\quad} \ * \ \text{line 1} \qquad \overset{(*) \text{ line 2}}{}$$

         The rule will delete secondary stress also if followed directly by a syllable with secondary stress.

The first to apply the metrical approach to Chinese phonology were Chen (1979, 1980, 1984, 2000) and Wright (1983) with their emphasis on Chinese poetry and the TS of Fuzhou, respectively; they were followed by Duanmu (1991, 1992, 2000a, 2007) and Hsiao (1991) with focus on Taiwanese folk songs and Mandarin Chinese phonology, respectively.

Theoretical issues of syntax-phonology interface 11

Duanmu first argues that standard Mandarin Chinese has word stress. When a heavy syllable is followed by a light syllable, the heavy syllable has stress while the light syllable does not, e.g., *maa-ma*[1] 'mother.' Thus, he proposes a weight-to-stress principle stated in (14).

(14) The weight-to-stress principle

If a syllable is heavy, then it is stressed.

He then argues that stress is sensitive to both moras and syllables. Since Duanmu advocates the idea that moraic and syllabic iambs either do not exist or can be analyzed in terms of trochees, thus he proposes that the foot contains both the moraic trochee and the syllabic trochee, which is called the dual trochee. Duanmu (1990, 2000a) proposes the non-head stress rule, shown in (15), for assigning compound and phrasal stress.

(15) Non-head stress principle

In the syntactic structure [X XP] (or [XP X]), where X is the syntactic head and XP the syntactic non-head, XP should be stressed.

Duanmu (2007) claims that the non-head stress rule is a consequence of the information-stress principle stated in (16).

(16) The information-stress principle

A word or phrase that carries more information than its neighbor(s) should be stressed.

Duanmu argues that by assuming this principle, many stress effects can be accounted for. For example, pronouns usually do not carry stress since they refer to obvious entities or entities that have been mentioned. Another example is the flexibility of the phrasal stress since the information load of a word depends on the context.

Duanmu extends his theory of stress to tones and TS in Mandarin Chinese. Based on the observation across languages that stressed syllables are always accompanied by tones or pitch accents, he proposes a tone-stress principle rule shown in (17).

(17) Tone-stress principle

A stressed syllable can be assigned a lexical tone or pitch accent.
An unstressed syllable is not assigned a lexical tone or pitch accent.

Duanmu also discusses the third TS rule in Mandarin Chinese. Different from Chen (2000) who proposes a new prosodic unit, i.e., the minimal rhythmic unit, Duanmu proposes an alternative analysis with the notion of the metrical foot that starts with a stressed syllable followed by an unstressed one. The stress is determined by the information-stress principle in (16). He suggests that the third TS

12 Theoretical issues of syntax-phonology interface

obligatorily applies over two syllables that belong to the same immediate syntactic constituent, do not belong to separated full feet (containing two or more syllables), and optionally applies over two syllables that belong to two full feet. The rules he proposes are given in (18).

(18) a. Build disyllabic feet left to right for polysyllabic words
b. Build feet cyclically based on phrasal stress
c. Build disyllabic feet left to right for free words
d. 3TS starts from each foot and then cyclically
e. In a 3Ts domain, T3 must change before T3, but can optionally change before the T2 that came from T3

Duanmu claims that his metrical approach is better than the stress-insensitive foot analysis (Shih 1986; Chen 2000) because he believes that his approach, which assumes a regular foot structure is consistent with his analysis of the word-length problem and the word-order problem in Mandarin Chinese, explains why T3 sandhi is sensitive to emphasis and obtains support from other Chinese dialects.

1.6 Early studies of prosodic phonology

The term "prosodic studies" in discussion here refers to the study of prosodic structure/prosodic units/prosodic hierarchies rather than that of prosodic (i.e., suprasegmental) patterns, which could be the contours and phenomena themselves.

It is Selkirk who did some pioneering work in prosodic studies (Selkirk 1978, 1980a, 1980b, 1981). Based on the idea of Liberman (1975) and Liberman and Prince (1977) that segments are dominated by a multilayered structure, which expresses rhythmic properties of the linear string and assigns relative prominence to individual chunks, Selkirk developed the first model of prosodic phonology. A six-layer prosodic hierarchy was proposed, as shown in (19).

(19)
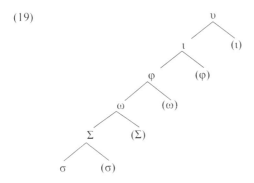

However, Selkirk soon abandons prosodic constituency under the influence of the grid-only approach (Prince 1983). She claims that the function of prosodic categories, except the intonational phrase, is taken over by the metrical grid (Selkirk 1984). Later, she returns to prosodic constituency, arguing that there is a "peaceful coexistence" of prosodic constituency and the metrical grid. She argues that the metrical grid is defined not with respect to syntactic domains but prosodic structure instead (Selkirk 1986). This system thus acknowledges two distinct mapping mechanisms that are serially ordered: prosodic constituency is the output of regular mapping rules, with Morphosyntactic structure as its input, and the metrical grid construction is performed on prosodic structure domains by a second set of mapping rules. In particular, following Chen (1985, 1987), Selkirk suggests that prosodic phrasing is constructed by referring to the ends of X' representations. In this end-based approach, she sets two parameters, each having two possible values, as given in (20).[2]

(20) a. # [X^{max} b. X^{max}] #
     c. # [X^{head} d. X^{head}] #

As can be seen from (20), the first parameter determines whether it is at the right or the left edge of a constituent, which is relevant to the construction rule. The second parameter indicates the nature of the constituent itself, which is possible values of X^{max} or X^{head}. Hence two parameters may have four logically possible phrasing types into which languages might fall. The cases found to conform to (20a) are TS in Ewe (Selkirk 1986) and TS in Shanghai (Selkirk & Shen 1990). The cases found to agree with (20b) are TS in Xiamen (Chen 1985, 1987, 1990; Selkirk 1986), vowel shortening in Chimwiini (Selkirk 1986), and the tonal phrasing in Papago (Hale & Selkirk 1987). As for (20c), Selkirk has not provided us with any examples, but Chen (1990) has found a supporting case in the cliticizing TS of Wenzhou, a southern Wu Chinese dialect. As for (20d), Selkirk (1986) offers the example of liaison in French, of which Chen (1990) holds a different opinion.

Following Selkirk's work, Nespor, Vogel, and others (Napoli & Nespor 1979; Nespor & Vogel 1979, 1982, 1983; Booij 1983, 1985a, 1985b, 1986; Hayes 1984b, 1989; Chen 1985, 1987, 1990, 2000; Neijt 1985; Nespor 1985, 1986; Vogel 1985, 1986; Ito 1986; Zec 1988) also made important contributions to the early studies of prosodic phonology. For example, a clitic group (CG) was added and inserted between the phonological word and the phonological phrase (Hayes 1984b; Nespor & Vogel 1986), and the mora was the lowest constituent (Zec 1988). Hence the fullest prosodic hierarchy of levels proposed so far can be shown as follows in (21).

(21)

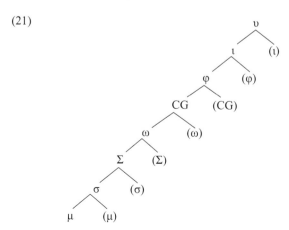

14 *Theoretical issues of syntax-phonology interface*

Different from the Edge/End-Based Approach, Nespor and Vogel (1986) (Selkirk 1986) propose the Category-Based Approach and make reference to X-bar notions of phrase structure, such as head-complement, modifier-head, and specifier-head relations, as well as syntactic branching (Inkelas & Zec 1990).

Part of what prosodic phonology is concerned with is the set of prosodic categories discussed earlier. A second concern of the prosodic theory is the hierarchical nature of prosodic domains. It is generally assumed that a unit at any given level in the hierarchy shown in (21) can never be composed of anything but the units at the next lower level. In the prosodic hierarchy, a prosodic constituent of a given level n immediately dominates only constituents of the lower-level $n-1$ and is exhaustively contained in a constituent of the immediately higher-level $n+1$. In other words, recursive prosodic structures are assumed not to occur. Thus comes the strict layer hypothesis proposed by Selkirk (1984, 1986), Nespor and Vogel (1986), and Hayes (1989), as given in (22).[3]

(22) a. A given nonterminal unit of the prosodic hierarchy, X^p, is composed of one or more units of the immediately lower category, X^{p-1}.

b. A unit of a given level of the hierarchy is exhaustively contained in the super-ordinate unit of which it is a part.

As seen from (22), PW may not dominate PW, and PW may not dominate CG, etc. It is a well-formedness condition on prosodic constituency. However, it has been noticed that the strict layer hypothesis might not be a universal principle, because in some languages, prosodic recursivity seems to be allowed (Ladd 1986, 1990; Hyman et al. 1987; Odden 1987; Inkelas 1989; and others). Selkirk (1996) has to suggest considering recursivity as a violable condition or constraint in the spirit of the Optimality Theory, which will be discussed later.

1.7 Prosodic studies in the optimality theory

Along with the birth of Optimality Theory in the 1990s (McCarthy & Prince 1993; Prince & Smolensky 1993), which abandons derivation-based phonology and embraces a constraints-based approach, came a new perspective in prosodic studies. Within the OT framework, prosodic phonology follows its basic principles and allows constraint violability, which is a language universal property, while the different rankings of constraints reflect a language-specific property. The mapping between syntax and phonology is interpreted as different ranking constraints in a hierarchy of different grammatical categories. Different rankings of constraints lead to different prosodic units in natural languages. Therefore, the prosodic studies with an OT framework is thought to be able to predict various types of prosodic units of different languages.

The constraints in the prosodic studies with an OT framework can be divided into three types: constraints mapping between syntax and phonology, prosodic constraints, and Morphosyntactic constraints, with the first type as faithfulness constraints while the other two are markedness constraints.

Theoretical issues of syntax-phonology interface   15

In the spirit of the Generalized Alignment theory of McCarthy and Prince (1993), Selkirk (1996) defines a class of constraints on edge alignment of syntactic units with phonological units as in (23) and (24).

(23) $W_D C_{ON}$

    a. A_{LIGN} (X°, L; ω, L)
    b. A_{LIGN} (X°, R; ω, R)

(24) $P_{HRASE} C_{ON}$

    a. A_{LIGN} (XP, L; φ, L)
    b. A_{LIGN} (XP, R; φ, R)

In (23), it is indicated that each lexical word needs to have its left or right edge align with the left or right edge of the prosodic word. Constraints in (24) state that the right or left edge of any XP in Morphosyntactic structure coincides with the right or left edge of some phonological phrase in prosodic structure.

Align constraints require that the edge of syntactic structure match that of the prosodic category. They target a group of conditions, thus, covering different levels of the mapping between syntax and phonology. These two constraints were later referred to as A_{LIGN}-XP, L and A_{LIGN}-XP, R or A_{LIGN}-XP in Truckenbrodt (1995, 1999), which asked that the right edge of a syntactic phrase align with the right edge of a phonological phrase and the left edge of a syntactic phrase align with the left edge of a phonological phrase, respectively. Alignment theory is actually derived from Edge-based theory (Chen 1985, 1987; Selkirk 1986).

Another theory related to the syntax interface study is the Wrapping constraint within the OT framework (Truckenbrodt 1999). It demands wrapping each syntactic phrase within a phonological phrase: Wrap (XP; φ). Both alignment constraint and wrapping constraint are typically the constraints of interface between syntax and phonology, besides which there is a Match theory (Selkirk 2006, 2009, 2011), as given in (25).

(25) Match theory of syntactic-prosodic constituency correspondence

    a.   Match (α, π) [S-P faithfulness]
    b.   Match (π, α) [P-S faithfulness]
    c.   Match clause

        A clause in a syntactic constituent structure must be matched by a corresponding prosodic constituent, call it *ι*, in phonological representation.

    d.   Match phrase

        A phrase in a syntactic constituent structure must be matched by a corresponding prosodic constituent, call it *φ*, in phonological representation.

16 *Theoretical issues of syntax-phonology interface*

   e.   Match word

        A word in a syntactic constituent structure must be matched by a corresponding prosodic constituent, call it ω, in phonological representation.

These Match constraints call for the constituent structures of syntax and phonology to correspond. It predicts a strong tendency for phonological domains to mirror syntactic constituents. The view to be argued is that the phonological constituent structure produced for individual sentences in individual languages is the result of syntactic constituency-respecting Match constraints. Moreover, in identifying distinct prosodic constituent types (ι, φ, ω) to correspond to the designated syntactic constituent types, the Match theory embodies the claim that the grammar allows the fundamental syntactic distinctions between clause, phrase, and word to be reflected in the phonological representation.

In addition to the constraints discussed in the OT framework, four general constraints that are entailed by the strict layer hypothesis (Selkirk 1984) are also proposed (Selkirk 1995), as given in (26).

(26) Strict layer hypothesis in OT
     (where C^n = some prosodic category)

   a.   Layeredness: no C^i dominates a C^j, iff j > i (e.g., no σ dominates a Σ)
   b.   Headedness: any C^i must dominate a C^{i-1} (e.g., a ω must dominate a Σ)
   c.   Exhaustivity: no C^i dominates C^j, iff j < i-1, (e.g., no ω immediately dominates a σ)
   d.   Non-recursivity: no C^i dominates C^j, iff j = i (e.g., no Σ dominates a Σ)

The strict layer hypothesis is the well-formedness condition for the tree diagram of prosodic hierarchy. The following prosodic structures in (27) are considered ill formed because they violate the strict layer hypothesis.

(27)   a. Multiple domination   b. Heterogeneous sisters

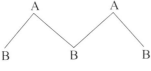

   c. Skipping of levels   d. Recursion

The strict layer hypothesis determines the organization of the prosodic hierarchical structure and constrains the prosodic constituents that serve as domains of

Theoretical issues of syntax-phonology interface 17

phonological rules application. The structural relationship existing among different prosodic constituents has a direct bearing on the construction principles of prosodic hierarchy.

Within the OT framework, there are many constraints for different types of prosodic units. For instance, BinMin (φ, ω) requires that a phonological phrase contains at least two prosodic words, while BinMax (φ, ω) demands that a phonological phrase can be formed by two prosodic words at the most. These two constraints can be summed up as follows in (28).

(28) a. W_{RAP}-XP, which requires that each XP is contained in the same phonological phrase

b. N_{ONREC}, which demands that phrases are not recursive (Truckenbrodt 1995, 1999)

c. A_{LIGN}-F_{OC}, which refers to each focused constituent being aligned with a phonological phrase boundary (Truckenbrodt 1995, 1999)

d. B_{INARY}-M_{AP}, which means that a major phrase must consist of at most and/or at least two minor phrases (Selkirk 2000; Prieto 2005, 2006)

e. $U_{NIFORMITY}$, which requires that a string is ideally parsed into units of the same length (Ghini 1993; Sandalo & Truckenbrodt 2002; Prieto 2005, 2006)

f. $I_{NCREASING}$ U_{NITS}, which indicates that phonological phrases on the recursive side are heavier than those in the non-recursive side (Ghini 1993)

The Align-Wrap theory and the Match theory reflect the most recent development in the study of the interface between syntax and phonology. They present different predictions to prosodic structures. When Wrap-XP, Align-XP, and non-recursivity interact, they might predict the different types of relations between syntax and phonology (Truckenbrodt 1999). In a non-recursive high-ranking language, for a VP with two internal arguments such as [NP NP V]VP, Wrap-XP and Align-XP can be applied to predict and derive the three different prosodic structures presented in (29).

(29) a. (NP NP Verb)φ   Wrap-XP >> Align-R/L-XP
    b. (NP) (NP) Verb   Align-R-XP >> Wrap-XP
    c. (NP) (NP Verb)   Align-L-XP >> Wrap-XP

In (29a), the ranking of Wrap-XP is higher than that of Align-XP, VP corresponds to a phonological phrase, and there is no other phonological phrase within VP. If any constraints of Align-XP, such as Align-XP-L or Align-XP-R, get its ranking higher than that of Wrap-XP, the whole VP phrase will have no phonological phrase to respond. Therefore, the Match theory seems able to derive only one type of prosodic structure: ((NP)φ (NP)φ Verb)φ. However, further cross-linguistics study is needed to determine which theory the domain of rule application sensitive to phonologic phenomena really supports.

18 *Theoretical issues of syntax-phonology interface*

1.8 Sum up

The domain of rule application of Chinese TS has been a major topic in the studies of the interface between syntax and phonology. The facts found in Xiamen and Shanghai dialects are among those lending the first support to the Edge-based theory under the derivation-based phonology. Selkirk has refurbished the Edge-based theory, from which she has developed the Match theory under the constraint-based phonology (i.e., the OT) and believes that the Match theory works not only to analyze those language facts originally supporting the Edge-based theory but also to determine the domain of phonological rule application by referring to both edges of syntactic category. However, with a large amount of TS data found in Chinese dialects, I will show in this book that the Match theory fails to make the correct prediction to the sandhi phenomena in some Chinese dialects. This is because the theories under the OT framework (such as the Align-Wrap theory and the Match theory) are all derived from the Indirect Reference theory, but TS in some Chinese dialects (such as Pingyao, Danyang, and Ruicheng) seems to support the Direct Reference theory (such as the c/m-command condition). Therefore, this book will try to prove, with the linguistic data from Chinese TS, that the interface theories under the OT framework do not have the explanation power superior to that of the interface theories proposed before the OT era.

Notes

1 Here I follow Duanmu's transcription for examples cited from his book (Duanmu 2000a).
2 The symbol '#' stands for the blockage of phonological process.
3 Adopted here is the interpretation by Nespor and Vogel (1986: 7).

2 Functional relations in tone sandhi

2.1 Introduction

Selkirk (1984) has already noticed how phonology is sensitive to the functional distinction between arguments and adjuncts. For example, in an adjunct-head structure in English, the stress of compounds falls on the head rather than the adjunct, while in argument-head structures, it falls on the argument instead of the head. In many cases, the stress assignment of English compounds depends on the functional relation to the head.

However, it is Chen (1985, 1987) who applies the concept of argument/adjunct dichotomy to the study of Chinese TS. Chen points out that the domain of TS in Xiamen depends in a crucial way on the functional distinction between arguments and adjuncts.

Huang (1982) and Tang (1990) have discussed the distinction between arguments and adjuncts from a syntactic perspective, and I will further my observation and analysis of how phonology is sensitive to functional relations. In the following, I am going to discuss how functional categories, such as adjunct, argument, and head, play their roles in phrasal phonology with detailed analyses of some Chinese dialects such as Xiamen, Fuzhou, Wu, and Pingyao.

2.2 Adjunct in Xiamen Chinese

Xiamen, a Southern Min dialect of Chinese, has rich and complicated TS phenomena, which has been thoroughly studied (Cheng 1968, 1973, 1991; Chen 1985, 1987, 1992c, 2000; Chung 1987; Hsiao 1991; Hsu 1992; Zhang 1992; Lin 1994). As for the domain of Xiamen TS rule application, the most important ones were made by Chen (1987, 1992c, 2000) and Cheng (1991). The former has provided us with almost all of the major TS data, while the latter is the first to discuss the domain of Xiamen TS from the viewpoint of functional relations. In this section, I will first discuss some of the previous analyses, especially the one made by Chen, and then reanalyze the TS domain of Xiamen.

2.2.1 Xiamen tonal system

There are seven citation tones in Xiamen Chinese, as shown in (1).[1]

(1) The citation tones in Xiamen
a. 44 b. 53 c. 21 d. 22 e. 24 f. 5 g. 3

The TS rule and the mode of rule application in Xiamen at the phrasal level are stated in (2) and (3), respectively.[2]

(2) Tone sandhi rule (TSR)
T → T' / ___ T]'α

(3) The mode of TSR
a. Free syllable

b. Checked syllable
(i) 5 → 21 (-p, -t, -k)
    21 (-q)
(ii) 3 → 5 (-p, -t, -k)
    53 (-q)

Generally speaking, there is a process whereby each citation tone assumes a sandhi form in a sort of chain shift. The "free" syllable tones form a closed circle as depicted in (3a). "Checked" syllable tones form a subsystem of their own, and the rules are given in (3b). If the phonetic details are disregarded, both "free" and "checked" syllable TS can be generalized as (2).

2.2.2 Chen's TG formation

According to functional relations, Chen proposes *tone group formation* (TG formation) for Xiamen TS, as seen in (4).

(4) TG formation (Chen 1985, 1987)
Mark the right edge of every XP with #, except where XP is an adjunct c-commanding its head.

The TG formation in (4) not only points out that Xiamen TS depends on functional categories but also combines two different approaches – namely, the end-based approach proposed by Selkirk (1986) and the relation-based approach claimed by Kaisse (1985). According to Chen, three conditions need to be taken

Functional relations in tone sandhi 21

into consideration in order to ascertain the domain of Xiamen TS: edge condition, adjunct/argument dichotomy condition, and c-command condition.

Since Reinhart (1981) discussed in detail the notion of c-command, two different definitions have been proposed: a) the preliminary definition given by Reinhart and b) the revised definition proposed by Chomsky (1986a), given, respectively, in (5a) and (5b).

(5) a. Preliminary definition
         α c-commands β iff
         every branching node dominating α dominates β.

     b. Revised definition
         α c-commands β iff
         every maximal projection dominating α dominates β.

To distinguish these two different c-command definitions, (5a) is generally called c-command, while (5b) is termed m-command. It should be noted that the notion of c-command according to Chen is in fact the preliminary definition of c-command according to Reinhart.

However, as noticed by Chen himself, the TG formation in (4) fails to explain why the adjunct within VP differs from the sentential adjunct.[3] In Xiamen, a VP-adjunct cannot form its own TS domain; instead, with its following head it forms one domain, as seen in (6). A sentential adjunct, on the other hand, must have its own domain, as seen in (7).[4]

(6) a. Ting   sio-tsia   yi-king   tsau   a
         33   55–53 #   55–33 =   53   n
         Ting   miss   already   go   ASP
         'Miss Ting has already left.'

     b. Ting   sio-tsia   kuah-kin   tsiaq   png
         33   55–53 #   55–55 =   21   33
         Ting   miss   quickly   eat   meal
         'Miss Ting quickly ate her meal.'

(7) a. Ting   sio-tsia   tai-k'ai   tsau   a
         33   55–53 #   21–21 #   53   n
         Ting   miss   probably   go   ASP
         'Miss Ting has probably left.'

     b. Ting   sio-tsia   tai-k'ai   yi-king   tsau   a
         33   55–53 #   21–21 #   55–33 =   53   n
         Ting   miss   probably   already   go   ASP
         'Miss Ting has probably already left.'

By virtue of the TG formation in (4), if an adjunct c-commands its head, a TG boundary '#' cannot be inserted. According to the definition of c-command, both *yi-king* 'already' in (6a) and *tai-k'ai* 'probably' in (7a) c-command the closely following *tsau* 'go,' but only the former forms one TG with *tsau*, while the latter and the following *tsau* form two different TGs. And this fact shows that there is some problem within the TG formation in (4).

2.2.3 Domain-c-command approach to Xiamen TS

After Chen (1987), Chung (1987) made a different analysis based on Hakka TS data. Following Kaisse's idea (1985), he considers the domain of TS an m-command domain with the K-condition instead of functional relations. The general idea of Kaisse's hypothesis is seen in (8a), and her definition of domain c-command is given in (8b).

(8) a. K-condition (Kaisse 1985)
For a rule to apply to a sequence of two words α and β,
(i) α must domain-c-command β or
(ii) β must domain-c-command α.
b. Domain c-command (Kaisse 1985)
In the structure [X^{max} ... x ...], X^{max} is defined as the domain of x. Then X c-commands any Y in its domain.

Kaisse's domain-c-command definition is, in fact, a refurbished version of that of m-command by Chomsky (1986a). According to the K-condition in (8a), TS rule applies between α and β, so long as they stand in a head-XP relation, where the XP is neutral between argument and adjunct.

However, Chung's analysis can solve the contradiction between (6) and (7) because the VP-adjunct's position in the syntactic tree is different from that of the sentential adjunct. The former is within the VP and is m-commanded by the head of the VP – namely, the verb, as seen in (9). But the latter is outside the VP and thus not m-commanded by the verb, as seen in (10).

(9)

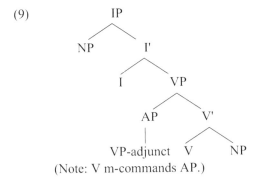

(Note: V m-commands AP.)

(10)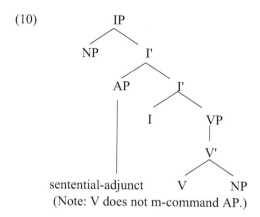
(Note: V does not m-command AP.)

Since *yi-king* 'already' in (6a) is a VP-adjunct m-commanded by the verb, the TS rule applies. But *tai-k'ai* 'probably' in (7a) is a sentential adjunct that is not m-commanded by the verb, so the TS rule does not apply. However, Chung's analysis cannot explain cases in which the verb and the preceding PP are divided into two different TGs in Xiamen, as seen in (11).

(11) a. Ting   sio-tsia   ti   hak-hau   tsiaq   png
         33   55–53 #   21   3–33 #   21   33
         Ting   miss   at   school   eat   meal
    'Miss Ting eats her meal at school.'

   b. Ting   sio-tsia   kuah-kin   ti   hak-hau   tsiaq   png
       33   55–53 #   55–55 =   21   3–33 #   21   33
       Ting   miss   quickly   at   school   eat   meal
    'Miss Ting ate her meal quickly at school.'

In the syntactic tree, the PP *ti hak-hau* 'at school' is m-commanded by the verb *tsiaq* 'eat,' as seen in (12).

(12)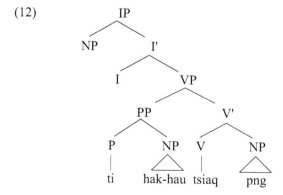

24 *Functional relations in tone sandhi*

According to the K-condition, *tsiaq* m-commands *hak-hau*, so the TS rule should apply between them. But as a matter of fact, this is a wrong TS output for Xiamen. Therefore, for Xiamen TS, Kaisse's hypothesis in (8), employed by Chung, is not a successful one.

2.2.4 Revised TG formation

In order to solve the problem left over by Chen (1987), Chung (1987) and Chen (1992c) revised the TG formation for Xiamen as shown in (13).

(13) Revised TG formation
    Mark the right edge of every XP with #, except where
    XP is an adjunct c-commanding its lexical head.

Compared with the preliminary version in (4), the revised version in (13) also considers that functional relations with the head, instead of m-command, are the key to the Xiamen TS. Different from (4), (13) emphasizes that the adjunct only c-commands its lexical heads, not all of its heads. Since a sentential adjunct is licensed by I (Infl), which is the head of a functional category, it is a non-lexical head; thus the TS rule must be blocked between a sentential adjunct and its following elements, although the sentential adjunct c-commands its following elements. But the adjuncts within the VP and NP are different because both of them modify lexical heads and thus the TS rule must be applied between adjuncts and their heads. As for the cases in which the TS rule must be blocked between the PP and the closely following verb, according to Chen (1992c), the NP (i.e., the XP between the P and verb) is an argument rather than an adjunct, although the PP is the adjunct of the verb, thus blocking the TS rule, as seen in (14).

(14)
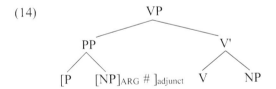

Thus it can be seen that the revised version in (13) by Chen not only solves the problem in (6) and (7) but also works out a solution for the problem in (11).

2.2.5 Re-revised TG formation

However, the hypothesis in (13) still contains some problems. First, let us consider the examples from (15) to (20).

(15) a. tso   tsit   ts'ut   liok-yah-p'ih   lai   k'uah
         33   3   5 =   3 – 55 – 21 #   33   21
         rent   one   Cl   video-movie   to   watch
         'Rent a video movie to watch'

b. liok-yah-p'ih   tso   tsit   ts'ut   lai   k'uah
3 – 55 – 21 #   33   3   5 =   33   21
video-movie   rent   one   Cl   to   watch
'Rent a video movie to watch'

(16) a. bue   tsap   kuah   be-a   tsiu   lai   lim
55   3   53 =   21–55   53 #   33   55
buy   ten   Cl   beer   wine   to   drink
'Buy ten bottles of beer to drink'

b. be-a   tsiu   bue   tsap   kuah   lai   lim
21–55   53 #   55   3   53 =   33   55
beer   wine   buy   ten   Cl   to   drink
'Buy ten bottles of beer to drink'

(17) a. tso   tsit   ts'ut   liok-yah-p'ih   tsin   kui
33   3   5 =   3 – 55 – 21 #   33   21
rent   one   Cl   video-movie   very   expensive
'It is very expensive to rent a video movie.'

b. liok-yah-p'ih   tso   tsit   ts'ut   tsin   kui
3 – 55 – 21 #   33   3   3 #   33   21
video-movie   rent   one   Cl   very   expensive
'It is very expensive to rent a video movie.'

(18) a. lim   tsap   kuah   be-a   tsiu   e   tsui
33   3   53 =   21–55   53 #   21   21
drink   ten   Cl   beer   wine   will   drunk
'To drink ten bottles of beer will cause drunkenness.'

b. be-a   tsiu   lim   tsap   kuah   e   tsui
21–55   53 #   33   3   21 #   21   21
beer   wine   drink   ten   Cl   will   drunk
'To drink ten bottles of beer will cause drunkenness.'

(19) ts'iuh   sah   pai   siuh   t'iam
53   33   53 #   33   53
sing   three   Cl   too   tired
'It is too tiring to sing three times.'

(20) ts'iuh   tsit   pai   hoo   yi   t'iah
53   3   55 =   44   22   44
sing   one   Cl   for   him   hear
'Sing once for him to hear.'

Chen (1992c) has made an analysis of case (15). In his opinion, the adnominal adjunct QP in (15a) for the NP *liok-yah-p'ih* 'video movie,' which occupies an object position, is reanalyzed as an adverbial phrase as well as a post-head adjunct in (15b) as a result of the topicalization of *liok-yah-p'ih*. The syntactic structure given by Chen for (15b) is shown in (21).

(21)
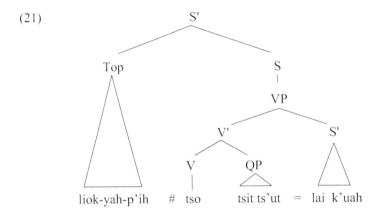

The first question we want to ask is how '=,' which is put at the right edge of the QP to symbolize the application of the TS rule, is obtained. According to the TG formation in (13), '#' should be assigned to the right edge of all of the XPs, except when an XP is an adjunct c-commanding its lexical head, in which case an '=' should be put there instead. But in (21), the QP c-commands only the verb *tso* 'rent' at its left without c-commanding any elements to its right. By Chen's analysis, the QP seems to be an adjunct c-commanding its left head, thus gaining an '=' at its right, although this QP does not have any c-command relation with its right elements. Such an analysis is also suitable for example (16b). But this analysis violates the locality conditions (Poser 1981, 1985; Steriade 1987), which maintain that the application of the TS rule to the right should have nothing to do with the syntactic condition to the left.

The second question is concerned with "lexical head." According to (13), the TS rule must be blocked between the XP and the following elements, except when the XP is an adjunct c-commanding its lexical head. Before discussing the problem involved in (13), let us briefly present Chinese phrase structures first (Huang 1982, 1991; Tang 1990). In the notation of X'-theory, every phrasal category is a projection of a zero-level category in terms of the following formalization.[5]

(22) a. X' = X X"*
     b. X" = X"* X'

Zero-level categories are assumed to be of two different types. One type consists of the lexical categories, including N, V, P, and A. Another type covers the non-lexical or functional categories such as complementizer (C) and Infl (I). Now let us come back to the problem in (13). According to (13), an adjunct can c-command its lexical head, excluding a non-lexical head or a functional head, i.e., Infl or Comp of CP (see Chen 1992c: 19). But *hoo* 'for' in (20) is the head of a functional category, i.e., the Comp of CP, instead of a lexical head, so the TS rule still applies between the QP *tsit pai* 'one' and *hoo*. Thus this shows that the TG formation in (13) needs further revision. That is why I propose in (23) a re-revised TG formation for Xiamen.[6]

(23) Re-revised TG formation (Zhang 1992)
Mark the right edge of every XP with #, except where XP is an adjunct m-commanding either its head or the head of XP on the right, except Infl.

The TG formation in (23) can account for, without any exception, all of the data mentioned earlier. Adjuncts in both examples (6) and (7) m-command their following heads, but since the head of the former is a verb while that of the latter is an Infl, the TS rule can be applied only to (6) and is blocked in (7), as shown, respectively, in (24) and (25).

(24)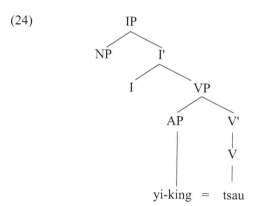

(Note: AP m-commands V, i.e. the head of VP.)

(25)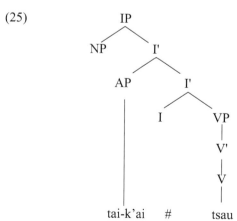

(Note: AP m-commands Infl, i.e. the head of IP.)

28 *Functional relations in tone sandhi*

In example (11a), the NP *hak-hau* 'school' is an argument, not an adjunct, for the preposition *ti* 'at,' so the TS rule is blocked between *hak-hau* and *tsiaq*. The example is reproduced in (26) for the sake of convenience.

(26)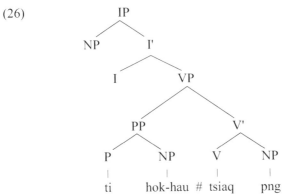

(Note: The XP before V, i.e. the head of VP, is an argument.)

As for example (11b), since the adjunct *kuah-kin* 'quickly' m-commands the head of PP, i.e., *ti* 'at,' on the right, the TS rule is applied between *kuah-kin* and *ti*, as seen in (27).

(27)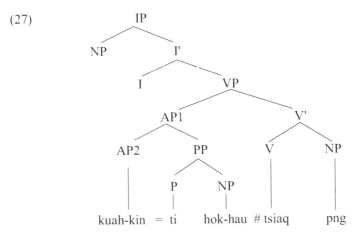

(Note: AP2 m-commands P, the head of PP on the right).

Now let us consider the examples (15)–(20) in accordance with the TG formation in (23).

In both (15b) and (16b), the QPs, as adjuncts, m-command the right head *lai* 'to.' Likewise, in example (20), the QP m-commands *hoo* 'for' the head of CP on the right. So the TS rule must be applied to (15b), (16b), and (20), in which the heads following the QPs are all complementizers and are all heads of CP. The syntactic structure of (20) can be repictured as (28).

(28)

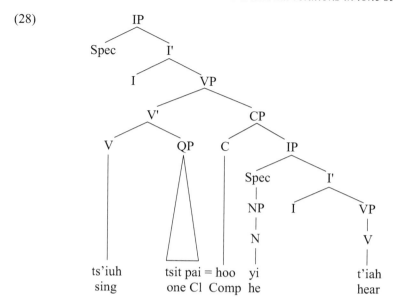

As for examples (17b), (18b), and (19), their syntactic tree structures are the same as illustrated in (29), in which the QP as an adjunct cannot m-command any of the elements on its right, thus blocking the TS rule.

(29)

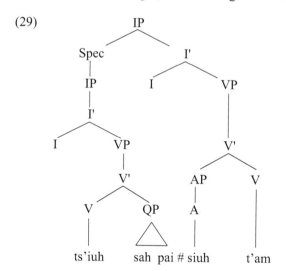

Therefore, it can be seen that the TG formation in (23) can account for all of the data here.

If we compare the TG formations in (23) and (13), we will see such differences between them as a) the syntactic condition of (23) is m-command, while the syntactic condition of (13) is c-command; b) (23) is concerned only with an adjunct's m-command relations to the right heads while ignoring its left elements (locality conditions are related to this point), but (13) sometimes depends on the relation between an adjunct and its left head in order to decide whether or not there is a boundary to the right of TG; and c) by (23), an adjunct can m-command all of the following heads, including C of CP, except Infl, but by (13), an adjunct can c-command only its lexical head, excluding all non-lexical heads or functional heads, i.e., either Infl or Comp of CP. One key point concerning (c) is the fact that Infl in Chinese is a trace, i.e., one of the empty categories, in S-structure. Based on the discussion of "A not A" question sentences, Huang (1990) has successfully proved that the AGR and verb in Chinese move, respectively, downward from I° and upward from VP to "VP shell," which is located between I' and VP. So after head-to-head movement, Infl, a head of IP, becomes a trace, as shown in (30).

(30)

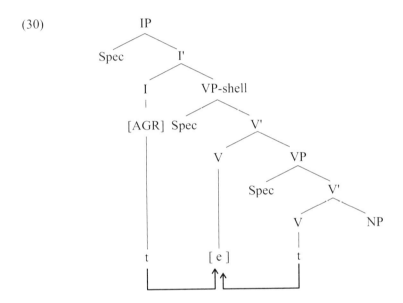

Thus it can be seen that the definition in (23) differs from that in (13) in that the former maintains that the TS rule is blocked by an empty category, while the latter holds that it is blocked by functional words. As I mentioned in the previous discussion, the TS rule is still applicable, even if functional heads on the right are m-commanded by an adjunct, and this has been proved by *lai* 'to' in (15b) and (16b), as well as *hoo* 'for' in (20). Therefore, whether TS should apply is not decided by the distinction between functional words and lexical words, but by the difference between empty and non-empty categories. However, it should be pointed out that in spite of such differences, definitions (23) and (13) share one thing in common. That is, like (13), definition (23) also claims that the functional relation (i.e., adjunct) to the head is one of the keys to Xiamen TS.

Functional relations in tone sandhi   31

2.2.6 OT analysis of Xiamen TS

Chen (2000) considers the domain of Xiamen TS as the phonological phrase, which in Truckenbrodt's proposal (1999) can be reanalyzed by the theory of syntax-phonology interface under the OT framework. According to Truckenbrodt, the ranking of prosodic constraints in Xiamen is Wrap-XP >> Align-R-XP.

Now let us check to see if the ranking of prosodic constraints of Wrap-XP, which is higher than that of Align-R-XP, can be applied to define the phonological phrase in Xiamen.

First, we need to check if the Wrapping theory and the Alignment theory can explain the inconsistency between AvP as the adjunct of the sentence and AvP as the adjunct of the VP. AvP as the adjunct of the VP is shown in (31).

(31) Syntactic structure: $[[yi]_{DP}[[yi\text{-}king]_{AvP} = tsau]_{VP} = a]_{IP}$
      Prosodic struture: (yi   yi-king   tsau)$_\varphi$
                           he   already   go   ASP
                           'He has already left.'

$[[yi]_{DP}[[yi\text{-}king]_{AvP}\,tsau]_{VP}\,a]_{IP}$	Exhausitivity	Wrap-XP	Align-R	*P-phrase
☞ a. (yi yi-king tsau)$_\varphi$			*	*
b. (yi yi-king)$_\varphi$ (tsau)$_\varphi$		*!		**
c. (yi)$_\varphi$ (yi-king tsau)$_\varphi$			*	**!
d. (yi)$_\varphi$ (yi-king)$_\varphi$ (tsau)$_\varphi$		*!		***
e. yi (yi-king tsau)$_\varphi$	*!		*	*

In tableau (31), the AvP *yi-king* in candidates (b) and (d) has no corresponding phonological phrase on its right. And, moreover, because *yi* is a DP, which belongs to the functional category, it works only with lexical items instead of functional items by the constraint of Lexical Category Condition (LCC) (Truckenbrodt 1999). To have no corresponding phonological phrase label on the right of DP does not violate any interface conditions. Therefore, these two candidates both fulfill the constraint requirement of Align-R. However, due to the fact that the AvP *yi-king* combines with the following verb *tsau* to form a VP, this VP should be analyzed as a phonological phrase by Wrap-XP, and, therefore, both of these candidates get eliminated because they violate Wrap-XP, which should have a higher ranking. As for candidates (a), (b), and (c), none of their AvP *yi-king* have a corresponding phonological phrase on the right, thus violating the constraint of Align-R. But since all of them meet the constraint of Wrap-XP, they come out even, if without any other constraints. Due to the fact that its *yi* is not considered in analysis at the prosodic phrasal level, candidate (31e) violates the constraint and gets eliminated. As can be seen, each of the phonological phrases listed violates *P-phrase, i.e., markedness constraint, at least once. If compared with (31a), (31c) obviously violates *P-phrase constraint more seriously. Therefore, (31a) stands out as the

32 *Functional relations in tone sandhi*

optimal form and the winner owing to the fact that the whole part in (31a) can be analyzed as one phonological phrase. Non-recursivity constraint cannot be violated in Xiamen TS. For the candidates given in the following examples, those violating the constraints of Recursivity and Exhausitivity and causing unncessary increase in the number of phonological phrases have already been eliminated.

The analyses of AvP as the adjunct of the sentences are also given.

(32) Syntactic structure: $[[yi]_{DP}[[tai\text{-}k'ai]_{AvP} \# tsau]_{VP} = a]_{IP}$
Prosodic struture:　(yi　tai-k'ai)$_\varphi$　(tsau)$_\varphi$
　　　　　　　　he　probably　go　ASP
　　　　　　'He has probably left.'

[[yi]DP [tai-k'ai]AvP # [tsau]VP a]IP	Wrap-XP	Align-R
☞a. (yi tai-k'ai)φ (tsau)φ		
b. (yi tai-k'ai tsau)φ		*!

In candidate (32a), AvP *tai-k'ai* corresponds to the right of the phonological phrase on its right, thus meeting the constraint of Align-R. Its *yi* is a DP, which is a functional element with the maximum projection and which has no corresponding relation to the edge of the phonological phrase on its right, thus tallying with the constraint of Align-R.

With the whole part containing the maximum projection of a functional word and, thus, not being covered within the domain of a phonological phrase, AvP *tai-k'ai* in (32b) does not correspond on its right to the right edge of the phonological phrase. The result of this assessment is that candidate (32a) is the optimal form with its whole part analyzed into two phonological phrases.

Thus it can be seen that with the ranking of the constraint hierarchy, Wrap-XP >> Align-R, the Wrap-Align theory, can explain the difference between the sentential adjunct and the VP adjunct in Xiamen while defining the domains of TS.

However, it should be pointed out that if the XP within a Wrap-XP is not an adjunct, we have to place restrictions on this type of XP. In other words, we must exclude such XPs as those belonging to an empty category defined by LCC and functional XP, as well as those lexical phrases such as NP, VP, and AP, which are embedded with functional phrases.

Now let us apply the Match theory to the case of the Xiamen TS domian and see if it can explain the prosodic structure of Xiamen at the level of the phonological phrase.

First, let us check on AvP as the VP adjunct in (33).

(33) a.　Syntactic structure: $[[yi]_{DP} [[yi\text{-}king]_{AvP} = tsau]_{VP} = a]_{IP}$
　　 b.　Prosodic struture:　yi　((yi-king)$_\varphi$　tsau)$_\varphi$　Match (XP; φ)
　　　　　　　　　　　he　already　go　ASP
　　　　　　　　'He has already left.'

Now, let us take a look at AvP as the adjunct of the sentence in (34).

(34) a. Syntactic structure: $[[\text{yi}]_{DP} [[\text{tai-k'ai}]_{AvP} \# \text{tsau}]_{VP} = a]_{IP}$
    b. Prosodic struture: yi $((\text{tai-k'ai})_\varphi$ tsau$)_\varphi$ Match (XP; φ)
        he   probably   go   ASP
        'He has probably left.'

As far as the tone group is concerned, the AvP used to modify the VP differs from that used to modify the sentence: (a) in (33) and (34) are syntactic structures, while (b) is a recursive prosodic structure, i.e., a phonological phrase. A syntactic phrase gets matched to a phonological phrase with its syntactic DP and IP being eliminated by the Match condition (XP; φ).

The data of Xiamen TS can only help define the right edge of phonological phrases, which means if a monosyllabic word keeps the form of its citation tone unchanged in TS, the right edge of this word will be the right edge of the phonological phrase. However, Xiamen TS cannot define the left edge of phonological phrases. While the Match theory requires that the phonological phrase and syntactic phrase correspond to each other on both right and left edges, it differs in essence from the other theories, such as the Wrap-Align theory and the Edge-based theory, in terms of defining phonological phrases. For instance, *yi yi-king tsau* is predicted by the Wrap-Align theory as (yi yi-king tsau)$_\varphi$, which is a phonological phrase, as seen in (31) $[[\text{yi}]_{DP} [[\text{yi-king}]_{AvP} = \text{tsau}]_{VP} = a]_{IP}$ 'he has already left.' But the same structure gets analyzed by the Match theory into two phonological phrases 'yi ((yi-king)$_\varphi$ tsau)$_\varphi$,' in (33), with one of them dominating the other, which is a recursive prosodic structure. And, moreover, the pronoun *yi* is not considered within the domain of any phonological phrases.

Thus, it can be seen, the domain of Xiamen TS is a phonological phrase, the defining of which needs to refer to the right edge of the syntactic phrase. To apply to Xiamen TS, the Wrap-Align theory needs to rank Wrap-XP before Align-R and to place restrictions on the types of XPs in the constraint of Wrap-XP. The Match theory faces the similar restriction in Xiamen on the XPs in its Match (XP; φ), and such XPs cannot be functional phrases, or an empty category, or the syntactic phrases embedded with the functional phrases.

It is true that Xiamen provides support to the proposal that the prosodic structure can be derived with reference only to one edge of the syntactic structure, thus leading to the Edge-based theory (Chen 1985, 1987; Selkirk 1986). The Wrap-Align theory under OT's framework, in fact, only furthers the idea of the Edge-based theory because both, in essence, claim that the defining of a phonological phrase needs to refer to only one edge (i.e., either right or left) of the syntactic phrase with different languages choosing different parameters to define their phonological phrases.

However, Xiamen TS can help only with defining the right edge of the phonological phrase, not the left. Since the Match theory requires that phonological phrase and syntactic phrase correspond to each on both right and left edges, it

34 *Functional relations in tone sandhi*

differs from the Wrap-Align theory and the Edge-based theory fundamentally with regard to the prediction of phonological phrases.

Moreover, as discussed in Section 2.2.5, whether TS should apply is not decided by the distinction between functional words and lexical words, but by the difference between empty and non-empty categories.

2.3 Asymmetry of functional relations in Fuzhou Chinese

Fuzhou Chinese is a northern Min dialect spoken in the northeastern part of Fujian, located in southern China. Fuzhou TS has also been thoroughly studied (Chan 1980, 1985; Wright 1983; Shih 1986; Hung 1987, 1990; Zhang 1992; Chan 1991; Li 2002). The most important work was done by Chan (1985), who has not only provided us with a wealth of data but also applied the non-linear approach to the analysis of citation tone, sandhi tone, stress, tonal domain condition, and vowel quality changes in Fuzhou. As for the tonal domain in question here, Chan has proposed a hypothesis according to which the syntactic head of phrase structure is a key to tonal domains, and based on that, Hung (1987) has raised the hypothesis from the view of functional relations. So the following two sections are dedicated to discussing the works done by Chan (1985) and Hung (1987).

2.3.1 Fuzhou tonotactic background

Based on the work of both Chan (1985) and Hung (1987), Fuzhou has seven CTs, as seen in (35).[7]

(35) The citation tones in Fuzhou
      a. 44 b. 52 c. 31 d. 213 e. 242 f. 23 g. 4

Fuzhou TS is quite complicated. As pointed out by Chan (1985) and Hung (1987), what determines the TS domain includes not only phonological conditions but also syntactic and prosodic conditions. But generally speaking, under certain circumstances, a syllable, if followed by another syllable, will have its tone changed from a citation tone into a sandhi tone. The disyllabic TS patterns can be summarized as seen in the following table.

(36) The sandhi tones of disyllables in Fuzhou

2nd syll. TS of 1st syll. 1st syll.	44	52	31	213	242	23	4
44, 213, 242	44	44	44	52	52	52	44
31, 23	31	31	45	44	44	44	31
52, 4	44	31	31	31	31	31	31

Functional relations in tone sandhi   35

In the cases of tri-syllabic TS and polysyllabic TS, the antepenultimate syllable and all preceding syllables (if any) change into the [31] sandhi tone. However, if the penultimate syllable is an original [52] or [4] tone, the antepenultimate syllable undergoes TS by virtue of the patterns given in (36) but triggered by the sandhi tone, instead of the citation tone, of the penultimate syllable. Roughly speaking, the Fuzhou TS rule can be stated as follows in (37).[8]

(37) Fuzhou TS rule

$$T \rightarrow T' / \_\_ T \,]\alpha$$

2.3.2 Tonal domain condition in Fuzhou

Now let us discuss the conditions that determine the domain of Fuzhou TS. In Fuzhou, TS seems to be sensitive to the direction of branching structure. Let us consider the following examples first.

(38)

[sie [kie - loung]]
eat   egg
'to eat eggs'

BT	4	44	242
TS ok	31 =	52	242

(39)

[[ing - ngai] k'ang]
should   see
'to ought to see'

BT	213	44	213
TS *	31	44 =	213
ok	44	44 #	213

Example (38) is a right-branching structure in which the TS rule applies between a monosyllable and an immediate constituent (IC). Example (39) is a left-branching structure with the TS rule blocked between a monosyllable and an IC. Thus the distinction between right/left branching in Fuzhou TS can be shown as follows in (40).

36 *Functional relations in tone sandhi*

(40) Right-branching Structure

[X = [X - X]]

(41) Left-branching Structure

[[X - X] # X]

With (40) and (41), we may assume that the domain of Fuzhou TS is a syntactic domain – namely, a c-command domain as defined by Reinhart (1981) – as shown in (42).

(42) TS domain in Fuzhou (preliminary)
   Given linearly ordered *a-b*, TS rule is applied right to left iff *a* c-commands *b*.

Hypothesis (42) provides an explanation for the difference between (40) and (41). That is because in (40), since the third syllable is c-commanded by the second one, which is c-commanded by the first, all of the three syllables belong to one TS domain. But in (41), since the second syllable does not c-command the third one, and only the first syllable c-commands the second one, there is only one TS domain formed by the first and second syllable. But hypothesis (42) fails in examples such as (43), which follows.

(43)

```
         [ keing   [ loey   zuo ] ]
           tall      six    foot
         'to be as tall as six feet'
BT        52         4      213
─────────────────────────────────
TS  *     31    =   31     213
    ok    52    #   31     213
```

As seen in (43), although the first syllable *keing* 'tall' also c-commands its following syllables, the TS rule must still be blocked, otherwise an ungrammatical output form will be produced. Comparing (43) with the previously mentioned (38) and (39), we may propose another hypothesis from the viewpoint of functional relations as follows in (44).

(44) Argument/adjunct dichotomy hypothesis
   The TS rule is applied to argument structure, but blocked in adjunct structure.

Since (38) is an argument structure, the TS rule is applied between its head and argument. As for (39) and (43), they are both adjunct structures, so the TS rule must be blocked between a monosyllable and an IC. But the hypothesis of argument versus adjunct in (44) cannot account for all of the Fuzhou data. In fact, we have some counterevidence to (44) in (45) and (46), which follow.

(45) a.

[zy [tsing ngui]]
book very expensive
'The book is very expensive.'

BT   44   242   213
─────────────────────────────
TS *   31 =   52   213
    ok   44 #   52   213

b.

[[suong-seing] nguai]
believe   me
'Believe me.'

BT   44   213   31
─────────────────────────────
TS   *   31   31   = 31
     ok   52   213 # 31

(46) a.

[kuo [lo - riq]]
too   honest
'too honest'

BT   213   31   4
─────────────────────────────
TS   *   213 # 31   4
     ok   31   = 31   4

b.

[[hi - ki] piu]
plane   ticket
'the air ticket'

BT   44   44   31
─────────────────────────────
TS   *   31   44 # 31
     ok   31   52 = 31

38   *Functional relations in tone sandhi*

Both (45a) and (45b) are argument structures to which the TS rule must be blocked instead of being applied as in (38). On the contrary, both (46a) and (46b) are adjunct structures to which the TS rule must be applied instead of being blocked as in (40) and (43). However, attention should be paid especially to cases (45a) and (46b). In (45a), the first syllable *zy* 'book' c-commands its following element *tsing* 'very,' but the TS rule is still blocked, while in (46b), neither the first nor the second syllable c-commands the third syllable, but the TS rule is applied between the second and third syllable. Thus it can be seen that to explain the complicated Fuzhou TS, we cannot rely wholly on syntax nor depend completely on functional relations. In fact, to ascertain the domain of Fuzhou TS, we need to take into consideration both functional categories and syntactic conditions. As far as the former is concerned, TS is sensitive to position between functional relations. In Fuzhou, the behaviors of argument and adjunct in TS is not a simple symmetrical phenomenon, as seen in (47), but a complicated asymmetrical phenomenon, as generalized by Chen (1990) and represented here in (48).

(47) a.   argument =/# head
      b.   adjunct #/= head
      c.   head =/# argument
      d.   head #/= adjunct

(48) a.   argument # head
      b.   adjunct = head
      c.   head = argument
      d.   head # adjunct

Previously mentioned (45a) is an example for case (48a), (46a) for case (48b), (38) for case (48c), and (43) for case (48d). All of these examples are tri-syllabic TS. The following represented in (49) are disyllabic TS examples.

(49) a. (for case (48a))

		i		ts'iu
		he		laugh
		'He laughs.'		
		argument		head
	BT	44		213
	TS	44	#	213

     b. (for case (48b))

		ia		ui
		very		expensive
		'very expensive'		
		adjunct		head
	BT	31		213
	TS	44	=	213

Functional relations in tone sandhi 39

c. (for case (48c))

	sie	puong
	eat	rice
	'to eat rice'	
	head	argument
BT	4	242

TS	31	=	242

d. (for case (48d))

	p'aq	p'uai
	hit	break
	'to break'	
	head	adjunct
BT	23	213

TS	23	#	213

Fuzhou TS is not only sensitive to the position between functional categories but also to syntactic branching structure. In a syllable that bears the functional relation shown in (48b) and (48c), only a right-branching structure will form a TS domain, as proved by case (38) and (46a), while a left-branching structure will turn out to have two domains, as proved by case (39) and (45b). As for (46b), why is it also one TS domain? That is because *hi-ki-piu* 'plane ticket' in Chinese is a lexical item instead of a phrase, and this can be tested by inserting a grammatical marker *de* 'of' between *hi-ki* and *piu*. In Fuzhou, all of the lexical items should be affected by the TS rule, no matter what kind of functional relations or syntactic conditions they possess. Therefore, although *hi-ki-piu* is a left-branching structure, it still belongs to one TS domain, simply because it is a lexical item. Thus it can be seen that, apart from functional relations and syntactic conditions, a *lexical integrity principle* also influences the formation of Fuzhou TS domains. In accordance with the complicated TS phenomena in Fuzhou, Hung (1987) proposes the principles shown in (50)–(53).

(50) Prosodic constraint on Fuzhou external TS (Hung 1987)
The constituent(s) of a tone group to the left of a determinant are monosyllabic.

(51) Fuzhou TS domains (Hung 1987)
XP [. . . tg [(M *) X (A)] tg (M)] XP

(where M stands for modifier, A for argument, XP for maximal projection of X (a lexical head), tg for tone group, () for optional, and * for any arbitrary number)

(52) Fuzhou foot formation rules (Hung 1987)

a. Link the syllables in polysyllabic lexical items into freely structured feet

40   *Functional relations in tone sandhi*

    b. Scanning from left to right, link heads to their arguments to form disyllabic or right-branching feet

    c. Scanning from left to right, link modifiers to their heads to form disyllabic or right-branching feet

(53) Lexical integrity principle (Hung 1987)
Lexical integrity takes precedence over other syntactic relationships.

The aforementioned principles basically cover all of the previously mentioned TS phenomena and insightfully analyze Fuzhou TS data in view of the distinction between argument and adjunct. Although in his analysis Hung already notices the difference between right/left-branching structures, he takes it as a prosodic constraint without giving any explanation for the existence of such a constraint. In my opinion, this is not a prosodic stipulation, but a syntactic condition, i.e., a c-command condition. In Fuzhou TS, the c-command relations affect functional categories (defined by Reinhart (1981)). According to my reanalysis of Fuzhou TS, Fuzhou does not need such a complicated description or so many principles as in (50)–(53). Instead, Fuzhou TS can be simply divided into two types: one is lexical TS, whose rule is shown in (54), and the other is phrasal TS, whose rule is given in (55).

(54) Lexical TS (LTS) rule
$$\text{T} \ \rightarrow \ \text{T'} / \ \underline{\quad} \ \text{T} \ ]_{\searrow \circ}$$

(55) Phrasal TS (PTS) rule
$$\text{T} \ \rightarrow \ \text{T'} / \ \underline{\quad} \ \text{T} \ ]_{\searrow P}$$

The domain formation of lexical TS (LTS) and phrasal TS (PTS) can be simply stated as (56) and (57), respectively.

(56) LTS domain formation
The LTS rule is applied iteratively right to left to lexical items.

(57) PTS domain formation
The PTS rule is applied iteratively right to left to the syllable that is either the adjunct or the head of an argument when the syllable c-commands a following syllable.

As for LTS, there is no necessity for any further discussion because the lexicon is sensitive only to the phonological environment. As for PTS, it is much more complicated by requiring consideration of such factors as phonological environment, functional categories, and the c-command condition, as well as the direction of rule application. Now, let us reanalyze the data mentioned previously with the application of (57).

Functional relations in tone sandhi 41

Let us start with disyllabic TS, where we do not have to take the c-command condition into consideration. The disyllabic example, i.e., *i* 'he' and *ts'iu* 'laugh,' in (49a) is an argument-head structure. According to (57), the PTS rule is applied only to the head of an argument. But the head, *ts'iu* 'laugh,' in (49a) is in the final position, and according to rule (55), the underlying tone of the final syllable should be kept in TS. So (49a) obviously does not conform to the phonological environment of TS, and as a result, both the argument and head remain unchanged in TS. The example in (49b) is an adjunct-head structure. According to (57), the PTS rule is applied to the adjunct of a head. Since the adjunct, *ia* 'very,' in (49b) is in the initial position, conforming to the phonological environment of rule (55), this adjunct has a sandhi tone. As for example (49c), it is a head-argument structure with its head, *sie* 'eat,' as the target to which the sandhi tone is assigned, thus conforming to the phonological environment required for the application of the PTS rule, so it receives a sandhi tone. The TS rule application in (49d) is somewhat similar to that in (49a), although (49d) is a head-adjunct structure. In (49d), the adjunct, *p'uai* 'break,' is the target for the assignment of a sandhi tone, but the position that it occupies does not conform to the phonological environment set by rule (55). As a result, the PTS rule cannot work in this case, and so the underlying tone is kept.

Now let us turn to tri-syllabic TS, starting with example (45a). According to (57), rule (55) is applied iteratively right to left. So in (45a), the first XP, i.e., *tsing* 'very' and *ngui* 'expensive,' which c-command each other, is an adjunct-head structure for the TS rule, and on the analogy of our analysis of case (49b), the adjunct *tsing* 'very' here obtains a sandhi tone. Moreover, since the first syllable *zy* 'book' in (45a) c-commands its following syllable *tsing* 'very,' the TS rule continues its iterative application right to left. Since at the second step of rule application *zy* 'book' is an argument of *tsing ngui* 'very expensive,' and also since an argument can never get a sandhi tone according to (57), *zy* 'book' in (45a) keeps its underlying tone by analogy with our analysis of case (49a), as repeated in (58).

(58) = (45a)

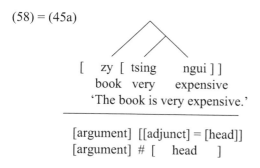

[zy [tsing   ngui]]
 book very   expensive
   'The book is very expensive.'

[argument] [[adjunct] = [head]]
[argument] # [head   ]

As for example (45b), since the final syllable *nguai* 'me' is not c-commanded by the penultimate *seing* 'believe,' the TS rule cannot be applied between the last two syllables, although the structure between *suong-seing* and *nguai* in (45b) is a head-argument structure, as repeated in (59).

42 *Functional relations in tone sandhi*

(59) = (45b)

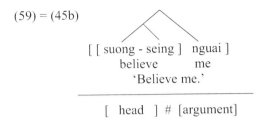

[[suong - seing] nguai]
believe   me
'Believe me.'

[head] # [argument]

Now let us consider example (46a). The last two syllables of (46a), i.e., *lo-riq* 'honest,' form a lexical item, thus causing the application of the LTS rule (54). And also because the first syllable *kuo* 'too' in (46a) c-commands the following syllables *lo-riq* and it is an adjunct-head structure, the adjunct *kuo* in (46a) gets its sandhi tone by analogy with our analysis of (49b), as repeated in (60).

(60) = (46a)

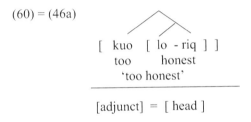

[kuo   [lo - riq]]
 too   honest
'too honest'

[adjunct] = [head]

As for example (46b), it is a lexical item, so it can be treated by the LTS rule in (54). Now let us go back to example (38). The last two syllables, i.e., *kie-loung* 'egg,' in (38) form one lexical item, so the LTS rule should be applied. And because the first syllable *sie* 'eat' in (38) c-commands its following syllables and also because the structure formed by *sie* and *kie-loung* is a head-argument structure, the head *sie* 'eat' obtains a sandhi tone in accordance with (57), as repeated in (61).

(61) = (38)

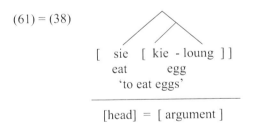

[sie   [kie - loung]]
 eat   egg
'to eat eggs'

[head] = [argument]

As for example (39), since the final syllable *k'ang* 'see' is not c-commanded by the penultimate syllable *ngai*, the TS rule is blocked between the adjunct *ing-ngai* 'should' and the head *k'ang* 'see,' although it is an adjunct-head structure, as repeated in (62).

(62) = (39)

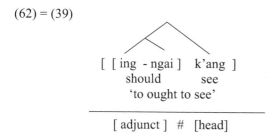

[[ing - ngai] k'ang]
   should   see
'to ought to see'

[adjunct] # [head]

Finally, let us take a look at example (43). In (43), the structure at the first step of rule application is an adjunct-head structure, so the adjunct *loey* 'six' gets sandhi tone by (57). The structure at the second step of rule application is a head-adjunct structure. With such functional relations, the head *keing* 'tall' must keep its underlying tone in spite of the fact that the first syllable in (43) c-commands its following element, as repeated in (63).

(63) = (43)

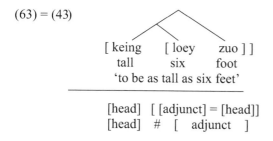

[keing [loey   zuo]]
   tall   six   foot
'to be as tall as six feet'

[head] [[adjunct] = [head]]
[head]   #   [adjunct   ]

Up till now, I have proved that the c-command condition is needed in Fuzhou TS, and I have also proved that the principle proposed in (57) can account for all of the Fuzhou TS. It should be pointed out that Fuzhou TS shows us that functional relations with the head play an important role, and Fuzhou is a typical case in which a syntactic process is effective within a functional domain.

2.3.3 On the hypothesis of head/non-head relations

2.3.3.1 Chan's head dominance condition

Apart from the influence of adjunct/argument structure, the head/non-head relation has also drawn attention in Chinese TS studies. And Chan (1980) is the first to try to relate TS directly to the function of syntactic head. For instance, when Chan analyzes Fuzhou dialect, she considers the head a key to explaining TS phenomena. According to Chan, Chinese phrase structure is typically head-final, and in Fuzhou, the head typically coincides with the last dominant syllable of a tone group. So she postulates for Fuzhou TS a principle called the head dominance condition as follows in (64).

44 *Functional relations in tone sandhi*

(64) Head dominance condition (Chan 1980)
Let 'y' be a monosyllabic word immediately dominated by a preterminal category symbol 'Y,' and let 'Y' be the head of 'X.' Daughters of 'Z' are within the TS domain of 'y' iff 'Z' is the first node to the left of 'Y' and the daughters of 'Z' are monosyllabic words.

The examples in (65) show us how the principle in (64) works.

(65)

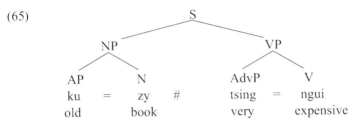

'Old books are very expensive.'

'Book' and 'expensive' are the heads of NP and VP, respectively, while 'old' and 'very' are monosyllabic words dominated by the first nodes under NP and VP to the left of their respective heads, hence the TS rule applies between 'old' and 'book,' as well as between 'very' and 'expensive.' On the other hand, the TS rule is blocked between 'book' and 'very' because 'very' is not the head of a phrasal node dominating both words.

But as pointed out by Hung (1987), the principle in (64) cannot explain the fact that the TS rule applies between verbs and their objects, with verbs being heads of VPs and objects being to their right, which is a counterexample of the head dominance condition proposed by Chan.

2.3.3.2 Non-head stress hypothesis

After Chan (1980), Duanmu (1990) cross-linguistically furthers the discussion of the head's influence on phonology and proposes a hypothesis that is called non-head stress (NHS), whereby in a syntactic head/non-head relation, the stress is assigned to the non-head.[9] According to Duanmu, the relation between head and non-head can be defined as follows in (66).

(66) In X^{n+1} Y is the non-head and X^n is the head.
      /\
     Y X^n (Y = any projection)

By his definition in (66), the head need not be an X° but could be any projection of X, and non-head covers what may be called modifier, complement, etc. Moreover, definition (66) does not distinguish adjunct versus argument non-heads. The NHS proposed by Duanmu is shown in (67).

(67) Non-head stress rule
In a head/non-head structure, stress the non-head.

Functional relations in tone sandhi   45

Having applied (66) and (67), respectively, to Chengdu Chinese and Shanghai Chinese, Duanmu concludes that NHS is an effective hypothesis for almost all of the Chinese dialects.

However, Duanmu's stress hypothesis will meet some difficulty in explaining the TS of Chinese dialects if it only relies on a single parameter such as a syntactic head. As mentioned earlier, Hung (1987) has correctly pointed out that Chan's (1980) inevitable problems in her analysis of Fuzhou TS result from the fact that she attaches importance only to the influence of the head. In the following, I am going to discuss some problems in the analysis by Duanmu (1990, 2000a, 2007).

Chengdu dialect is the chief evidence that Duanmu has employed to support his NHS hypothesis. According to Duanmu's analysis, in Chengdu TS, the stress pattern for a modifier-head (MH) structure, i.e., an adjunct-head relation, is *S-s*,[10] as shown in (68), and the stress pattern for the verb-object (VO) structure, i.e., a head-argument relation, is *s-S*, as seen in (69).

(68) a. niu   nai
          cow   milk
          'cow's milk'
          _____
          S - s   Stress pattern

      b. ji   dan
          chicken egg
          'egg'
          _____
          S - s   Stress pattern

      c. hong shao
          red   cook
          'to cook with brown sauce'
          _____
          S - s   Stress pattern

      d. shen   lu
          dark   green
          'dark green'
          _____
          S - s   Stress pattern

(69) a. chao   fan
          fry   rice
          'to fry rice'
          _____
          s - S   Stress pattern

      b. pao   cai
          pickle vegetable
          'to pickle vegetable'
          _____
          s - S   Stress pattern

46 *Functional relations in tone sandhi*

Both (68a)–(68b) are adnominal MH, while (68c)–(68d) are both adverbial MH, and all of them have the same stress pattern: *S-s*. Both (69a)–(69b) are VO structures with the same stress pattern: *s-S*. In MH, the modifier is the stress syllable, but in VO, the object is the stress syllable. Neither in MH nor in VO will the stress be assigned to the head syllable. Therefore, Duanmu concludes that in Chengdu, the non-head is stressed. However, the Chengdu data provided by Duanmu are not sufficient for the discussion of the NHS hypothesis because he has only discussed the MH and VO cases without providing us with the data for some other important structures such as subject-predicate (SP) structure, i.e., an argument-head relation and verb-resultative (VR) structure, i.e., a head-adjunct relation. If the hypothesis in (67) is correct, the expected results will be as follows in (70).

(70) a.   S-s type: MH and SP
     b.   s-S type: VO and VR

As a matter of fact, the classification in (70) is unusual in most Chinese dialects. The TS of SP is sometimes grouped with that of VO instead of MH, as seen in Wu dialects, and sometimes not. In the latter case, the TS of VO is often classified with that of MH, while the TS of SP is classified with the other group, as seen in Min dialects. It rarely occurs that MH is grouped with SP instead of VO, while SP and VO belong to different groups. Furthermore, the Shanghai dialect, which Duanmu has employed as the supporting evidence for his hypothesis, turns out to be just the opposite and serves as the counterevidence to his own hypothesis, which is unfolded in the next section.

2.3.3.3 Counterevidence from Shanghai Chinese

It is well-known that there are two types of TS in Shanghai dialect: one is called *guang-yong shi bian-diao* 'TS in broad used form,' and the other is called *zhai-yong shi bian-diao* 'TS in narrow used form.'[11] For convenience's sake, let us name the former 'TS type G' (TS-G) and call the latter 'TS type Z' (TS-Z).[12] Generally speaking, the difference in tonal representation between them lies in the fact that TS-G is a spreading case, while TS-Z is a case of direct mapping. Roughly speaking, the sandhi tone form for the whole domain of TS-G results from the tone spreading left to right from the first syllable, thus leading many Wu linguists to regard such TS as left-prominent type, which is indicated by T-t. As for TS-Z, the last syllable keeps its underlying tone, while the preceding syllable changes by dropping the latter half of its base tone. As a result, the original contour tone changes into a level tone, thus causing some linguists to take such TS as a right-prominent type, indicated by t-T. Now let us see how various different structures are classified in the Shanghai dialect.

In Shanghai, the TS behavior of structures such as SP, as seen in (71); VO, as seen in (72); and adverbial MH, as seen in (73) belong to the TS-Z (i.e., t-T) type. And all of the adnominal MH structures belong to the TS-G type (i.e., T-t), as seen in (74).[13]

(71) SP structure

a.

		ming	da
		life	big
		'(You) are lucky.'	
	BT	LM	LM
	TS-Z	L	LM
	pattern	t -	T

b.

		tian	leng
		sky	cold
		'It is cold.'	
	BT	HM	LM
	TS-Z	H	LM
	pattern	t -	T

(72) VO structure

a.

		ban	shu
		move	book
		'to move books'	
	BT	HM	HM
	TS-Z	H	HM
	pattern	t -	T

b.

		suo	men
		lock	door
		'to lock the door'	
	BT	MH	LM
	TS-Z	M	LM
	pattern	t -	T

(73) Adverbial MH structure

a.

		lao	du
		very	big
		'very big'	
	BT	LM	LM
	TS-Z	L	LM
	pattern	t -	T

48 *Functional relations in tone sandhi*

b.

	ji	huai
	extremely	bad
	'very bad'	
BT	LMq	LM
TS-Z	L	LM
pattern	t -	T

(74) Adnominal MH structure

a.

	da	shu
	big	tree
	'big trees'	
BT	LM	LM
TS-G	L	M
pattern	T -	t

b.

	xiao	yu
	small	rain
	'light rain'	
BT	MH	LM
TS-G	M	H
pattern	T -	t

c.

	san	yu
	mountain	taro
	'Sweet potato'	
BT	HM	LM
TS-G	H	M
pattern	T -	t

d.

	kuai	xin
	fast	letter
	'express mail'	
BT	MH	MH
TS-G	M	H
pattern	T -	t

Syntactically, SP is a head-final structure, VO is a head-initial structure, and MH is a head-final structure. If the NHS hypothesis in (67) is correct, SP should

Functional relations in tone sandhi 49

be grouped with MH, while VO should be classified all by itself as the other group. But as shown earlier, SP is grouped with VO and, moreover, although both adverbial MH and adnominal MH are head-final, the former is grouped with SP and VO (i.e., TS-Z), while the latter forms its own group belonging to TS-G. Counterevidence for the NHS hypothesis can be found even in the data used by Duanmu himself. For instance, since both *chi bao* 'to eat till full' and *da lan* 'to hit (sth.) broken' are both head-initial structures, the stress (or prominent tone) is assigned to *bao* and *lan*, which are both non-head, respectively (Duanmu 1990: 180). However, both *chi le* 'ate' and *lai guo* 'came' are also head-initial structures, so the stress, in accordance with the NHS hypothesis, should be assigned to *le* and *guo*, but the stress is assigned to *chi* and *lai*, which are both heads. Thus it can be seen that the Shanghai dialect cannot serve as the supporting evidence for the NHS hypothesis; instead, it works as counterevidence.

2.3.3.4 Further argumentation from other Wu dialects

The fact that SP and VO in the Shanghai dialect have the same TS behavior refutes the hypothesis that claims that TS is only sensitive to head/non-head relations. And based upon this, we may wonder whether Shanghai TS is sensitive to functional structures. We may suppose that SP and VO have the same TS behavior because they are both argument structures, although they have different head/non-head relations. This supposition seems to get us somewhere. SP and VO have the same TS behavior in most of the Wu dialects such as Chongming (Zhang 1988), Huinan (Z. Chen 1987), Xinzhuang, and Wenzhou. But this hypothesis concerning the pure functional relations of TS is, anyway, not the key to dealing with the TS of Wu dialects, although SP and VO are classified together in Wu TS. In Shanghai, as seen in (73) and (74), not only do the TS of SP and VO belong to the same group (TS-Z) but also the TS of adverbial MH (MHa)[14] joins in the same group with that of SP and VO instead of adnominal MH (MHb), which goes to the other group (TS-G), although MHa and MHb share the same adjunct-head functional relation. So it is hard to believe that it is pure functional relations that cause SP, VO, and MHa to go to the same TS group. SP, VO, and MHa versus MHb is not only seen in Shanghai; as a matter of fact, it is commonly seen in other Wu dialects mentioned earlier. In Wu dialects, TS can be divided into three types: a) lexical TS (hereafter LTS), b) clitic TS (hereafter CTS), and c) phrasal TS (hereafter PTS).[15] Roughly speaking, lexical items belong to LTS, where one content word plus a functional element forms a CG that belongs to CTS, and a phrase, unique in its style, belongs to PTS. Comparatively speaking, PTS is much more complicated than the other two types of TS because not all of the syntactic phrases will undergo PTS. For example, in many Wu dialects, such phrases as SP, VO, and MHa will undergo PTS, while the phrases of adnominal MH will be subject to LTS. The following examples are Chongming (75), Huinan (76), Xinzhuang (77), and Wenzhou (78), respectively.

50 *Functional relations in tone sandhi*

(75) Chongming dialect (Zhang 1988)

a. PTS case

SP		shu	da	
		tree	big	
		'The tree is big.'		
	BT	MLM	MLM	
	*	MLM	H	by LTS
	ok	L	MLM	by PTS
		jiao	chang	
		foot	long	
		'The legs are long.'		
	BT	Hq	LM	
	*	H	H	by LTS
	ok	H	LM	by PTS
VO		kan	gao	
		read	draft	
		'to read a draft'		
	BT	M	HMH	
	*	M	n	by LTS
	ok	M	HMH	by PTS
		sha	gou	
		kill	dog	
		'to kill a dog'		
	BT	Hq	HMH	
	*	H	M	by LTS
	ok	H	HMH	by PTS
MHa		zai	nao	
		again	stir up trouble	
		'to stir up trouble again'		
	BT	M	MLM	
	*	M	n	by LTS
	ok	M	MLM	by PTS
		zhen	mang	
		real	busy	
		'really busy'		
	BT	H	LM	
	*	H	H	by LTS
	ok	H	LM	by PTS

Functional relations in tone sandhi 51

b. LTS case

MHb

		xiao	niu	
		small	ox	
		'calf'		
BT		HMH	LM	
ok		HMH	H	by LTS
*		M	LM	by PTS

		hao	ma	
		good	horse	
		'good horse'		
BT		HMH	LML	
ok		HMH	M	by LTS
*		M	LML	by PTS

		hong	shu	
		red	tree	
		'red tree'		
BT		LM	MLM	
ok		LM	n	by LTS
*		L	MLM	by PTS

		lao	dian	
		old	store	
		'old store'		
BT		LML	M	
ok		LML	n	by LTS
*		L	M	by PTS

(76) Huinan dialect (Z. Chen 1987)

a. PTS case
SP

		tian	qing	
		sky	clear	
		'The sky is clear.'		
BT		HM	MLM	
*		H	HM	by LTS
ok		H	MLM	by PTS

		shou	chang	
		hand	long	
		'The hands are long.'		
BT		H	MLM	
*		MH	HM	by LTS
ok		H	MLM	by PTS

52 *Functional relations in tone sandhi*

VO

		bu	tong	
		mend	bucket	
		'to mend bucket'		
	BT	H	MLM	
	*	MH	HM	by LTS
	ok	H	MLM	by PTS

		yang	xiang	
		raise	elephant	
		'to raise elephants'		
	BT	MLM	LM	
	*	ML	MH	by LTS
	ok	L	LM	by PTS

MHa

		kuai	fang	
		quickly	set off	
		'to set off quickly'		
	BT	MH	MH	
	*	H	H	by LTS
	ok	M	MH	by PTS

		lao	bian	
		often	change	
		'to be changing all the time'		
	BT	MLM	MH	
	*	ML	MH	by LTS
	ok	L	MH	by PTS

b. LTS case
MHb

		xiao	mi	
		small	rice	
		'millet'		
	BT	H	MLM	
	ok	MH	ML	by LTS
	*	H	MLM	by PTS

		leng	han	
		cold	sweat	
		'cold sweat'		
	BT	MLM	LM	
	ok	ML	MH	by LTS
	*	L	LM	by PTS

Functional relations in tone sandhi   53

	ji	mu	
	step	mother	
	'stepmother'		
BT	MH	MLM	
ok	H	H	by LTS
*	M	MLM	by PTS

	nei	di	
	inner	brother	
	'brother-in-law'		
BT	LM	LM	
ok	ML	MH	by LTS
*	L	LM	by PTS

(77) Xinzhuang dialect (Zhang 1986)

a. PTS case

SP

	shui	shao	
	water	little	
	'The water is little.'		
BT	H	H	
*	MH	ML	by LTS
ok	H	H	by PTS

	gua	tian	
	melon	sweet	
	'The melon is sweet.'		
BT	HM	ML	
*	H	HM	by LTS
ok	H	ML	by PTS

VO

	jia	bei	
	add	blanket	
	'to add blanket'		
BT	HM	LM	
*	H	ML	by LTS
ok	H	LM	by PTS

	liu	yan	
	leave	message	
	'to leave message'		
BT	ML	ML	
*	LM	HM	by LTS
ok	L	ML	by PTS

54 *Functional relations in tone sandhi*

MHa

		sao	hou	
		a bit	thick	
		'a little bit thicker'		
	BT	H	LM	
*		H	ML	by LTS
ok		H	LM	by PTS
		gan	tou	
		dare	steal	
		'dare to steal'		
	BT	H	HM	
*		MH	ML	by LTS
ok		H	HM	by PTS

b. LTS case
MHb

		hong	tang	
		red	sugar	
		'brown sugar'		
	BT	ML	ML	
ok		LM	HM	by LTS
*		L	ML	by PTS
		huang	deng	
		yellow	lamp	
		'yellow lamp'		
	BT	ML	HM	
ok		LM	HM	by LTS
*		L	HM	by PTS
		jiu	shu	
		old	book	
		'old book'		
	BT	LM	HM	
ok		M	H	by LTS
*		L	HM	by PTS
		da	chuang	
		big	bed	
		'big bed'		
	BT	LM	ML	
ok		M	H	by LTS
*		L	ML	by PTS

(78) Wenzhou dialect (Pan 1989)

a. PTS case

SP

		tian	qing	
		sky	clear	
		'The sky is clear.'		
	BT	M	ML	
	*	L	L	by LTS
	ok	M	L	by PTS
		shou	leng	
		hand	cold	
		'The hands are cold.'		
	BT	MH	MH	
	*	HM	MH	by LTS
	ok	MH	MH	by PTS

VO

		da	qiu	
		beat	ball	
		'to play ball'		
	BT	MH	ML	
	*	HM	ML	by LTS
	ok	L	ML	by PTS
		ti	tou	
		shave	head	
		'to cut hair'		
	BT	HM	ML	
	*	L	L	by LTS
	ok	L	ML	by PTS

MHa

		kuai	zou	
		quickly	walk	
		'to walk quickly'		
	BT	HM	MH	
	*	HM	MH	by LTS
	ok	HM	L	by PTS
		hao	chi	
		good	eat	
		'to taste good'		
	BT	MH	Lq	
	*	HM	Lq	by LTS
	ok	MH	Lq	by PTS

56 *Functional relations in tone sandhi*

b. LTS case

MHb

		zhu pig 'pork'	rou meat	
BT		M	Lq	
ok		HM	Lq	by LTS
*		M	Lq	by PTS
		da big 'rice'	mi rice	
BT		L	MH	
ok		HM	MH	by LTS
*		L	L	by PTS
		xiao small 'small house'	wu house	
BT		MH	Lq	
ok		HM	Lq	by LTS
*		MH	Lq	by PTS
		hong red 'red paper'	zhi paper	
BT		ML	MH	
ok		HM	MH	by LTS
*		ML	L	by PTS

As seen from the earlier Wu dialects, SP, VO, and MHa have their TS behaviors grouped together, while the TS of MHb alone belongs to the other group. Although they both are phrases, the former reads PTS, while the latter reads LTS.[16] Thus it can be seen that it is neither only argument/adjunct nor only head that is responsible for such a classification. In a word, functional categories do not cast any influence on Wu TS. As for what causes such a TS classification in Wu dialects, it is something related to a syntactic condition with a functional relation.

2.4 Summary

Although it was quite long ago when Selkirk caught sight of the issue of how phonology is sensitive to the functional distinction between arguments and adjuncts

Functional relations in tone sandhi   57

(Selkirk 1984), Chan (1985), Chen (1985, 1987), and Hung (1987) have all discussed the role of functional relations in TS. Since the 1990s, such discussions have not made much progress in spite of OT becoming a fashion in the study of phonology. The aim of this chapter was to bring up the interests in and reassessment of the values of functional relations in the interface studies of syntax-phonology through the discussion of functional categories, such as adjunct, argument, and head, as well as what roles these relations play in the TS of some Chinese dialects such as Xiamen, Fuzhou, Wu, and Pingyao. The following chapters will continue this discussion with further observation and analysis of how phonology is sensitive to functional relations.

Notes

1 Here tone shapes are symbolized by a numerical notation, where five equals the highest and one equals the lowest on a five-point scale. The last two tones are restricted to 'checked' syllables, while the other five co-occur with 'free' syllables.
2 T stands for base tone, T' for sandhi tone, and α for sandhi domain.
3 For a detailed discussion of the distinction between VP-adjunct and sentential adjunct, see Tang (1990).
4 Here the symbol '#' stands for the boundary between tone groups (TG), and the TS rule is applied within TG but blocked across TG; the symbol '=' is used occasionally for highlighting the obligatory application of TS rule at certain junctions and the letter 'n' for neutral tone.
5 In (22), where $X°$ stands for zero or more occurrences of some maximal projection, X is called a zero-bar projection, X' a single-bar projection, and X" a double-bar (or maximal) projection.
6 This TG formation is suitable only to TS above the Xiamen phrasal level. As for the TS of pronoun or grammatical markers, they are different because they belong to the clitic group TS.
7 Both tone f and g are short and accompanied by a glottal stop ending.
8 This TS rule is applied iteratively from right to left.
9 In Chinese linguistics, some problems, such as whether there is word stress in Chinese and, if there is, what properties such stress possesses, still remain unsolved. In this section, I am not going to argue about the properties of stress in Chinese. Instead, for the sake of discussion, I simply adopt Duanmu's term because there is no direct connection between the property of suprasegmental elements and the conditions for forming phonological domains.
10 The capitalized S stands for main stress, and the small letter s for stresslessness. Here I only follow Duanmu in using the term *stress*. However, the stress pattern can be replaced by the tonal pattern with S-s taken as a left-prominent tone type, i.e., T-t, and s-S regarded as a right-prominent tone type, i.e., t-T. No matter which term is more acceptable, the result will be the same and will not affect the discussion of the conditions for TS domains.
11 These two terms are widely accepted by Wu Chinese linguists.
12 As a matter of fact, the difference between TS-G and TS-Z is that the former is lexical TS (LTS), while the latter is phrasal TS (PTS).
13 Here tone shapes are symbolized by a letter notation (where L = low, M = middle, H = high, LM = low rising, and so on). And, moreover, due to typographical considerations, the Pinyin system, instead of the IPA, is adopted here for transcription.
14 For convenience's sake, I term adverbial MH as MHa and adnominal MH as MHb hereafter.

58 *Functional relations in tone sandhi*

15 As for these three types of TS, the detailed discussions can be seen in Zhang (1988, 1989), Chen (1989, 1990), and Chen and Zhang (1990).

16 In the aforementioned Wu dialects, SP, VO, and MHa basically read PTS, some of which sometimes may read LTS, while some others may read both PTS and LTS. It should be noted, however, although some of SP, VO, and MHa may read LTS, MHb, in a normal unmarked situation, will never read PTS; instead, MHb always reads LTS. Therefore, MHb's TS behavior is indeed different from that of SP, VO, and MHa.

3 The c-command condition in phonology

3.1 Introduction

As covered in the previous discussion, the domain of TS rules in some dialects is found or determined by the c-command condition. In this chapter, a detailed analysis will be made of the important role played by the c-command notion in determining the domains, types, and modes of sandhi rule application in Chinese dialects.

Since Reinhart (1976, 1983) discussed in detail the notion of c-command, several different definitions concerning c-command have been proposed. Among them only two can be considered to be particularly influential: a) the preliminary definition given by Reinhart and b) the revised version proposed by Chomsky (1986a), shown, respectively, as follows in (1).

(1) a. Preliminary definition (Reinhart 1976, 1983)
    α c-commands β iff
    every branching node dominating α dominates β.

   b. Revised definition (Chomsky 1986a)
    α c-commands β iff
    every maximal projection dominating α dominates β.

To differentiate these two different c-command definitions, (1a) is generally called c-command while (1b) is termed m-command, as illustrated in (2).

(2)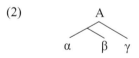

Suppose that structure A is a maximal projection, then by (1a), α only c-commands β and not γ, but γ c-commands both α and β. Yet by (1b), α m-commands both β and γ. It should be pointed out that almost all mentions of 'c-command' concerning current issues refer to the revised definition, i.e., m-command, thus, abandoning the original version. Therefore, in the Direct Reference Approach, the notion of c-command according to Kaisse (1985) is in fact the definition of m-command according to Chomsky. However, I will show that in many Chinese dialects, when TS is sensitive to c-command, this c-command is the c-command of the preliminary

60 *The c-command condition in phonology*

definition instead of the revised definition, i.e., m-command. The following sections will present evidence obtained from some Chinese dialects.

3.2 Danyang Chinese: Case study (1)

The first type of c-command refers to one that determines the domain of tonal spreading, and Danyang Chinese is just such a typical case. Some Chinese linguists have covered the tonal patterns of Danyang in their discussions (Chen 1986a; Chan 1989; Yip 1989; Bao 1990, 1999; Duanmu 1990, 1991; Zhang 1992, 1996). Here the discussion is confined to a simple analysis of particular relevant cases.

3.2.1 Spreading tones in Danyang

Spoken in the midsouth of Jiangsu province in east China, a place where Wu dialect and eastern Mandarin dialect intersect, Danyang possesses properties of both Wu dialect and Mandarin. Danyang has two different sets of citation tones found in literary and colloquial speech, respectively. The one in literary speech has four citation tones, as seen in (3), and the other in colloquial speech has six citation tones, as seen in (4) (Lü et al. 1980; Ting 1984).

(3)   The citation tones in Danyang literary speech

     a. M b. LH c. H d. Hq

(4)   The citation tones in Danyang colloquial speech

     a. M b. LH c. H d. L e. Mq f. Hq

    Danyang has two TS rules as shown in (5a) and (5b), where rule (5a) must be applied before rule (5b).

(5)   Danyang TS rules

    (5a). H → Ø / __ H
    (5b). H → Ø / __ LH #

    In Danyang Chinese, there are six spreading patterns derived from six base melodies (hereafter BM), as shown in (6).[1]

(6)   Spreading patterns in Danyang

	BM	Disyllable	Tri-syllable	Quadrisyllable
a.	H	H – H	H – H – H	H – H – H – H
b.	M	M – M	M – M – M	M – M – M – M
c.	L	L – L	L – L – L	L – L – L – L
d.	HL	HL – L	HL – L – L	HL – L – L – L
e.	LH	LH – H	LH – H – H	LH – H – H – H
f.	HLH	HL – LH	HL – HL – LH	HL – HL – HL – LH

The c-command condition in phonology 61

Descriptively, the polysyllabic tone patterns in (6) can be seen as being derived from the corresponding base melodies by left-to-right association and the spreading of the first tone, as illustrated by the derivations of the quadrisyllabic patterns in (6d) and (6f), as shown in (7).[2]

(7) a. Base melody: HL (=(6d))

  1) Association and spreading (left to right)

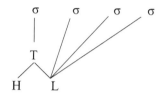

  2) Tier conflation

b. Base melody: HLH (=(6f))

  1) Association and spreading (left to right)

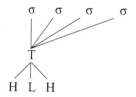

  2) Tier conflation

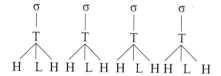

  3) Simplification
    i. HL HL HL HLH by rule (5a)
    ii. HL – HL – HL – LH by rule (5b)

3.2.2 *Patterns of the spreading domains*

It has been noticed that Danyang's spreading domain in right-branching structures differs from that in left-branching structures. The former is the whole phrase structure, as illustrated in (8a), while the latter covers only the first two syllables – namely, IC – as shown in (8b).

62 *The c-command condition in phonology*

(8) a.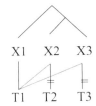

b.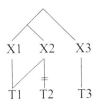

In (8a), the citation tones of X2 and X3 are deleted, but T1 is spread rightward to unlinked tone-bearing units. In (8b), only X2's citation tone is deleted, and T1 is spread only to X2, not to X3, which keeps its citation tone without any change. Some examples of such right-branching and left-branching structures are given in (9).[3]

(9) a.

b.

The c-command condition in phonology 63

Domain of rule application is an everlasting topic. According to the Indirect Reference Approach (Selkirk 1984, 1986), a TS domain is a prosodic domain determined by an edge condition, but according to the Direct Reference Approach (Kaisse 1985), it turns out to be an m-command domain (defined by Chomsky (1986a)). But how about the spreading domain of Danyang Chinese? Before discussing what actually determines the tonal domain of Danyang, let us first take a look at the patterns of Danyang's spreading domain. According to the data provided by Lü et al. (1980), I have summed up the patterns of the quadrisyllabic spreading domain of Danyang's unmarked reading at the phrasal level, as given (10).

(10) a.
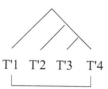

b.
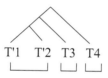

c.
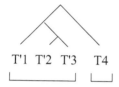

d.
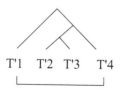

Found in (11) are the examples relevant to the patterns in (10).

(11) a.
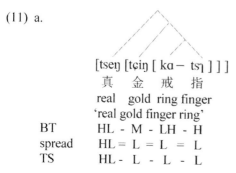

[tseŋ [tɕiŋ [kɑ – tsɿ]]]
真　金　戒　指
real　gold　ring　finger
'real gold finger ring'

BT　　　　HL - M - LH - H
spread　　HL = L = L = L
TS　　　　HL - L - L - L

64 *The c-command condition in phonology*

b.

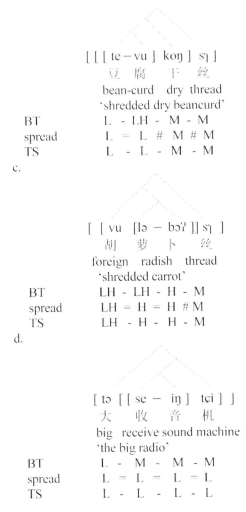

```
                    [ [ [ te – vu ] koŋ ] sղ ]
                        豆  腐    干    丝
                     bean-curd  dry  thread
                     'shredded dry beancurd'
BT                   L  -  LH  -  M  -  M
spread               L  =  L   #  M  #  M
TS                   L  -  L   -  M  -  M
```

c.

```
                    [ [ vu  [lə – bɔʔ ] ] sղ ]
                      胡    萝    卜      丝
                    foreign radish thread
                    'shredded carrot'
BT                  LH  -  LH  -  H  -  M
spread              LH  =  H   =  H  #  M
TS                  LH  -  H   -  H  -  M
```

d.

```
                    [ tɔ [ [ se – iŋ ] tɕi ] ]
                      大    收    音    机
                    big  receive sound machine
                    'the big radio'
BT                  L  -  M  -  M  -  M
spread              L  =  L  =  L  =  L
TS                  L  -  L  -  L  -  L
```

3.2.3 Hypotheses on condition of the spreading domains

3.2.3.1 Metrical condition

Now let us discuss the decisive factor for the Danyang spreading domain. With the metrical approach, Duanmu (1990, 1991) considers the spreading domain of Danyang to be a metrical domain, i.e., a stress domain, and thus proposes for the formation of the Danyang spreading domain such principles and rules as follows in (12).

(12) Stress principles in Danyang (Duanmu 1991)

   a.   Stress equalization convention (SEC)
        Assign left-headed stress cyclically, starting from every morpheme.

The c-command condition in phonology   65

b. Stress clash rule (SCR)
On each cycle, if the highest column of asterisks is adjacent to a lower column, remove the lower column.
c. Column lowering rule (CLR)
If a metrical domain has only one column of asterisks, delete all the asterisks except the top one.
d. Stress reduction rule (SRR)
When there is more than one line of asterisks, delete the bottom line (post-cyclic and optional).
e. Tonal domain formation (TDF)
The tonal domain starts from a stressed syllable and includes all stressless syllables to the right, until just before the next stressed syllable.

The principles and rules in (12) look insightful. However, when we apply these metrical principles to Danyang data, they do not work as expected. The following are the results of such a check on the patterns in (10) with the principles in (12).

(13) = (10a)
   a. By SEC in (12a)
```
( *                        )
( * )  ( *                 )
( * )  ( * )  ( *          )
[ T1 [ T2  [ T3  T4 ]]]
```

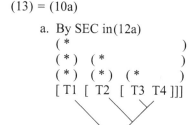

   b. By SCR in (12b)
```
( *                    )
( * )  (               )
( * )  (    ) (        )
 T1    T2    T3    T4
```

   c. By CLR in (12c)
```
( *                    )
 T1    T2    T3    T4
```

   d. By TDF in (12e)
```
       *
    T'1   T'2   T'3   T'4
    |_____|    (Correct output)
```

66 *The c-command condition in phonology*

(14) = (10b)

a. By SEC in (12a)

```
( *                    )
( *            ) ( * )
( *        ) (  *  ) ( * )
[[[ T1      T2 ]  T3 ]  T4 ]
```

b. By SRR in (12d)

```
( *                  )
( *            ) ( * )
  T1    T2    T3    T4
```

c. By TDF in (12e)

```
    *                 *
  T'1    T'2    T'3    T
  |_____| |___|      (Wrong output)
```

or a'. By SEC in (12a)

```
  ( *                    )
  ( *            ) ( * )
  ( *        ) ( * ) ( * )
  [[[ T1    T2 ]  T3 ]  T4 ]
```

b'. By TDF in (12e)

```
    *              *      *
  T'1      T'2    T3      T4
  |_____| |__| |__|      (Correct output)
```

(15) = (10c)

a. By SEC in (12a)

```
    ( *                    )
    ( *              ) ( * )
    ( * ) ( *        ) ( * )
    [[ T1  [ T2     T3 ]] T4 ]
```

The c-command condition in phonology   67

b. By SCR in (12b)

```
( *                   )
( *            ) ( * )
( * ) (        ) ( * )
 T1    T2    T3    T4
```

c. By SRR in (12d)

```
( *                   )
( *            ) ( * )
 T1    T2    T3    T4
```

d. By TDF in (12e)

```
  *                *
 T'1    T'2    T'3    T4
 |_____|  |__|      (Correct output)
```

(16) = (10d)

a. By SEC in (12a)

```
    ( *                   )
    ( * ) ( *             )
    ( * ) ( *        ) ( * )
    [ T1 [[ T2    T3 ]  T4 ]]
```

b. By SCR in (12b)

```
    ( *                   )
    ( * ) (               )
    ( * ) (          ) ( * )
     T1     T2    T3    T4
```

c. By TDF in (12e)

```
    *                *
   T'1    T'2    T'3    T4
   |_____|  |__|      (Wrong output)
```

or a'. By SEC in (12a)

```
    ( *                   )
    ( * ) ( *             )
    ( * ) ( *        ) ( * )
    [ T1 [[ T2    T3 ]  T4 ]]
```

68 *The c-command condition in phonology*

b'. By SCR in (12b)
```
(  *                              )
( * ) (                           )
( * ) (              ) ( * )
  T1    T2      T3      T4
```

c'. By SRR in (12d)
```
(  *                              )
( * ) (                           )
  T1    T2      T3      T4
```

d'. By CLR in (12c)
```
(  *                              )
  T1    T2      T3      T4
```

e'. By TDF in (12e)
```
   *
  T'1   T'2    T'3    T'4
  |_____|
```
                              (Correct output)

As we can see, the application of the principles in (12) will produce the correct output only from (10a) and (10c) as shown by (13) and (15), respectively, but both (10b) and (10d) are problematic. In (10b), SRR is not applied obligatorily, while in (10d), it is obligatorily applied. Otherwise, the wrong output will be produced for (10b) and (10d), as shown by (14) and (16), respectively. Therefore, the first flaw in metrical analysis is a mechanical problem. Second, the nature of stress is also a problem worthy of discussion. As a matter of fact, it is still an open question as to whether or not there is word stress in Chinese (Lin 1985; Zhang 2014; Ma 2015).[4] So far, we have got no experimental evidence which can prove that there is a word stress in Chinese besides the focus stress. Even among those phonologists who argue for the existence of stress in Chinese, their views are greatly divergent concerning problems such as the nature of stress and the way to determine stress. For instance, although Chan (1989, 1991) also claims that the TS domain of Danyang is a stress domain, she considers the right-branching case an initial-stress pattern and the left-branching case a final-stress pattern, as seen in (17).[5]

(17) a. Initial-stress pattern

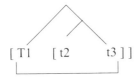

b. Final-stress pattern

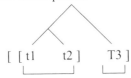

The c-command condition in phonology   69

According to Chan, since T1 in (17a) determines the tonal pattern of both t2 and t3, it is the stress locus of the whole structure, and since T3 in (17b) remains unaltered and reserves its original citation tone form, the stress will be T3. But, controversially, there will be two possibilities for the stress in (17b) in accordance with the stress principles in (12) proposed by Duanmu (1991). One is that if the SRR in (12d) is applied, (17b) will have only one domain with the stress placed on the first syllable, as seen in (18). But this is a wrong output. The other possibility is that SRR cannot apply because based on the stress principle in (12d) the application of SRR is optional. Thus (17b) has two domains with two stresses: one on the first syllable and the other on the third syllable, as seen in (19).

(18) One domain analysis

a. By SEC in (12a)

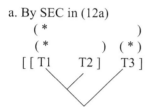

b. By SRR (optional) in (12d)
```
     ( *                     )
      T1     T2     T3
```

c. By TDF in (12e)
```
      *
     T'1    T'2    T'3
      └─────────────┘           (Wrong output)
```

(19) Two domain analysis

a. By SEC in (12a)

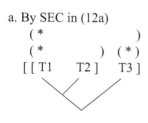

b. By TDF in (12e)
```
      *             *
     T'1    T'2    T3
      └──────┘      └──┘
```

It should be noted that both Chan and Duanmu claim that there is stress in Danyang and, accordingly, Danyang's TS domain is the stress domain. But according to Chan, the stress of the tri-syllabic left-branching structure is placed on the third syllable, as seen in (17b), while according to Duanmu, it is laid either on the first syllable, as seen in (18), or on both the first and the third syllable, as shown in (19). Thus it can be seen that the so-called stress is still a puzzle, which we, including those arguing for the existence of stress, are still unable to perceive and define precisely. Therefore, we cannot consider the stress analysis a reliable approach for Danyang TS.

3.2.3.2 C-command condition

As a matter of fact, the difference between different branching structures in Danyang TS is not that between different stress patterns, but a difference in tonal spreading domains. The so-called stress is actually a prominent tone. The tonal spreading domain of unmarked reading in Danyang Chinese is the domain defined in terms of c-command (as defined by Reinhart), and, accordingly, I propose the following principle.

(20) Spreading domain formation in Danyang

  α spreads rightward to β iff
  β is c-commanded by α

Now let us use the c-command approach, the principle proposed in (20), to reanalyze the examples in (11), repeated in (21) for convenience.

(21) a.

[X1 [X2 [X3 - X4]]]
[T1 = T2 = T3 = T4]
[c-command domain]

a'.   [tseŋ [tɕiŋ [kɑ − tsʅ]]]
       real gold ring finger
       'real gold finger ring'
BT   HL - M - LH - H
spread   HL = L = L = L
TS   HL - L - L - L

b.

[[[X1 - X2] X3] X4]
[T1 = T2 # T3 # T4]
c-command
  domain

b'. [[[te − vu] koŋ] sɿ]
        bean-curd   dry   thread
        'shredded dry beancurd'
BT   L - LH - M - M
spread   L = L   # M # M
TS   L - L   - M - M

c.

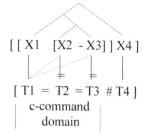

[[X1 [X2 - X3]] X4]

[T1 = T2 = T3 # T4]
     c-command
      domain

c'. [[vu [lə − bɔʔ]] sɿ]
        foreign radish   thread
        'shredded carrot'
BT   LH - LH - H - M
spread   LH = H   = H # M
TS   LH - H   - H - M

d.

[X1 [[X2 - X3] X4]]

[T1 = T2 = T3 = T4]
[c-command domain]

d'. [tə [[se − iŋ] tɕi]]
        big receive sound machine
        'the big radio'
BT   L - M - M - M
spread   L = L = L = L
TS   L - L - L - L

As shown in (21), the spreading domain of Danyang Chinese is a c-command domain as defined by Reinhart (1983). In (21a), X1 c-commands X2, X3, and X4, so the spreading domain is from T1 to T4. In (21b), X1 only c-commands X2, not X3 and X4, thus its spreading domain covers only T1 and T2. This conclusion is also borne out by (21c) and (21d). In (21c), X1 c-commands X2 and X3, not X4, so X1's spreading domain is from T1 to T3, not including T4. In (21d), X1 c-commands X2, X3, and X4, thus its spreading domain is from T1 to T4. Thus it can be seen that the TS domain of Danyang Chinese is a typical case of the c-command domain.

72 *The c-command condition in phonology*

3.3 Ruicheng Chinese: Case study (2)

The second type of c-command, supported by the evidence from Ruicheng Chinese, is the one that determines whether the TS rule is applied or blocked. In Ruicheng, there are two TS rules, as represented here in (22).

(22) Ruicheng TS rules

    a.   ML → LM / __ ML
    b.   HM → ML / __ HM

3.3.1 Condition of tonal domain in Ruicheng

Ruicheng seems identical to Danyang Chinese in the sense that it also has the whole phrase structure as the domain in its uniform right-branching structures and the ICs as the domain in its left-branching structures. However, it actually differs from Danyang in the fact that the TS of the former is a cyclic case, while the TS of the latter is a spreading case. As far as Ruicheng is concerned, the TS rule applies in every cycle of the right-branching structures, but only in the first cycle of its left-branching structures and never vice versa; otherwise, it will only produce the wrong output forms, as seen in (23).

(23) a.

$$[X1 \quad [X2 \quad [X3 \ - \ X4]]]$$
$$[T3 \ = \ T4]$$
$$[T2 = T3]$$
$$[T1 \ = \ T2]$$

———————

$$[T1 = T2 = T3 = T4]$$

a'.   [tɕʰy [ɕiɑu [tɕieĩ − pei]]]
             取   小   金   笔
             take small gold   pen
         'to take the small golden pen'

BT   HM - HM - ML - ML
(i)   [LM   ]
               [NA   ]
       [ML   ]

———————

ok   ML - HM - LM - ML (cycle)

━━━━━━━━━━━━━

(ii)   [LM   ]
           [blocked]
      [blocked]

———————

*   HM - HM - LM - ML (block)

The c-command condition in phonology   73

b.

```
           /\
          /  \
         /   /\
        /   /  \
[ [ [ X1  -  X2 ]  X3 ]  X4 ]
  [  T1  =  T2  ]
          [  T2  #  T3  ]
                  [  T3  #  T4  ]
_____
  [  T1  =  T2  #  T3  #  T4  ]
```

b'.   [[[kaŋ – tʰiɛ] tʂʰaŋ] ɕiɑu]
          钢   铁   厂   小
         steel   iron   works small
         'the steel and iron works is small'

BT   ML - ML - HM - HM
(i)   [LM   ]
              [NA   ]
                   [ML   ]
     _____
*   LM - ML - ML - HM (cycle)
     ============================
(ii)   [LM   ]
              [blocked]
                   [blocked]
     _____
ok   LM - ML - HM - HM (block)
```

c.

```
           /\
          /  \
         /\   \
        /  \   \
[ [ X1 [ X2  -  X3 ] ]  X4 ]
       [  T2  =  T3  ]
  [  T1  =  T2  ]
                 [  T3  #  T4  ]
_____
  [  T1  =  T2  =  T3  #  T4  ]
```

c'.   [[ɕiẽ [liŋ – tɑu]] xɑu]
          新   领   导   好
         new   leader   good
         'the new leader is good'

BT   ML - HM - HM - HM
(i)   [ML   ]
         [LM   ]
                   [ML   ]
     _____
*   LM - ML - ML - HM
     ============================
```

74 *The c-command condition in phonology*

(ii)

```
                      [ ML          ]
        [ LM          ]
                      [  blocked  ]
```
_____

ok   LM - ML - HM - HM

d.

```
[ X1 [ [  X2  -  X3  ]  X4 ]
       [  T2  -  T3  ]
              [  T3  #  T4  ]
[ T1  -   T2 ]
```
_____

```
[ T1  =  T2  -  T3  #  T4   ]
```

d′.   [ai [[tcʰiŋ − xai   ] ʂɔŋ]]
             挨   青   海   省
             be next to Qing-hai   province
             'to be next to Qing-hai Province'

BT   ML - ML - HM - HM
(i)   [NA   ]
                               [ML   ]
            [LM   ]
_____

*   LM - ML - ML - HM
_____

(ii)   [NA   ]
                               [blocked]
            [LM   ]
_____

ok   LM - ML - HM - HM

Comparing Danyang with Ruicheng, we see that these two dialects have in fact different sandhi domains. Danyang has a c-command domain as in the original definition, but Ruicheng seems not to. In (23a), since X3 and X4 c-command each other, they form the first cycle TS domain, but since X3 does not c-command X2, which does not c-command X1 in the following second and third cycles, while T3 and T2, as well as T2 and T1 form their own cycles, respectively, the TS domain in (23a) stretches from T1 to T4. So can we adopt the m-command hypothesis, as held by Kaisse, to account for the Ruicheng case? The answer is negative because in (23a), X1 and X2 still form a TS domain, although the former is not m-commanded by the latter, and in (23d), on the contrary, the TS rule is still blocked between X3 and X4 in spite of the fact that X4 m-commands X3. Hence m-command fails as a hypothesis for Ruicheng.

It seems that none of the current m/c-command hypotheses can offer us a satisfactory explanation of Ruicheng data. However, Ruicheng's TS domain is also the c-command domain as defined by Reinhart, and the only thing that makes it different from all of the others is its left-to-right stipulation in application, illustrated in (23).

(24) C-command principle in Ruicheng
The TS rule applies cyclically iff
   i. α c-commands β;
   ii. β is the constituent adjacent to α at its right side.

Since (24) is distinguished from all of the other c-command hypotheses only in its special stipulation in application of left to right, instead of in its definition as a c-command, the principle given in (24) is able to account for all of the cases in Ruicheng. In (23a), X1 commands X2, X2 commands X3, and X3 commands X4, thus its TS domain is from T1 to T4. In (23b), X1 commands X2, and neither X2 commands X3 nor X3 commands X4, thus its TS domain covers only T1 and T2. In (23c), X1 commands X2, which commands X3 but not X4, so its TS domain stretches from T1 to T3, not including T4. In (23d), X1 commands X2, and X2 commands X3, which does not command X4, so its TS domain is from T1 to T3 without including T4.

3.3.2 Comparison between Ruicheng and Danyang

It should be noted that the Ruicheng case in (23d) and the Danyang case in (21d) in Section 3.2 are two crucial examples. With exactly the same syntactic branching structure, (23d)'s TS domain is from T1 to T3, while (21d)'s TS domain stretches from T1 to T4. That is because they have different sandhi domains. TS rules in Ruicheng Chinese apply cyclically to a command domain from left to right, but rules in Danyang are directly applied to a c-command domain. In *[X1[[X2-X3] X4]]*, X1 c-commands X4, while X3 does not command X4. So, in the Danyang case in (21d), X4 is a TS domain, but in (23d), X4 is not a TS domain in Ruicheng. This shows that the different stipulations for c-command bring about different TS domains in Danyang and Ruicheng, reproduced as follows in (25).

(25) a. = (21d)

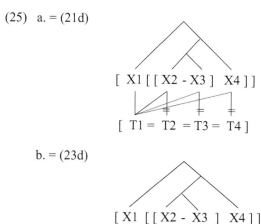

   b. = (23d)

76   *The c-command condition in phonology*

$$[\text{T2} = \text{T3}]$$
$$[\text{T3} \ \# \ \text{T4}]$$
$$[\text{T1} = \text{T2}]$$

$$[\text{T1} = \text{T2} = \text{T3} \ \# \ \text{T4}]$$

3.4 Pingyao Chinese: Case study (3)

The earlier discussion on Danyang and Ruicheng is confined to the relationship between c-command conditions and sandhi domains, but this section probes into the relationship between c-command conditions and the modes of rule application through the case study of Pingyao Chinese.

3.4.1 Tonological background

Spoken in the central part of Shanxi province in north China, Pingyao belongs to the Jin dialect. More precisely, it is a subdialect of central Jin. Pingyao Chinese has five citation tones (Hou 1980, 1982), as given in (26).[6]

(26) The citation tones in Pingyao Chinese

Tonal Category	Phonetic Value	Examples	
1. Ping Tone	LM	iŋ	"overcast"
2. Shang Tone	HM	ɕiɔ	"small"
3. Qu Tone	MH	ts`æ	"dish"
4. Yin Ru Tone	LMq	ʂʌʔ	"lose"
5. Yang Ru Tone	HMq	ɣʌʔ	"moon"

In connected speech, Pingyao TS is divided into two types (Hou 1980, 1982). What tonal sequences actually emerge depends upon both the combination of citation tones (CT) and the functional relations holding between tone-bearing units across the sandhi site. All of the argument structures belong to type A (TSA), while all of the others fall under type B (TSB). Summaries of disyllabic tonal patterns of TSA and TSB are given in (27) and (28), respectively.

(27) Disyllabic TSA patterns of Pingyao

T_1 / T_2	LM	LMq	MH	HM	HMq
LM	LM-LM	LM-LMq	ML-MH	MH-MLM	MH-MLM
LMq	LMq-LM	LMq-LMq	MLq-MH	MHq-MLM	MHq-MLM
MH	LM-LM	LM-LMq	ML-MH	MH-MLM	MH-MLM
HM	HM-LM	HM-LMq	HM-MH	MH-MLM	MH-MLM
HMq	HMq-LM	HMq-LMq	HMq-MH	MHq-MLM	MHq-MLM

(28) Disyllabic TSB patterns of Pingyao

T_1 / T_2	LM	LMq	MH	HM	HMq
LMa(yang)	LM-LM	LM-LMq	ML-MH	MH-MLM	MH-MLM
LMb(yin)	ML-MH	ML-MHq	ML-LM	ML-HM	ML-HMq
LMq	MLq-MH	MLq-MHq	LMq-LM	MLq-HM	MLq-HMq
MH	MH-HM	MH-HMq	MH-HM	MH-HM	MH-HMq
HM	HM-LM	HM-LMq	HM-MH	HM-HM	HM-HMq
HMq	HMq-LM	HMq-LMq	HMq-MH	MHq-HM	HMq-HMq

In the two tables, the leftmost column and the top row show the form of the CTs of the first and the second syllable, respectively. The intersections of the columns and the rows indicate the sandhi tone forms of bi-tonal sequences.

The tones of LMq and HMq can be considered as the allotones of LM and HM, respectively, because they have the same TS patterns. Thus the patterns of TSA can be simplified as (29).

(29)

T_1 / T_2	LM	MH	HM
LM	LM-LM	ML-MH	MH-MLM
MH	LM-LM	ML-MH	MH-MLM
HM	HM-LM	HM-MH	MH-MLM

As for TSB, the tonal behavior of LM in sandhi position is divided into two types that indicate the two different historical sources of the citation tone LM. One is the *yin ping* tone and the other the *yang-ping* tone.[7] The contrast of *yin ping* and *yang-ping* gets lost when merged in the citation tonal system, but preserved at the sandhi level. In addition, the sandhi forms of LMq are realized as falling tones just like its counterpart LM of *yin ping* tones, except for those marked out in the shaded cell, which remain as rising tones. So the patterns of TSB in table (28) can be simplified as (30).

(30)

T_1 / T_2	LM	MH	HM
LMa (yang)	LM-LM	ML-MH	MH-MLM
LMb(yin)	ML-MH	ML-LM/LMq-LM	ML-HM
MH	MH-HM	MH-HM	MH-HM
HM	HM-LM	HM-MH	HM-HM

As shown by the data, Pingyao exhibits a very complicated case of TS patterns. The mode of rules for TSA is a regressive one, and the rules of TSA are proposed in (31).

78 *The c-command condition in phonology*

(31) Regressive rules for TSA

    a. LM → ML / ____ MH
    b. LM → MH / ____ MLM (HM)[8]
    c. MH → LM / ____ LM
    d. MH → ML / ____ MH
    e. HM → MH / ____ HM

The rules of TSB are more complicated. Besides the regressive rules, progressive rules and bidirectional rules will also be applied, as shown in (32).

(32) a.   Regressive rules for TSB

        a.   LMa → ML / ____ MH
        b.   LMa → MH / ____ MLM (HM)
        c.   LMb → ML / ____ HM

    b.   Progressive rules for TSB

        a.   LM → HM / MH ____
        b.   MH → HM / MH ____

    c.   Bidirectional rules for TSB

        a.   LMb-LM → ML-MH
        b.   LMb-MH → ML-LM

This argument (TSA) versus non-argument (TSB) dichotomy in TS patterns can be summarized and illustrated as (33) and (34), respectively.

(33)

CT	*TSA*	*TSB*
M(q) – MH	ML(q) – MH	LM(q) – LM
MH – LM(q)	LM – LM(q)	MH – HM(q)
HM – LM	LM – LM	MH – HM
MH – MH	ML – MH	MH – HM

(34)

	a. kəŋ ti	b. tɕyə təu
	耕 地	豇 豆
	'till soil'	'cowpea'
Functional type	argument	non-argument
Syntactic type	verb-object (VO)	modifier-noun (MH)
Tone sandhi type	type A (TSA)	type B (TSB)
Citation tone	LM - MH	LM - MH
Sandhi tone	ML - MH	LM - LM

The examples in (34) show that the citation tones for type A and type B are exactly the same, but the sandhi tones are different because of the difference in functional relations.

This fact becomes even more intriguing when we consider the effect of TS on more complex structures exhibiting hierarchical structure and allowing for possible interaction between TSA and TSB. Some examples show that the internal structure is visible for rule application, since TS rules apply cyclically, and the rule selection (TSA or TSB) depends on the functional relation that holds for each cycle, as seen in (35).

(35)

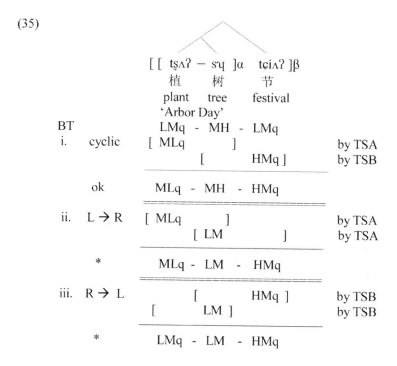

As shown in (35), only the cyclic mode will bring about the correct output form. In the derivations, labeled brackets [. . .]A and [. . .]B stand for functional units of type A or type B, which select for TSA or TSB, respectively, on each cycle. Some other examples, however, suggest a non-cyclic mode, as seen in (36).

80 *The c-command condition in phonology*

(36) a.

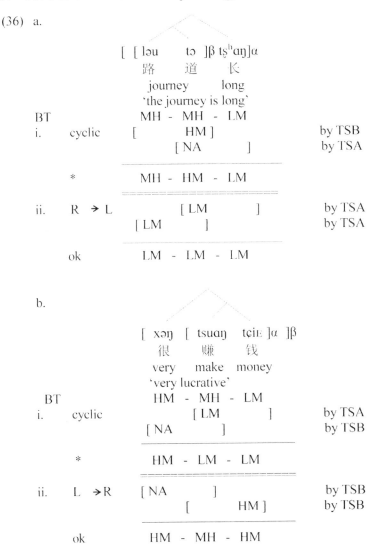

                [[lɔu   tɔ]β tʂʰaŋ]α
                 路   道   长
                journey   long
                'the journey is long'

BT   MH - MH - LM
i.   cyclic   [HM]   by TSB
                 [NA   ]   by TSA

     *   MH - HM - LM

ii. R → L   [LM   ]   by TSA
             [LM   ]   by TSA

   ok   LM - LM - LM

b.

                [xəŋ [tsuaŋ tɕiɛ]α]β
               很   赚   钱
               very   make money
               'very lucrative'

BT   HM - MH - LM
i.   cyclic   [LM   ]   by TSA
               [NA   ]   by TSB

    *   HM - LM - LM

ii. L → R [NA   ]   by TSB
                 [HM]   by TSB

   ok   HM - MH - HM

Apparently, in the cases of (35) and (36), the functional information for internal structures is ignored. Moreover, TS rules apply iteratively, with the functional relation holding on the outer structures that determine both the applicable rule (TSA or TSB) and the direction of application (right to left or left to right). Without going into the detail, (37) lays out the overall patterns of Pingyao TS.

(37)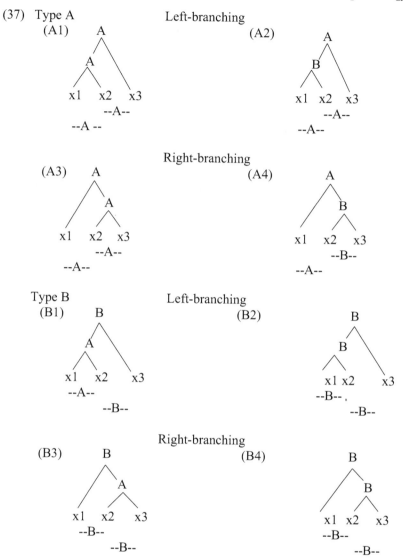

The figures in (37) exhaust all logical possibilities: right/left-branching structures, and A- or B-type grammatical constructions on the inner/outer cycle. The trees represent the IC hierarchy in the usual manner, with node labels A/B indicating the argument structure types (argument/others), and x's standing for the syllables. – A – and – B – indicate which TS applies to which pair of adjacent syllables.

82 *The c-command condition in phonology*

3.4.2 Early analyses

The early analyses of (37) have been made by Chen (1990) and Shen (1988). Shen proposes the prosodic domain formation principle, reproduced in (38).

(38) Prosodic domain formation principle

    a.   Scanning direction
        Scan SP (subject-predicate) and VO (verb-object) from right to left, elsewhere left to right.
    b.   Minimal prosodic domain
        Scan the largest construction in accordance with (a), if the first two syllables constitute a Morphosyntactic unit, then they constitute the minimal prosodic domain; otherwise, the whole tri-syllabic string is the minimal prosodic domain.

As a matter of fact, the principle laid out in (38) is mainly concerned with the formation of TS domains instead of with the application of TS rules. Therefore, Chen (1990) proposes the directional cyclicity principles concerning the application of Pingyao TS rules seen in (39).

(39) Principles of directional cyclicity

    a.   TS applies to two to three syllable feet.
    b.   Directionality
        TS scans A constructions from right to left.
        TS scans B constructions from left to right.
    c.   IC constraint
        TS applies between ICs.
    d.   Rule selection
        TSA/B applies to A/B constructions, respectively.
    e.   Bracket erasure
        When TS fails on account of (c), try the next larger construction (erasing inner structures in the process).

3.4.3 Present analysis

As mentioned earlier, Pingyao's TS domain is a functional/syntactic domain. In Pingyao, type A and type B constructions are different types of functional structures determined by functional categories. More precisely, it is the syntactic factors with functional relations that determine the application of TS rules. Hence I propose here a new hypothesis for Pingyao TS, which I name the edge c-command principle, as given in (40).

(40) Edge c-command principle

    Within argument structure, TSA applies iteratively right to left if X3 c-commands both X2 and X1, and in non-argument structure where X1 c-commands both X2 and X3, TSB applies iteratively left to right. Otherwise, TSA/B applies cyclically.

It should be noted that TSA applies right to left, therefore it takes the rightmost element X3 as the dominant element, which then determines the mode of rule application by virtue of the c-command condition; TSB works in the same way as TSA, but in a different direction. As seen from the principle in (40), in Pingyao, a functional relation (argument structure versus non-argument structure) determines the type of TS rule (TSA versus TSB), while a syntactic condition (c-command) determines the mode of TS rule application. Now let us use the principle in (40) to test all of the patterns illustrated in (37).

In both (A1) and (A2) of (37), TSA applies iteratively right to left because X3 c-commands both X2 and X1, illustrated by (41a). In (A3) and (A4), since X3 does not c-command X1, TSA and TSB apply cyclically, which is seen as (41b). In (B1) and (B2), TSA/B applies cyclically because X1 does not c-command X3, as shown in (41c). In (B3) and (B4), since X1 c-commands both X2 and X3, TSB applies iteratively left to right, as presented in (41d).

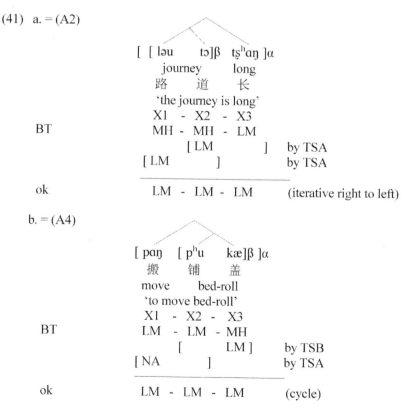

84   *The c-command condition in phonology*

c. = (B1)

$$[\ [\ ts_{\Lambda}? \ - \ s\gamma \ ]\alpha \ tci_{\Lambda}? \ ]\beta$$

植　　　树　　　节

plant　　tree　　festival

'Arbor Day'

X1 - X2 - X3

BT   　　LMq - MH - LMq

| MLq　　　　　| by TSA

　　　　　| HMq | by TSB

ok   　　MLq - MH - HMq   (cycle)

d. = (B3)

$$[\ x\partial \eta \ [\ tsu\alpha\eta \ \ tciE \ ]\alpha \ ]\beta$$

很　　　赚　　　钱

very　　make　money

'very lucrative'

X1 - X2 - X3

BT   　　HM - MH - LM

| NA　　　　| by TSB

　　　　　[HM | by TSB

ok   　　HM - MH - HM   (iterative left to right)

Thus it can be seen that the principle in (40) can explain all of the cases in (37), which shows that Pingyao uses a typical functional/syntactic condition instead of a foot condition as claimed by Shen and Chen.

3.5 OT analysis of Pingyao TS

3.5.1 OT analysis of disyllabic TS in Pingyao

J. Zhang (1999) revisited the case of Pingyao TS and gave an OT analysis of both TSA and TSB. The constraints under the OT framework he proposed for disyllabic TSA of Pingyao are given in (42).

(42) Constraints for TSA of Pingyao

a. Pres(σ_2, T): Preserve the tonal property of the second syllable
b. Pres(σ_1, C): Preserve the tonal contour of the first syllable
c. Pres(σ_1, R): Preserve the tonal register of the first syllable

The c-command condition in phonology   85

d. Word final rise: There must be a pitch rise word finally
e. Pres(HM): Preserve the property of a base high falling tone in the sandhi form
f. Num(Inf) ≤ 2: A word with two syllables can carry at most two tonal inflection points
g. Num(Inf) ≥ 1: A word with two syllables should have at least one tonal inflection point
h. Dur(B): A pitch rise or a sharp pitch fall is disallowed
i. Reg(2) H: No adjacent high registers

The ranking of the constraints for TSA is summarized in (43).

(43) Pres(σ_2, T), WFR, Num(Inf) ≤ 2, Num(Inf) ≥ 1

$\downarrow$

Pres(HM)

$\downarrow$

Reg(2) H

$\downarrow$

Dur(B), Pres(σ_1, C)

$\downarrow$

Pres(σ_1, R)

Some of the constraints for TSA are also available to TSB, which are Num(Inf) ≤ 2, Num(Inf) ≥ 1, Dur(B), Pre(σ_1, C), Pre(σ_1, R), and Pres(HM). Nevertheless, the constraints specifically for TSB are given in (44).

(44) Constraints for TSB of Pingyao

a. *Yin/Yang* preservation: In sandhi forms, *yin* tones are falling and *yang* tones are rising
b. Num(Inf) ≤ 1: A word cannot have more than one tonal inflection point
c. Pre(σ_2, C): Preserve the tonal contour of the second syllable
d. Pre(σ_2, R): Preserve the tonal register of the second syllable
e. Reg(2)L: Two adjacent low registers is disallowed
f. *Non-lexical tone: A tone not in the lexical inventory is not allowed in the sandhi form

The ranking of the constraints for TSB in Pingyao is shown in (45).

(45) *Yin/Yang* preservation, Num(Inf) ≤ 2, Num(Inf) ≥ 1

$\downarrow$

Pres(σ_1, C), Pres(σ_1, R), Pres(HM)

$\downarrow$

Num(Inf)≤ 1, Reg(2)L

$\downarrow$

Dur(B), * Non-lexical Tone, Pres(σ_2, C)

$\downarrow$

Pres(σ_2, R)

86 *The c-command condition in phonology*

However, Zhang's constraint-based analysis contains several problems. First, some language-specific constraints adopted are not compatible with OT by which constraints are universal. And such cases include Pres(HM) and Dur(B), i.e., *yin/yang* preservations, which are unusual to the Pingyao case and not better than an ad hoc stipulation. Second, Zhang's analysis enjoys too much freedom. For example, he treats the data in the shaded cell in (46) as an anomaly and leaves it without explanation.

(46)

T_1/T_2	LM	LMq	MH	HM	HMq
LMa(yang)	LM-LM	LM-LMq	ML-MH	MH-MLM	MH-MLM
LMb(yin)	ML-MH	ML-MHq	ML-LM	ML-HM	ML-HMq
LMq	MLq-MH	MLq-MHq	LMq-LM	MLq-HM	MLq-HMq
MH	MH-HM	MH-HMq	MH-HM	MH-HM	MH-HMq
HM	HM-LM	HM-LMq	HM-MH	HM-HM	HM-HMq
HMq	HMq-LM	HMq-LMq	HMq-MH	MHq-HM	HMq-HMq

Third, because *yang-ping* LM in TSB has the same TS behavior as in TSA, he regards it as an idiosyncrasy of Pingyao. The fact is that if the OT framework can satisfactorily capture bi-tonal sandhi in Pingyao, the *yang-ping* having the same sandhi behavior in TSA or TSB should not be ignored and must be accounted for. If *yang-ping* in TSB is taken into consideration, the ranking constraints proposed for TSB fail to predict all the attested sandhi forms.

3.5.2 OT analysis of tri-syllabic TS in Pingyao

In tri-tonal sequence, the TS domain (TSD) in Pingyao will undergo the restructuring. Let us use OT constraints to delimitate the TSD and account for the modes of rule application first (i.e., cyclical mode vs. iterative mode). The TSD in Pingyao is disyllabic, and, therefore, we could come up with the binary constraint seen as (47).

(47) Binary: TSD must be binary under syllabic analysis.

Under this constraint, the three syllables will be parsed as either (σσ)σ or σ(σσ) in order to prevent those unparsed structures from being chosen, and a constraint that demands every syllable in the input be parsed into a TSD is needed, as shown in (48).

(48) Parse σ: Every syllable should be parsed into TSD.

Ranking the Parse constraint higher than the binary constraint, the unparsed structures will be ruled out.

The c-command condition in phonology 87

Chen (1990, 2000) discussed the directionality of TS rules for type A and type B constructions: TS scans construction A right to left and scans construction B left to right. If we redefine that constructions A and B correspond to the phonological phrase and prosodic word, respectively, the directionality of TS in Pingyao can be rewritten because the TS rule scans phonological phrase from right to left and scans prosodic word from left to right. Then we can propose the alignment constraints, under the OT framework, stated in (49) and (50), respectively.[9]

(49)   Align (TSD, φ')R: The right edge of every TS domain is aligned with the right edge of the maximal phonological phrase.

(50)   Align (TSD, ω')L: The left edge of every TS domain is aligned with the left edge of the maximal phonological word.

Following Ito and Mester (2009), I refer to the larger structure of the tri-syllabic string as the maximal prosodic category. It should be noted that these two alignment constraints are not dominated in the prosodic hierarchy, and, consequently, the ranking of constraints for the tri-tonal sandhi in Pingyao is as shown in (51).

(51)   Align (TSD, ω')L / Align (TSD, φ')R >> Parse σ >> Binary

The constraints ranking in (51) can predict the domain of tri-syllabic TS, as illustrated in (52) and (53), respectively.

(52)

[σ σ σ] φ'	*Align (TSD, φ') R*	*Parse σ*	*Binary*
σ (σ σ)		*!	
(σ σ) σ	*!	*	
(σ) (σ σ)	*!		*
(σ σ) (σ)	*!		*
☞ (σ (σ σ))			*
((σ σ) σ)	*!		*

(53)

[σ σ σ] ω'	*Align (TSD, ω') L*	*Parse σ*	*Binary*
σ (σ σ)	*!	*	
(σ σ) σ		*!	
(σ) (σ σ)	*!		*
(σ σ) (σ)	*!		*
(σ (σ σ))	*!		*
☞ ((σ σ) σ)			*

88 *The c-command condition in phonology*

In (53), the two alignments make different decisions on parsing the TSD. If the input of tri-syllabic TS is a prosodic word, the TSD will be $((\sigma\ \sigma)\ \sigma)$; if the tri-syllabic TS input is a phonological phrase, the TSD will be $(\sigma\ (\sigma\ \sigma))$.

A tri-syllabic string will form two TSDs. If the internal TSD formed by two syllables is congruent with the intermediate prosodic category, it is the prosodic category that determines what type of TS rule will be chosen (i.e., phonological phrase or prosodic word). Otherwise, it is a maximal prosodic category. Tableaux (54)–(57) illustrate the formation of TSD for cases of A1, A4, B2, and B4 in (37).

(54) A1: $[[\sigma\ \sigma]_\varphi\ \sigma]_{\varphi'} \rightarrow (\sigma\ (\sigma\ \sigma))_{\varphi'}$.

$[[\sigma\ \sigma]_\varphi\ \sigma]_{\varphi'}$	*Align (TSD, φ') R*	*Parse σ*	*Binary*
$\sigma\ (\sigma\ \sigma)$		*!	
$(\sigma\ \sigma)_\varphi\ \sigma$	*!	*	
$(\sigma)\ (\sigma\ \sigma)$	*!		*
$(\sigma\ \sigma)_\varphi\ (\sigma)$	*!		*
☞ $(\sigma\ (\sigma\ \sigma))_{\varphi'}$			*
$((\sigma\ \sigma)_\varphi\ \sigma)_{\varphi'}$	*!		

(55) A4: $[\sigma\ [\sigma\ \sigma]_\omega]_{\varphi'} \rightarrow (\sigma\ (\sigma\ \sigma)_\omega)_{\varphi'}$.

$[\sigma\ [\sigma\ \sigma]_\omega]_{\varphi'}$	*Align (TSD, φ') R*	*Parse σ*	*Binary*
$\sigma\ (\sigma\ \sigma)_\omega$		*!	
$(\sigma\ \sigma)\ \sigma$	*!	*	
$(\sigma)\ (\sigma\ \sigma)_\omega$	*!		*
$(\sigma\ \sigma)\ (\sigma)$	*!		*
☞ $(\sigma\ (\sigma\ \sigma)_\omega)_{\varphi'}$			*
$((\sigma\ \sigma)\ \sigma)_{\varphi'}$	*!		*

(56) B2: $[[\sigma\ \sigma]_\omega\ \sigma]_{\omega'} \rightarrow ((\sigma\ \sigma)_\omega\ \sigma)_{\omega'}$.

$[[\sigma\ \sigma]_\omega\ \sigma]_{\omega'}$	*Align (TSD, ω') L*	*Parse σ*	*Binary*
$\sigma\ (\sigma\ \sigma)$	*!	*	
$(\sigma\ \sigma)_\omega\ \sigma$		*!	
$(\sigma)\ (\sigma\ \sigma)$	*!		*
$(\sigma\ \sigma)_\omega\ (\sigma)$	*!		*
$(\sigma\ (\sigma\ \sigma))_{\omega'}$	*!		*
☞ $((\sigma\ \sigma)_\omega\ \sigma)_{\omega'}$			*

(57) B4: $[\sigma\,[\sigma\,\sigma]_\omega]_{\omega'} \rightarrow ((\sigma\,\sigma)\,\sigma)_{\omega'}$.

$[\sigma\,[\sigma\,\sigma]_\omega]_{\omega'}$	Align (TSD, ω') L	Parse σ	Binary
$\sigma\,(\sigma\,\sigma)_\omega$	*!	*	
$(\sigma\,\sigma)\,\sigma$		*!	
$(\sigma)\,(\sigma\,\sigma)_\omega$	*!		*
$(\sigma\,\sigma)\,(\sigma)$	*!		*
$(\sigma\,(\sigma\,\sigma)_\omega)_{\omega'}$	*!		*
☞ $((\sigma\,\sigma)\,\sigma)_{\omega'}$			*

The constraints and recursive prosodic structures proposed here can predict the TSD to account for all eight TS patterns listed in (37) through restructuring. However, there are two problems in this analysis. The first problem is the property of the alignment. Normally, the term alignment refers to the correspondence of different domains, i.e., the correspondence between the Morphosyntactic category and the prosodic category. But if the Align-L (i.e., the domain of TS; maximal prosodic word) adopted in the analyses considers the domain of TS a prosodic unit, the alignment constraint here will be a correspondence between prosodic units only, rather than between Morphosyntactic units and prosodic units.

Another problem is the different TS behaviors of the embedded disyllabic units in the tri-syllables. Of the eight tri-syllabic patterns, the performance of the embedded disyllabic TS in the tri-syllable presents different properties. Some have it made up by a prosodic word with the application of TSB. Some get it consisting of a phonological phrase with the application of TSA, and some others contain no prosodic unit and, therefore, have their application of TS rule decided by the property of outer maximal prosodic units. The situation leads to the difficulty in defining the domain of the embedded disyllabic units in the tri-syllables as a consistent unit in prosodic hierarchy. So the OT approach fails to capture the TA patterns in Pingyao Chinese by brutal force or ad hoc constraints.

3.5.3 Summary

This section has reviewed all the previous studies on the domain issue of Pingyao TS rule application and reanalyzed the Pingyao TS with the Align theory. The following is the summary of the questions the TS domain of Pingyao Chinese has posed to current phonological theories.

First, if the domain of Pingyao TS is considered a prosodic unit with the perspective of the Indirect Reference Approach, this prosodic unit still has its syntactic information retained if analyzed with the rule-based phonology, and this retained syntactic structure will decide the direction as well as the mode of rule application.

90 *The c-command condition in phonology*

Second, the strict layer hypothesis in the OT framework is no longer a principle that cannot be violated. This is because to define the types A and B in Pingyao Chinese as a phonological phrase and a prosodic word, respectively, will result in the prosodic structure, which violates the strict layer hypothesis and cannot help to predict the mode of rule application. If the alignment constraint is brought in for the restructuring of tri-syllabic prosodic units, it will be difficult to define the property of the embedded disyllabic TS domain in the tri-syllabic units, thus making it impossible to be consistent in categorizing the hierarchical prosodic unit.

Third, based on the case study of the TS domain of rule application, Pingyao seems to support the view that phonology refers to the syntactic relations, which is in favor of the Direct Reference Approach.

3.6 Shanghai Chinese: Case study (4)

3.6.1 Basics of Shanghai TS

Shanghai Chinese is a subdialect of Wu Chinese, and it has five citation tones, as given in (58).

(58) The citation tones in Shanghai

    a. HL b. MH c. LM d. Hq e. LMq

As mentioned previously, there are two different types of TS in Shanghai dialect: one is *Guang-yong shi bian-diao* 'TS type G' (TS-G), i.e., 'TS in broad used form,' and the other is *zhai-yong shi bian-diao* 'TS type Z' (TS-Z), i.e., 'TS in narrow used form.' Phonologically, TS-G's mode of rule application is tonal spreading. That means in a given TS domain, all but the leftmost morpheme lose their underlying tones or base tones, and the base tone of the leftmost morpheme is associated in one-to-one fashion from left to right across the entire TS domain (Sherard 1972; Yip 1980; Zee & Maddieson 1980; Wright 1983; T. Shen 1985; Jin 1986; Zee 1988; Selkirk & Shen 1990; Duanmu 1992). The process of TS-G rule application can be summed up in (59).

(59) Process of TS-G rule application

    a.   Tone deletion (TD)
          In each TS domain, delete all underlying tones, except an initial syllable.
    b.   Association convention (AC)
          Associate tones to syllables one-to-one from left to right.
    c.   Default tone (DT)
          Assign default tone L to the remaining syllables.

Although no conclusion has yet been reached on such questions as how many base tones the Shanghai dialect has, how citation tones are derived from base tones, and how these base tones are represented, the focus here is not on these open questions, but on what conditions the TS domain of the Shanghai dialect is determined by. So here I just follow T. Shen (1985) and Jin (1986) and consider that, at the underlying level, Shanghai has only three base tones and that their corresponding relationship to citation tones is given in (60).[10]

(60) CT   a. HL   b. MH   c. LM   d. Hq   e. LMq
      BT   a. HL   b. MH   c. LH   d. MH   e. LH

Now let us take, for example, in (61) the base tone forms in (60) to illustrate how the principle in (59) works.[11]

(61) Example for TS-G rule application

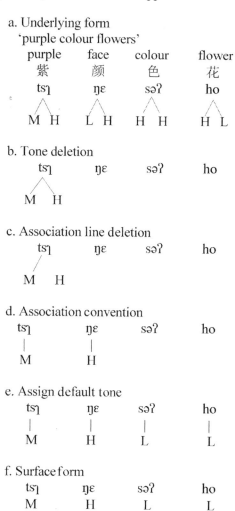

92 *The c-command condition in phonology*

As for the TS-Z type, Selkirk and Shen (1988) take it as a non-TS case. Some others, such as Duanmu (1992), consider it a case in which the TS rule is blocked with T1 and T2 belonging to two tonal domains, respectively. In fact, TS-Z is just another type of TS, in which the last syllable keeps its underlying tone, while the preceding syllable changes by dropping the latter half of its base tone. As a result, the original contour tone changes into a level tone. If TS-G is taken as a spreading case, TS-Z can be considered as a direct mapping case. The tonal representations of these two different cases are shown in (62).[12]

(62) a. TS-G case (spreading)

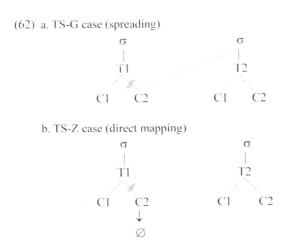

b. TS-Z case (direct mapping)

Given in (63a) and (63b) are the examples for (62a) and (62b), respectively.

(63) a.

		商 sã trade	品 pʰiŋ article	
		'commodity'		
BT		HL	MH	
ok	TS-G	H	L	by (62a)
*	TS-Z	H	MH	by (62b)

b.

		打 tã beat	狗 ky dog	
		'to beat dog'		
BT		MH	MH	
*	TS-G	M	H	by (62a)
ok	TS-Z	M	MH	by (62b)

3.6.2 Hypothesis on conditions for the association domain in Shanghai

3.6.2.1 Selkirk's edge principle

Now let us discuss what condition determines the spreading domain in the Shanghai dialect.

According to Selkirk and Shen (1990), the prosodic structure assigned to a sentence in Shanghai is the minimal structure consistent with the well-formedness constraint and the mapping rules. For any particular level of prosodic structure, only the bracketing of the sentence into constituents of one particular X-bar type is relevant and precisely only at the left or right edge of such a constituent. No syntactic relations govern the mapping at all. Thus there is no guarantee that the words included in a prosodic constituent should bear any consistent syntactic relation to each other. In particular, a lexical item is not required to c-command its companion function words[13] within a prosodic domain, nor is a function word required to c-command the lexical item within a prosodic domain. In Shanghai, Selkirk and Shen argue that the left edge of a syntactic word belonging to the category noun, verb, or adjective (= a 'lexical item') always coincides with the edge of a prosodic unit. Moreover, they propose that the tonal domain in Shanghai is the 'prosodic word' that is defined in (64).

(64) Shanghai Chinese prosodic word rule
  Prosodic word: {left, Lex°}

According to (64), a PW starts from the left end of a lexical word or a compound and extends till right before the left end of another lexical word (Lex°), as exemplified by (65).

(65)

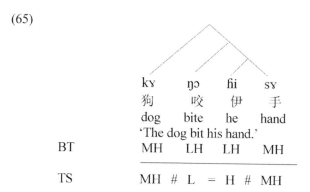

In (65), kɣ 'dog,' ŋɔ 'bite,' and sɣ 'hand' are lexical words, each starting a PW, and ɦi 'he' is a function word. Therefore, according to (64), there are three PWs in this whole sentence. They are kɣ, ŋɔ, and sɣ.

It should be noted that ɦi 'he' and sɣ 'hand' in (65) are immediate constituents (IC). Although they c-command each other, ɦi does not form a TS domain with sɣ.

94   *The c-command condition in phonology*

Instead, it forms a TS domain with ɲɔ on the left. Thus Selkirk and Shen claim that the ascertaining of a phonological domain is not sensitive to syntactic structure but to the edge of X^o or X^{max}.

Although a correct output can be produced from (65) when it is subject to the rule for prosodic word proposed by Selkirk and Shen, there are some problems in their theory. First, they cannot explain why within Shanghai the TS behavior of adnominal MH differs from that of adverbial MH, SP, and VO, although all of them are syntactic phrases. The examples of MH phrases that follow show the difference in TS behavior between adnominal MH in (66) and adverbial MH in (67).[14]

(66) a.

		老	树	
		lɔ	zɿ	
		old	tree	
		'old tree'		
	BT	LH	LH	

ok	L	=	H		(by spreading)
*	LH	#	LH		(by blocking)

b.

		老	房	子
		lɔ	vã − tsɿ	
		old	house	
		'old house'		
	BT	LH	LH	MH

ok	L	=	H	=	L	(by spreading)
*	LH	#	L	=	H	(by blocking)

(67) a.

		老	远
		lɔ	ɦy
		old	far
		'far away'	
	BT	LH	LH

*	L	=	H	(by spreading)
ok	LH	#	LH	(by blocking)

b.

		lɔ	zəŋ − tɕʰi	
		老	神 气	
		old	spirited	
		'very cocky'		
	BT	LH	LH	MH

*	L	=	H	=	L	(by spreading)
ok	LH	#	L	=	H	(by blocking)

All the examples in both (66) and (67) are phrases formed by two lexical words. According to the hypothesis in (64) proposed by Selkirk and Shen, each of them should have two TS domains as well as two prosodic words. But, as a matter of fact, there is only one TS domain and only one prosodic word in (66a) and (66b). And this is where the theory proposed by Selkirk and Shen fails.

Second, the discussion by Selkirk and Shen (1990) about the TS of function words also seems to be on the wrong track. According to Selkirk and Shen, a function word necessarily loses its base tone (obligatory tone deletion) and receives sandhi tone either from the preceding lexical item (left-to-right association) or by being assigned the default tone. Although this analysis can find support from (65) and (68), the counterevidence provided in (69) and (70) can easily make it lose its effectiveness.

(68)

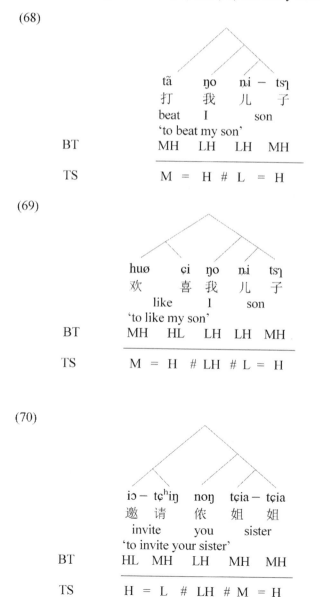

(69)

(70)

96   *The c-command condition in phonology*

According to Selkirk and Shen, personal pronouns, such as *No* 'I' in (69) and *voN* 'you' in (70), embedded as a possessive in a post-verbal noun phrase should join the verb in a prosodic word, just as /ɪ/ 'he' in (65) and *No* 'I' in (68). But as a matter of fact, none of the pronouns in (69) and (70) forms a TS domain with the lexical items to its left. Thus it can be seen that the analysis of Shanghai TS by Selkirk and Shen is not tenable.

3.6.2.2 Duanmu's metrical analysis

After Selkirk and Shen proposed the edge-condition approach, Duanmu (1992), following the theory proposed by Halle and Vergnaud (1987) and Hayes (1995), suggested a metrical approach to analyze the domain of tonal association for the Shanghai dialect. The rules and principles suggested by Duanmu are given in (71).

(71) Metrical rules in Shanghai

    a.   Morpheme level

        Line 0: trochee, left to right, ignore degenerate foot
        Line 1: left-headed, unbounded stress

    b.   Above the morpheme level

        Assign cyclic left-headed stress

    c.   Stress reduction

        Optionally delete line 1 stress

    d.   Clash resolution

        Remove the stress column next to a higher column

    e.   Stress Equalization Convention
    f.   Contrastive stress

        Add an asterisk to the given syllable

(72) Domain formation

    An association domain starts from a stress syllable till just before the next stressed syllable

Shanghai TS examples are provided in (73), including disyllable and tri-syllable ones. In (74), (75), and (76), the workings of the rules and principles in (71) and (72) are illustrated.

The c-command condition in phonology 97

(73) a.

	老	树
	lɔ	z̩
	old	tree
	'old tree'	
BT	LH	LH

| ok | L | = | H | | (one domain) |
| * | LH | # | LH | | (two domains) |

b.

	老	房	子
	lɔ	vã —	ts̩
	old	house	
	'old house'		
BT	LH	LH	MH

| ok | L | = | H | = | L | (one domain) |
| * | LH | # | L | = | H | (two domains) |

c.

	老	虎	头
	lɔ —	fu	dɣ
	tiger	head	
	'the head of a tiger'		
BT	LH	MH	LH

| ok | L | = | H | = | L | (one domain) |
| * | L | = | H | # | LH | (two domains) |

(74) = (73a)

a. By (71a) and (71b)

```
        *
     *       *
   ( X1 )  ( X2 )
         \   /
          \ /
```

b. By (71d)

```
     *
     *
   ( X1  X2 )
```

c. By (72)

```
       *
       *
   ( X1 = X2 )      output
   |_____|       one domain
```

98 *The c-command condition in phonology*

(75) = (73b)

    a. By (71a) and (71b)

            *

       *   *

     (X1) (X2 - X3)

    b. By (71d)

          *

       *

     (X1 X2 - X3)

    c. By (72)

         *

       *

     (X1 = X2 = X3)   output
                            one domain

(76) = (73c)

    a. By (71a) and (71b)

         *

      *   *

     (X1 - X2) (X3)

    b. By (71a), degenerate foot

        *

       *

     (X1 - X2 X3)

    c. By (72)

         *

       *

     (X1 = X2 = X3)   output
                            one domain

The metrical approach proposed by Duanmu (1992) can explain the cases in (66a) and (66b), which Selkirk and Shen fail to account for. According to Selkirk and Shen, there are two domains in the TS of both (66a) and (66b). But according to Duanmu, there is only one, which is correct.

However, although Duanmu can solve the problem of adnominal MH phrase, it fails in cases such as adverbial MH phrase, SP phrase, and VO phrase. Counterevidence for Duanmu's metrical analysis is given in (77)–(79).

The c-command condition in phonology   99

(77) Adverbial MH structure

a.	老	远		
	lɔ	ɦiɣ		
	old	far		
	'far away'			
BT	LH	LH		

*	L	=	H		(one domain)
ok	LH	#	LH		(two domains)

b.	老	神	气	
	lɔ	zən —	tɕʰi	
	old	spirited		
	'very cocky'			
BT	LH	LH	MH	

*	L	=	H	=	L	(one domain)
ok	LH	#	L	=	H	(two domains)

c.	努	力	做	
	nu —	liɿʔ	tsu	
	try hard	do		
	'to work hard'			
BT	LH	LH	MH	

*	L	=	H	=	L	(one domain)
ok	L	=	H	#	MH	(two domains)

(78) SP structure

a.	天	晴		
	tʰi	ziŋ		
	sky	clear		
	'The sky is clear.'			
BT	HL	LH		

*	H	=	L		(one domain)
ok	HL	#	LH		(two domains)

b.	姐	姐	笑	
	tɕia —	tɕia	ɕiɔ	
	sister	smile		
	'The sister smiles.'			
BT	MH	MH	MH	

*	M	=	H	=	L	(one domain)
ok	M	=	H	#	MH	(two domains)

100   *The c-command condition in phonology*

(79) VO structure

a.   搬   书
  bø   sɿ
  move   book
  'to move books'

BT   HL   HL

---

*   H = L   (one domain)
ok   HL # HL   (two domains)

b.   看   小   说
  kʰø   çiɔ — sɔʔ
  read   novel
  'to read novels'

BT   MH   MH   MH

---

*   M = H = L   (one domain)
ok   MH # M = H   (two domains)

If the principles in (71) and (72) proposed by Duanmu are correct, there should be only one TS domain in all the cases from (77) to (79). The stress assignment for (77a), (78a), and (79a) can be worked out by referring to (74), for (77b) and (79b) by referring to (75), and for (77c) and (78b) by referring to (76). But as a matter of fact, all of those predictions are wrong because there are two sandhi domains in the cases given in (77), (78), and (79). Therefore, Duanmu's metrical analysis cannot solve the problem in Shanghai either. Moreover, whether the compounds in Shanghai dialect have stress or not is still an open question.

3.6.2.3 *C-command within functional relations*

According to my analysis, it is neither the edge condition nor the metrical condition that determines the TS domain in Shanghai at the phrasal level. Instead, what influences or determines the TS domain in Shanghai includes both functional and syntactic conditions. There are three factors determining the TS domains in the Shanghai dialect: (i) the status of word-hood, (ii) functional relations, and (iii) syntactic conditions. Since the Shanghai dialect is a word-tone-sensitive language,[15] the concept of word is important. Roughly speaking, all of the lexical items, i.e., syntactic words, must undergo TS no matter what internal structures they have possessed. As for function words and syntactic phrases, the situation will be much more complicated. Not every function word will form a TS domain with the lexical item to its left; this fact goes against the claim of Selkirk and Shen. Only in some cases will a function word cliticize with its preceding lexical item; in other cases, it will form a TS domain all by itself. Likewise, not every syntactic phrase can be divided, as supposed by Selkirk and Shen, into several TS domains, nor can it form, as hypothesized by Duanmu, one tonal domain if its branching structure satisfies the requirements for TS rule application. As a matter of fact, a syntactic phrase in some cases forms one TS domain and in others splits into several TS domains. And all of these are decided completely by the functional relation and syntactic condition that a syntactic phrase belongs to.

The picture of TS at the phrasal level in Shanghai is like this: an adnominal MH structure generally undergoes TS-G – i.e., one syntactic phrase is one sandhi domain – and the TS-G rule is blocked in adverbial MH structures, SP structures, VO structures, etc., i.e., one phrase structure can split into several sandhi domains. The examples are given in (73), (77), (78), and (79).

What is the motivation for such a classification for the different types of TS in the Shanghai dialect? In my opinion, it is functional relation and syntactic condition that determine the TS at the phrasal level. To be more specific, it is the operation of c-command condition within functional relations. The principle that I propose for Shanghai TS at the phrasal level is stated in (80).

(80) TS condition in Shanghai dialect
 The TS rule is applied iff
 the adjunct is c-commanded by its head.

Now let us reanalyze the TS of phrase structures in Shanghai using the principle in (80). As seen in (73), (77), (78), and (79), the TS rule is applied to adnominal MH structures, but blocked in adverbial MH, SP, VO, and other structures. This can be accounted for by the principle in (80). The TS rule cannot be applied to SP and VO structures because they involve an argument-predicate relation instead of an adjunct-head relation required by the principle in (80). The TS rule is applied to an adnominal MH structure because it has both the functional condition (i.e., an adjunct-head relation) and the syntactic condition (i.e., the adjunct is c-commanded by its head) required by the principle in (81), which is illustrated as follows.

(81) Adnominal MH phrase structure[16]

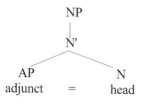

102 *The c-command condition in phonology*

However, an adverbial MH structure still causes some trouble. According to the traditional analysis, an adverbial MH structure conforms to the principle in (80) in both functional and syntactic conditions. In other words, the adjunct is c-commanded by its head, i.e., the verb. So it seems that the TS rule should be applied to it, as shown in (82).

(82) Adnominal MH phrase structure[17]

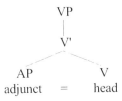

In fact, (82) makes a wrong prediction, and in the Shanghai dialect, the TS rule cannot be applied to an adverbial MH structure, as illustrated by (77). Although (82) seems to be counterevidence to the principle in (80), it is a verb-movement to result in a difference in the syntactic structures between adverbial MH in (83) and adnominal MH in (81).

(83) Adnominal MH phrase structure[18]

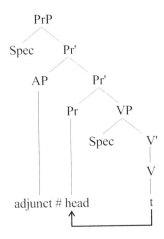

In (83), we see that the TS rule is blocked between the adjunct and the head in the adverbial MH structure because the adjunct in this case is not c-commanded by its head, thus violating the syntactic condition required by the principle in (80). So far, I have solved all the remaining problems in the hypotheses made by Selkirk and Shen, Duanmu, and others. Thus it can be seen that the c-command condition plays an important role in the Shanghai dialect and that the TS at the phrasal level in Shanghai is a case in which the c-command condition operates within a functional relation, i.e., an adjunct-head relation.

3.7 Sum up

Based on the evidence obtained from Chinese dialects, I have shown in this chapter the accessibility of syntax to phonology with an analysis of different types of c-command (as defined by Reinhart). Generally speaking, TS reacts in many ways to the c-command condition. Specifically, c-command determines what domain a tone will spread to, as in the Danyang case; whether the TS rule is applied or blocked, as in the Ruicheng case; what kind of rule application mode will be chosen, as in the Pingyao case; and how the c-command condition operates within functional relations, as in the Shanghai case. Moreover, I have also discussed some analyses under the OT framework, by applying them to some Chinese dialects, such as Pingyao, only to prove how null these analyses are as well as how effective the Direct Reference Approach (i.e., c-command condition) is in contrast.

Notes

1 For a detailed discussion on Danyang citation tones, base melodies, and spreading patterns, as well as the relationship among them, see Ting (1984), Chan (1989, 1991), Bao (1990, 1999), and Zhang (1992, 1996).

2 It should be noted that the spreading tier of (7a) differs from that of (7b). Example (7a) spreads from the tonemic tier, while (7b) spreads from the tone root tier. The spreading tier in Danyang is complicated; however, it is not directly relevant to the problems under discussion here. What we are concerned with is the spreading domain rather than the spreading tier. For a detailed discussion about the spreading tier, see Chan (1989, 1991), Bao (1990, 1999), and Zhang (1992, 1996).

3 *CT* stands for citation tones, *TS* for tone sandhi, symbol '#' for the spreading rule blocked, and symbol '=' for the rule applied.

4 The stress at the intonational level and the atonic tone, i.e., the neutral tone, which is relative to general tones, are not relevant to the problem in question.

5 Here the capital letter 'T' refers to Chan's stress syllable and the small letter 't' to her non-stress syllable.

6 Here *q* stands for the glottal ending of the checked syllable.

7 The ancient Chinese tonal system consists of four tonal categories, which underwent a register split into *yin* and *yang* tonal registers in middle Chinese due to the loss of voice distinction. *Yin* tone comes from the originally voiceless onset obstruent, while *yang* tone comes from the voiced obstruent. Originally, the tonal value of *yin* tones is higher in pitch than that of *yang* tones, but later in some Chinese dialects, *yin* tone and *yang* tone underwent register reversal.

8 In (29), the tone HM in TS position changes to the concave tone MLM. The first half of MLM retains the high falling property of HM; if we treat the rising property at the end of the tone as details of phonetic implementation, then all the TSA rules in (29) are progressive.

9 The notation φ' and ω' are used for the maximal prosodic phrase and prosodic word, respectively.

10 CT here refers to citation tones and BT stands for base tones. According to Zee (1988), there are four base tones in Shanghai, but according Duanmu, there are only two. Since my focus is not on these different views about base tones, I am not going to discuss them here.

11 For the sake of typographic convenience, the Pinyin system, instead of the IPA, is adopted here for transcription. Anyhow, it will not hinder nor affect our discussion on tonal phenomena if Pinyin is used to transcribe segmental elements.

104 *The c-command condition in phonology*

12 As for the tonal representation in Chinese, Yip (1980, 1989), Chan (1989, 1991), Duanmu (1990) and Bao (1999) have already discussed it. For convenience, I adopt the tonal representation by Yip and Chan, seen as follows.

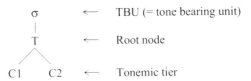

The tree expresses the contour tone formed by C1 and C2, with C1 referring to the preceding half of the contour tone, while C2 stands for its latter half. For instance, if C1 is *H* and C2 is *L*, this tone will be *HL*, a falling tone. Likewise, if C1 is *L* and C2 is *H*, this tone is *LH*, a rising tone.

13 According to Selkirk and Shen, prepositions, personal pronouns, complementizers, indefinite determiners, and classifiers are all function words.

14 The so-called spreading case and blocking case exemplified here are in fact two different types of TS, i.e., TS-G and TS-Z, which have been covered in the previous discussion. Since I am not going to argue with Selkirk and Shen, Duanmu, and others about the mode of tonal rules in Shanghai, here I just follow them, for convenience, in treating TS-Z as a blocking case belonging to different tonal domains as different prosodic units. This does not mean that I agree with their views about these two cases.

15 For a detailed discussion on word-tone-sensitive versus syllable-tone-sensitive, see Shih (1986), Zhang and Chen (1990), and Zhang (1992, 1996, 2008a).

16 Adjunct is c-commanded by a noun, i.e., the head of NP in (81).

17 Adjunct is c-commanded by a verb, i.e., the head of VP in (82).

18 Adjunct is not c-commanded by its head in (83).

4 Some issues in Mandarin interface studies

4.1 Introduction

Over the last two decades, the interface and prosodic studies have become the hottest research issues in Mandarin phonology (Zhang 1992, 1997, 2008a, 2008b, 2014; Chen & Zhang 1997; Feng 1997, 2009, 2013; Duanmu 2000a; Cao 2001; Ye 2001; Wu 2006; Li 2008; Wang 2008; Cao 2010; Deng 2010; Dong 2011; Zhou 2011). The most popular topic under discussion is the domain of rule application for the third TS (hereafter 3TS) and word-length preferences. Therefore, this chapter centers on these two topics and starts with the first, i.e., the domain of 3TS rule application.

4.2 The third tone sandhi in Mandarin

Mandarin Chinese has four citation tones – namely, even tone (H), rising tone (MH), dipping tone (MLM), and falling tone (HL), as seen in (1).

(1)   The citation tones in Mandarin

Tonal Categories		1 Yin Ping	2 Yang-Ping	3 Shang	4 Qu
Tonal contour		even	rising	dipping	falling
Tonal value	High register	H (55)	MH (35)		HL (51)
	Low register			MLM (214)	

For the sake of convenience, these four tones are also termed as first tone, second tone, third tone, and fourth tone. At the phonological level, Mandarin has a famous TS rule for having its dipping tone *MLM* (T3) changed into a rising tone *MH* (T2), as shown in (2).

(2)   The 3TS rule in Mandarin
       T3 → T2 / ____ T3

106 *Some issues in Mandarin interface studies*

However, as can be seen in (3), when more than two syllables get involved, not all of any two T3s will follow the pattern of T2+T3 in spite of the fact that the 3TS rule application requirement given in (2) has been met.

(3) a.   ling-dao dang 领导党 'to lead the party' (T3 T3 T3 → T2 T2 T3)
  b.   ling-dao hao 领导好 'leader (is) good' (T3 T3 T3 → T2 T2 T3)
  c.   qu-shui kou 取水口 'intake' (T3 T3 T3 → T2 T2 T3)
  d.   zong-tong fu 总统府 'presidential palace' (T3 T3 T3 → T2 T2 T3)
  e.   zhan-lan guan 展览馆 'exhibition hall' (T3 T3 T3 → T2 T2 T3)
  f.   xuan zong-tong 选总统 'to elect president' (T3 T3 T3 → T3 T2 T3)
  g.   dang ling-dao 党领导 'the party leads' (T3 T3 T3 → T3 T2 T3)
  h.   li zong-tong 李总统 'President Li' (T3 T3 T3 → T3 T2 T3)
  i.   chao mi-fen 炒米粉 'fried rice noodles' (T3 T3 T3 → T3 T2 T3)
  j.   zhi lao-hu 纸老虎 'paper tiger' (T3 T3 T3 → T3 T2 T3)

All the cases given in (3) begin with the same citation tones of T3+T3+T3, but end with the different TSs. Some of them turn to become T2+T2+T3, such as in (3a)–(3e), and some become T3+T2+T3, such as (3f)–(3j). Even for those reading the same as T2+T2+T3, there is still a difference, syntactically speaking, because some of them are a syntactic word, such as (3d)–(3e), and some are a syntactic phrase, such as (3a)–(3c). The same situation is found with those reading T3+T2+T3 with some of them being a syntactic word, such as (3i)–(3j) and some others a syntactic phrase, such as (3f)–(3h).

Therefore, how to determine the domain of the 3TS rule application has always been an issue in Mandarin phonology (C. Cheng 1970, 1973; Kaisse 1985; Shih 1986, 1997; L. Cheng 1987a, 1987b; Hung 1987; Z. Zhang 1988; Xu 1991; Chen 2000; Wee 2008; and others). In other words, the questions are whether the 3TS rule application in Mandarin should refer to syntactic information, or prosodic information, or both. Therefore, in this chapter, I will start with an overview of the syntax-phonology interface study in rule-based phonology, lay out the existing issues, discuss the result if the OT framework gets applied to the case study of Mandarin TS, compare two different interface approaches – i.e., rule-based versus constraint-based – and, finally, propose some solutions to the remaining issues.

4.2.1 The direct reference approach to Mandarin 3TS

C. Cheng (1973) and Kaisse (1985) are among those pioneers in the study of the 3TS rule application in Mandarin. According to them, the domain of the 3TS rule application in Mandarin is directly under the control of syntactic structure, in which the 3TS rule application is cyclic or it applies cyclically, and the 3TS rule applies across the syntactic structures from the smallest to the larger.

4.2.1.1 C. Cheng (1973)

C. Cheng determines the domain of the 3TS in Mandarin by the depth of syntactic boundaries and the speed of the conversation. He uses the figures of (1), (2), and

(3) to indicate, from close to remote, the approximate closeness of the syntactic relationships. (1) indicates the closest relationship while (3) the most remote. When the speed is slow, only the T3, which is labeled with 1, undergoes TS and turns to read T2, just as shown by (4a). When the speed is faster, those T3s labeled with (1) and (2) will have TS and turn to read T2, as seen in (4c). When the speed is the fastest, all of the T3s, except the last one in the tone sequence that remains unchanged and still reads T3, will have TS and turn to read T2, as shown by (4d). And, moreover, when the speed is fast but the conversation is causal, other than the fact that T1 turns to read T2 and the last syllable remains reading T3, all the other syllables in the middle of the tone sequence turn to read first tone, as shown by (4e).

(4)

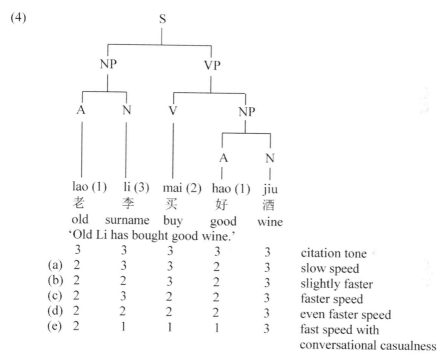

Based on the previous discussion, C. Cheng proposes that the domain of 3TS is influenced by two factors: (i) speed and (ii) syntactic relationships. However, C. Cheng's proposal is unable to account for the case in (4b) in which *Li* 'surname,' labeled with 3, has TS, while *mai* 'buy,' labeled with 2, remains unchanged. This obviously violates the principle of the depth of syntactic boundaries proposed by C. Cheng, even though he explains it by saying that (4b) is derived on the basis of (4a), which first gets its output form labeled as 3 before continuing TS until finally getting (4b). However, such an explanation is actually in conflict with the explanation of its phonetic representation because the TS of (4b) will need to skip the form with the structure labeled as 2 so as to get the TS with the structure labeled as 3. Thus it can be seen that C. Cheng's analysis can hardly predict the correct TS form for (4).

108 *Some issues in Mandarin interface studies*

4.2.1.2 Kaisse (1985)

Kaisse also considers that the domain of the 3TS rule application in Mandarin is directly influenced by syntactic structure and that the sandhi rule gets blocked between two sister branches. The Branch Condition proposed by Kaisse (1985: 174–175) for Mandarin 3TS is cited in (5).

(5)   The branch condition:

Tone sandhi may apply between two words *a* and *b* if *a* is the left branch of the constituent that contains *b* or if *b* is the right branch of the constituent that contains *a*; in other words, tone sandhi applies if the sandhi pair is on an edge of the constituent that contains it.

According to (5), if the tonal combinations are located, respectively, at the positions of *a* and *b* in (6), which follows, the TS rule cannot be applied because the boundaries of the element C, which contains both *a* and *b*, are F or G, respectively.

(6)

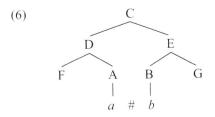

However, Kaisse's Branch Condition, as seen in (6), fails to explain a number of 3TS phenomena in Mandarin. For instance, if *a* and *b* are of the different TS domains but both are T3, they still have TS, even though such TS is not obligatory or a must. Check the case in (7).

(7)

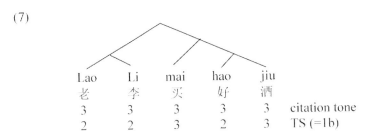

In (7), both *Li* 'surname' at position *a* and *mai* 'buy' at position *b* have TS, neither of which are allowed by the Branch Condition.

A similar case is given in (8). Both *xiang* 'think' at position *a* and *mei* 'beauty' at position *b* can have TS, as shown in (8a), and they also may not have TS, as shown by (8b). Both are possible and correct, but by Kaisse's Branch Condition, (8a) is not allowed.

(8)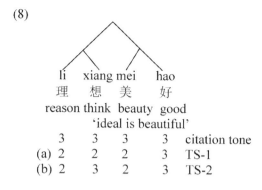

li   xiang mei   hao
理   想   美   好
reason think beauty good
            'ideal is beautiful'
        3   3   3   3   citation tone
(a)   2   2   2   3   TS-1
(b)   2   3   2   3   TS-2

Thus it can be seen that the problem with 3TS in Mandarin will remain unsolved if we rely solely on the direct syntax-sensitive approach.

4.2.2 The indirect reference approach to Mandarin 3TS

Now let us check to see if the indirect syntax-sensitive approach can solve the domain issue of 3TS rule application in Mandarin. According to the indirect syntax-sensitive approach, the domain of 3TS rule application is the prosodic structure; the prosodic structure in 3TS is sensitive to Morphosyntactic structure, and the prosodic structure can, thus, be derived from the Morphosyntactic structure, but is not necessarily identical to it. More linguists seem to be in favor of the indirect syntax-sensitive approach, but they hold different views as to which prosodic unit in a prosodic structure the domain of Mandarin TS rule should correspond to and how to define it (Shih 1986; L. Cheng 1987b; Hung 1987; Chen 2000). However, the discussion that follows focuses on the viewpoints proposed by Shih (1986), L. Cheng (1987b), and Chen (2000).

4.2.2.1 Shih (1986, 1997)

Shih believes that prosodic levels of foot, super-foot, and phrase are necessary for predicting the application of the Mandarin 3TS rule. She holds that the domain of 3TS is the foot in prosodic structure and, thus, proposes the Foot Formation Rule (FFR), which is cited in (9) (Shih 1986: 110; 1997: 98).

(9) Foot formation rule
   i) Foot (f) construction
       a. IC (immediate constituent): Link immediate constituents into disyllabic feet.
       b. DM (duple meter): Scanning from left to right, string together unpaired syllables into binary feet, unless they branch to the opposite direction.
   ii) Super-foot (f′) construction
       Join any leftover monosyllables to a neighboring binary foot according to the direction of syntactic branching.

110 *Some issues in Mandarin interface studies*

According to Shih, 3TS applies cyclically: first to feet (f), to super-feet (f'), and, finally, to phrases (p), as seen in (10).

(10)

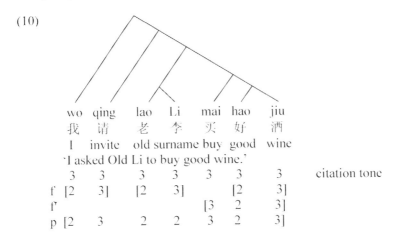

```
        wo    qing   lao   Li    mai   hao   jiu
        我    请     老    李    买    好    酒
        I     invite old   surname buy  good  wine
     'I asked Old Li to buy good wine.'
        3     3      3     3     3     3     3      citation tone
     f  [2    3]    [2     3]         [2    3]
     f'                          [3    2     3]
     p  [2    3      2     2     3     2     3]
```

At foot level, as shown in (10), IC divides *lao Li* 'Old Li' and *hao jiu* 'good wine' into separate feet, and DM sets *wo qing* 'I invite' as another foot. With TS applied at the foot level, *mai* 'buy' at the super-foot level forms a super-foot with the foot right next to it because *hao* 'good' has already turned into a T2 at the foot level, thus unable to satisfy the requirement for TS. And, as a result, *mai* 'buy' remains a T3 and only *Li* 'surname' continues TS at the phrasal level in the end.

Although Shih's FFR can explain some of the TS in Mandarin, it fails in the cases in (11) and (12).

First of all, it cannot explain the right-branching, fast-speed tri-syllabic TS patterns seen in (11b) and (12b).

```
(11)   gou_NP [[yao_V gou_NP]_VP]_IP
       dog    bite   dog
       'dogfight'
       狗     咬     狗
       3      3      3           citation tone
   (a) 3     [2      3]_IC       slow speed
   (b) 2      2      3           fast speed


(12)   xiang_V [[yang_V gou_NP]_VP]_IP
       想      养      狗
       think   raise   dog
       'Want a dog.'
       3       3       3          citation tone
   (a) 3      [2       3]_IC      slow speed
   (b) 2       2       3          fast speed
```

Some issues in Mandarin interface studies 111

Based on the prediction of FFR, both forms in (11b) and (12b) are wrong because the first syllables are not allowed for TS. But as a matter of fact, they both are correct as forms of fast speed used for emphasis.

Second, FFR fails to predict the correct form for quadrisyllabic TS, such as (13).

(13)　　[[shui guo]N jiuN]NP haoV
　　　　水　果　酒　好
　　　　water fruit wine　good
　　　　'Fruit wine is good.'
　　　　　3　　3　　3　　　3　　　citation tone
　　　* [2　　3]IC　[2　　　3]DM　incorrect TS form predicted by FFR

　　　　　2　　2　　2　　　3　　　correct TS form

To account for the aforementioned exceptional cases, Shih proposes the lexical integrity principle, by which she argues that the foot formation cannot influence the lexical internal structure (Shih 1986:138). Since *shui-guo-jiu* 'fruit wine' is a compound word, it cannot be split into two feet. However, (14) provides a counter example.

(14)　　　dangNP [[[ling dao]V]IC wo]VP
　　　　　党　　　领　导　　　我
　　　　　party　lead　guild　I
　　　　　'The Party leads me.'
　　　　　　3　　　3　　3　　　　3　　　citation tone
　　　(a) 3　　　[2　　2]IC　　3　　　slow speed
　　　(b) 2　　　2　　2　　　　3　　　fast speed

Ling-dao 'lead' in (14) is also a compound word. When *ling* 'lead' has changed to T2, *dang* 'party' in the front has lost the phonological environment for TS and, therefore, should remain unchanged, yet the fact is that it is still allowed for TS, as shown in (14b).

Third, FFR cannot explain the TS forms of some prepositional phrases, such as (15). Of the four TS forms given in (15), FFR can predict only one, (15a).

(15)　　[gou]N [[bi]P maN]PP xiaoV
　　　　狗　　比　马　　小
　　　　dog　　than horse　small
　　　　'Dog is smaller than horse.'
　　　　　3　　　3　　3　　　3　　　citation tone
　　　(a) 3　　　2　　3　　　3　　　TS-1
　　　(b) 3　　　2　　2　　　3　　　TS-2
　　　(c) 2　　　2　　2　　　3　　　TS-3
　　　(d) 2　　　3　　2　　　3　　　TS-4

112   *Some issues in Mandarin interface studies*

Shih believes that the difference in speed causes different TS forms. When the speed is normal, TS rules apply to the foot level; when the speed is faster, TS rules apply to the super-foot level, and when the speed is very fast, TS rules apply to the phrasal level. But (15) shows that when the 3TS rule gets applied to the super-foot or even the phrasal level, it brings out only (15b) and never produces (15c) or (15d).

Fourth, foot is an important concept in Shih's analysis, but she has never touched the issue of how to define the foot in Chinese from the perspective of general phonology. Neither has she discussed the similarities and differences between the Chinese foot in her FFR and the foot in Indo-European languages. Foot is a prosodic unit that is higher than syllable but lower than prosodic word in prosodic hierarchy. Whether foot as a prosodic unit exists in a language or not is determined by the metrical property of binary contrast such as strong versus weak, heavy versus light, long versus short, and high versus low. In Mandarin Chinese, however, the phonological structures are lacking a metrical binary contrast at the lexical-word level, and, therefore, the existence of such metrical foot is questionable (Zhang 2014).

Although Shih's FFR cannot successfully explain the 3TS patterns in Mandarin, her analysis has noticed the difference between syntactic structure and the domain of TS.

4.2.2.2 L. Cheng (1987b)

L. Cheng (1987b) divides 3TS in Mandarin into two categories: lexical level and post-lexical level. In other words, she believes that the 3TS rule applies to not only the lexical level but also to the post-lexical level. As for the phrasal level, she holds that the 3TS rule applies within prosodic word, phonological phrase, and intonational phrase. According to her, to determine the domain of TS rule application in Mandarin, one needs to refer to two prosodic parameters, i.e., the End-Based condition, proposed by Selkirk (1986), and the [±branchingness], proposed by Cowper and Rice (1987), as seen on (16).

(16) Mandarin end settings

PWd- word[, [branchingness +]
PPh- X^{head}[, [branchingness +]

The analytic process is illustrated in (17).

(17) wo   zhao xiao ming ɪᴘ[PRO da ni]
      我   找   小 明   打 你
      I   ask   person name   hit you
      'I ask Xiao-ming to hit you.'

3	3	3	2		3	3	citation tone
2	2	3	2		2	3	sandhi tone
3	3	3	2		3	3	lexical level
w[2	3	3	2		2	3	PWd level
X^{head}[2	2	3	2		2	3	PPh level
2	2	3	2		2	3	output

Some issues in Mandarin interface studies 113

According to L. Cheng, the case in (17) can be segmented into three prosodic words at the level of prosodic word (PWd). The pronoun *ni* 'you' is a function word. It, by Selkirk's definition, cannot be a prosodic word by itself, and, therefore, it adheres to the word at its front (i.e., *da* 'hit') and forms with it a prosodic word at the PWd level. As an internal branching unit, *xiao-ming* 'person name' forms a prosodic word by itself. Likewise, *wo* 'I' adheres to *zhao* 'look for,' thus forming a prosodic word with the latter. The 3TS rule applies at the prosodic level and *wo* 'I' turns to read T2. At the level of phonological phrase (PPh), since *zhao* 'look for' is the head of the branching verb phrase *zhao Xiao-ming* 'look for Xiao-ming,' it has a boundary label for the PPh at its left edge, and the 3TS rule applies at this level, thus turning *zhao* 'look for' into T2. Since there are no more neighboring T3s at the PPh level, the output form at this level is the final phonetic representation. If the neighboring T3s still exist at the PPh level, the 3TS rule will continue to apply at the level of intonational phrase (IPh), where the variant TS forms will be produced, as seen in (18).

(18)　xiao mei xiang IP[PRO da ta]
　　　　小　美　想　　　　打 他
　　　person name want　　　hit him
　　　'Xiao Mei wants to hit him.'

3	3	3	3	1	citation tone
2	2	2	3	1	TS-1
2	3	2	3	1	TS-2
2	3	3	3	1	lexical level
w[2	3	3	3	1	PWd level
X^{head}[2	3	3	3	1	PPh

a. [2	2	2	3	1]	IPh
b. [2	3	2	3	1]	IPh

At the PPh level, the existence of neighboring T3s is a fact. Therefore, at the IPh level, the whole sentence can form one domain and produce a TS form such as (18a) or the subject of the sentence forms one domain with the whole verb phrase forming another domain, thus producing the TS form such as (18b).

However, the End-Based Condition and the Branching Condition have some problems. First of all, they predict that the same syntactic structures produce the same TS forms. This prediction does not reflect the facts in (19).[1]

(19) a. ling-dao dang
　　　领　导　党
　　　lead guild party
　　　'to lead the party'

3	3	3	citation tone
(2	3)	(3)	*PWd
(2	2	3)	PPh

114 *Some issues in Mandarin interface studies*

b. ling-dao dang-wei
领 导 党 委
lead guild party committee
'to lead the party committee'

3	3	3	3	citation tone
(2	3)	(2	3)	PWd & PPh
(2	2	2	3)	IPh

As can be seen from the earlier discussion, (19a) has only one TS form while (19b) has two, but by End-Based Condition and Branching Condition, they should have the same TS form. Since the disyllabic noun *dang-wei* 'the party committee,' just like the monosyllabic noun *dang* 'party,' constitutes a bare noun, a non-branching constituent, these two syllables should be counted as one single prosodic unit and undergo TS. This shows that L. Cheng's approach is unable to account for the difference between (19a) and (19b).

Second, although L. Cheng claims that she analyzes Mandarin 3TS with the prosodic approach by using such terms as prosodic word, phonological phrase, and international phrase, she does not define these prosodic units. For instance, she takes *wo zhao* 'I look for,' *Xiao-ming* 'person name,' and *da ni* 'hit you' all as the same prosodic units, with the thought that they are all prosodic words. As a matter of fact, they are not the same prosodic units: *wo zhao* is a phonological phrase, *Xiao-ming* a prosodic word, and *da ni* a clitic group.

4.2.2.3 Chen (2000)

Now let us take a look at Chen's analysis. In his early works, Chen adopted Shih's principle of Foot Formation Rule (FFR). He gave up the term foot later and proposed "the Minimal Rhythmic Units" (MRU) with a set of constraints for determining MRU: {No Straddling, IP-Bound} >> Binarity >> Boundedness >> Congruence >> L-to-R (Chen 2000: 366–380). The detailed description of these constraints is given in (20) with sample cases given in (21a)–(21c).

(20) No straddling (NoStr): Immediate constituents must be MRU-mates.

IP-Bound: MRUs are IP-bound.
Binarity: The MRU is at least disyllabic.
Boundedness: The MRU is at most disyllabic.
Congruence: Group X forms an MRU with its closest Morphosyntactic mate.
L-to-R: MRUs are constructed from left to right.

(21) a. [wu wu wu wu wu]
五. 五. 五. 五. 五.
five five five five five
'5-5-5-5-5'

| 3 | 3 | 3 | 3 | 3 | citation tone |
| (2 | 3) | (2 | 2 | 3) | TS |

Some issues in Mandarin interface studies   115

	NoStr	Binarity	Boundedness	Congruence	LtoR
a. (wu.wu)(wu.wu)(wu)		*!			
☞b.(wu.wu)(wu.wu.wu)			*		O, 2
c.(wu.wu.wu)(wu.wu)			*		O, 3
d.(wu)(wu.wu)(wu.wu)		*!			

b. [[nei zhong] jiu] [you-hai]
　　那　　种　　酒　　有害
　　that　kind　wine　have harmful
　　'That kind of wine is harmful.'
　　　4　　3　　3　　3　　4　　citation tone
　　(4　　2　　3)　(3　　4)　　TS

	NoStr	Binarity	Boundedness	Congruence	LtoR
a. (nei zhong)(jiu you-hai)			*	*	O, 2
☞b. (nei zhong jiu)(you-hai)			*		O, 3
c. (nei zhong)(jiu)(you-hai)		*!			O, 2, 3
d. (nei zhong jiu you-hai)			***!		O

c. [[nei zhong] jiu] hao
　　哪　　种　　酒　　好
　　which kind wine good
　　'Which kind of wine is better?'
　　　3　　3　　3　　3　　citation tone
　　(2　　3)　(2　　3)　　TS

	NoStr	Binarity	Boundedness	Congruence	LtoR
a. (nei zhong jiu)(hao)		*!	*		O, 3
b. (nei zhong jiu hao)			*		O
☞c. (nei zhong)(jiu hao)				*	O, 2

According to Chen, TS rules need to be applied within MRU, within which, 3TS is optional. If a unit within MRU is a Morphosyntactic structure, the 3TS rule applies cyclically within MRU. In other words, the 3TS rule applies first to the lexical level and then the phrasal level, as shown by the derivation given in (22).

(22) [zhi-[lao-hu]] pao
　　纸　老　虎　　跑
　　paper　tiger　run
　　'The paper tiger runs.'
　　　3　3　3　3　　　　citation tone
　　　　(2　3)　　　　lexical MRU, 3TS
　　(3　2　3)　　　　lexical MRU, TS not applicable

　　(3　2　2　3)　　phrasal MRU, 3TS

116 *Some issues in Mandarin interface studies*

As can be seen from the previous discussion, the 3TS rule applies first to the inner-bracketed *lao-hu* 'tiger' and then to the outer-bracketed *zhi-[lao-hu]* 'paper tiger.' Due to the fact that the *lao* "prefix" already turns to read T2 as a result of the first cycle, thus making the neighboring T3 disappear for this cycle, the 3TS rule does not apply. And when the 3TS rule gets applied at the phrasal level, the correct phonetic representation gets produced. If a unit within MRU is not a morphological structure, the 3TS rule applies cyclically from left to right, as shown in (23).

(23) [wu wu wu]
　　五　五　五
　　five five five
　　'5-5-5'
　　3　　3　　3　　　　　　citation tone
　　(2　　2　　3)　　　　　MRU, TS

Chen also points out that prepositions, classifiers, and object pronouns are all clitics, which form the clitic groups with the elements that they adhere to on their left. In (24), we will see some cases of the clitic groups with the preposition *bi* 'than' and *wang* 'toward.'

(24) a.　gou [[bi ma]ₚₚ xiao]ᵥₚ
　　　　狗　　比　马　　小
　　　　dog than horse small
　　　　'The dog is smaller than the horse.'
　　　　gou = bi [ma xiao]ᵥₚ　　　cliticization
　　　　　3　　3　3　　3　　　　　citation tone
　　　　　(2　　3)　　　　　　　　lexical MRU
　　　　　(2　　3) (2　　3)　　　　phrasal MRU, 3TS

　　　b.　wo [[wang bei]ₚₚ zou]ᵥₚ
　　　　　我　　　往　　北　　走
　　　　　I　　toward north walk
　　　　　'I walk toward the north.'
　　　　　wo = wang [bei　zou]ᵥₚ　　cliticization
　　　　　　3　　3　　3　　3　　　　citation tone
　　　　　　(2　　3)　　　　　　　　lexical MRU, 3TS
　　　　　　(2　　3) (2　　3)　　　　phrasal MRU, 3TS

To determine MRU in Mandarin, what needs to be taken into consideration includes not only the clitic elements but also the edge of intonational phrases. This is because MRUs are IP-bound and can, thus, be segmented only within the intonational phrases instead of crossing their edge. Therefore, Chen's model of the domain of TS rule application in Mandarin is as provided in (25) (Chen 2000: 404).

(25) S-structure

       ↓

Cliticization → Intonation phrasing
                    (including emphatic boundary, etc.)

                      ↓

                  Lexical MRU, TS

                      ↓

                  Phrasal MRU, TS

(morphosyntax)   (phonology)

In both word-size units and sentential units, the MRU's segmentation within the parsing of connected speech abides by a single set of hierarchically ranked constraints: No Straddling, IP-Bound >> Binarity >> Boundedness >> Congruence >> L-to-R.

However, it must be pointed out that, although Chen (2000) adopts the OT concept in his analysis, he still relies on the orderly derivation for the phonetic representation, and, therefore, it is in essence an approach with the rule-based interface theory. Besides, Chen has analyzed 3TS with normal speed only. And even if this analysis succeeds in segmenting prosodic elements, i.e., MRUs, it still needs to refer to the Morphosyntactic structure and determine which mode of rule application will be chosen, i.e., iterative mode (from left to right) or cyclic mode. Another problem related to Chen's analysis is data. Taking the case *nei zhong jiu hao* 'Which kind of wine is better?' for example, Chen's handling, as seen in (26), is problematic.

(26)=(21c) [[nei zhong] jiu] hao
          哪   种   酒   好
        which kind wine good
        'Which kind of wine is better?'

3	3	3	3	citation tone
(2	3)	(2	3)	*TS-1
(2	2	3)	(3)	ok TS-2
(2	2	2	3)	ok TS-3

TS-1 proposed by Chen is actually a wrong output form. The correct forms should be TS-2 and TS-3.

4.2.3 OT approach to Mandarin 3TS

Now let us review the interface study under the OT framework. All three sentences given in (27) are spoken with the normal speed and in the most natural way without any focus. The OT analyses might cast some light on the issue of the domain of the 3TS rule application in Mandarin. The syntactic structure of the sentences given in (27) is presented in (28).

118 *Some issues in Mandarin interface studies*

(27) a. gou yao gou
    狗 咬 狗
    dog bite dog
    'Dogfight.'
    3   3   3   citation tone
    2   2   3   TS

   b. gou yao xiao-mei
      狗 咬 小美
      dog bite person name
      'The dog bites Xiao-mei.'
      3   3   3   3   citation tone
      2   3   2   3   TS

   c. xiao gou yao xiao-mei
      小 狗 咬 小美
      small dog bite person name
      'The puppy bites Xiao-mei.'
      3   3   3   3   3   citation tone
      2   3   3   2   3   TS

(28)

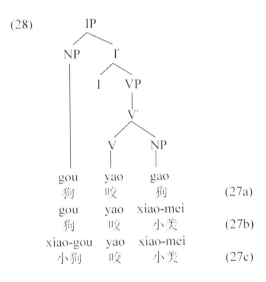

As shown by the syntactic tree in (28), the sentences given in (27) share the same structure but differ in syllable length. Both the subject and object of (27a) are monosyllabic words, the object of (27b) is a disyllabic word, and both the subject and object of (27c) are disyllabic words.

Let us check the most conventional TS patterns in (27) with the Align theory and Wrap theory to see if we may get the correct output forms. Since the Mandarin 3TS rule can be applied iteratively based on Morphosyntactic structures,

Some issues in Mandarin interface studies   119

the constraint ranking of the non-recursivity is comparatively low. Other than the non-recursivity, we need such conditions as Align-L (XP, PP) and Wrap (XP, PP). Let us check the TS pattern of (27c) first with the ranking of constraints, i.e., Wrap-XP, Align-L >> Non-recurisivity. According to the syntactic tree in (28), *xiao-mei* 'person name' is an NP, so it has an edge label of a phonological phrase on its left by the condition of Align-L. *Yao xiao-mei* 'bite Xiao-mei' is a VP, so it has an edge label of a phonological phrase on its left, too. The subject *xiao-gou* 'puppy' is an NP, so it has an edge label of a phonological phrase on its left as well. With Wrap-XP, both NP and VP should be wrapped within a phonological phrase, and, thus, we can have the prosodic structure of (27c), as illustrated in (29).

(29) (xiao-gou)$_\varphi$ (yao (xiao-mei)$_\varphi$)$_\varphi$ prosodic structure

3	3	3	3	3	citation tone
2	3		2	3	first cycle (3TS)
3	2	3			second cycle (3TS)
2	3	3	2	3	output (correct TS form)

According to (29), 3TS applies cyclically within the recursive phonological phrase and produces the correct output form *2–3–3–2–3*. The evaluation of the prosodic structure of (27c) is given in (30).[2]

(30) Syntactic structure: $_{IP}[_{NP}$[xiao-gou] $_{VP}$[yao $_{NP}$[xiao-mei]]]

     Prosodic structure: (xiao-gou)$_\varphi$ (yao (xiao-mei)$_\varphi$)$_\varphi$

$_{IP}[_{NP}$*[xiao-gou]* $_{VP}$*[yao* $_{NP}$*[xiao-mei]]]*	*Align-L*	*Wrap-XP*	*Non-Recursivity*
☞ a. (xiao-gou)$_\varphi$ (yao (xiao-mei)$_\varphi$)$_\varphi$			*
b. (xiao-gou yao xiao-mei)$_\varphi$	**!		
c. (xiao-gou)$_\varphi$ (yao xiao-mei)$_\varphi$	*		

Candidate (b) in the tableau gets eliminated because it violates Align-L twice: neither the left edge of the NP *xiao-mei* 'person name' nor that of the VP *yao-xiao-mei* 'bite Xiao-mei' correspond to the respective left edge of the phonological phrase. Candidate (c) in the tableau violates Align-L once and, thus, gets eliminated, too. Therefore, only candidate (a) wins out because the 3TS rule can be applied to its prosodic structure cyclically and ends up with the correct form.

However, the ranking of constraints can hardly help predict the prosodic structure of the phonological phrase in (27b) in which *xiao-mei* 'person name' at the object position is an NP, which, according to the condition of Align-L, should have an edge label corresponding to the phonological phrase at its left edge; *yao xiao-mei* 'bite Xiao-mei' is a VP, which should also have an edge label corresponding to the phonological phrase at its left edge, and *gou* 'dog' at the subject position is an NP, the left edge of which corresponds to the edge of the phonological phrase. Since Wrap-XP requires that NP and VP be wrapped within the phonological phrase, we will get the prosodic structure shown as (31).

120 *Some issues in Mandarin interface studies*

(31) (gou)$_\varphi$ (yao (xiao-mei$_\varphi$)$_\varphi$ prosodic structure

3	3	3	3	citation tone
3		2	3	first cycle (3TS)
	3	2	3	second cycle
*3	3	2	3	output (incorrect TS form)

| 2 | 3 | 2 | 3 | correct TS form |

Applied cyclically in the prosodic structure of (31), the 3TS rule results in the wrong output form. To acquire the correct phonetic representation, we need to add another constraint, i.e., Wrap (IP, PP). In other words, we need to wrap the whole IP within the prosodic phrase. Only in this way shall we come up with the prosodic structure for (27b), shown as (32).

(32) ((gou)$_\varphi$ (yao (xiao-mei)$_\varphi$)$_\varphi$)$_\varphi$ prosodic structure

3	3	3	3	citation tone
3		2	3	first cycle (3TS)
	3	2	3	second cycle
2	3	2	3	third cycle (3TS)

| 2 | 3 | 2 | 3 | output (correct TS form) |

As can be seen from (32), with the 3TS rule applied cyclically three times, the correct output form could be derived. However, this analysis has two problems. The first one is that the Wrap (IP, PP) approach violates the generally accepted view of the interface study, i.e., the maximal projection of functional category in the syntax-prosody mapping is invisible. And the second problem is that if added into the constraint-ranking hierarchy, Wrap (IP, PP) will lead to the wrong output form such as 2–3–3–2–3 in (27c).

Now, let us take a look at (27a). If Align-L and Wrap-XP get applied, *gou* 'dog' at the subject and object positions are NPs, and then the left edges of both should correspond to their respective phonological phrases' edge boundaries. And for *yao gou* 'bite a dog,' which is a VP, its left edge should correspond to its phonological phrase's edge boundary, too. The prosodic structure thus gained will look like (33).

(33) (gou)$_\varphi$ (yao (gou)$_\varphi$)$_\varphi$ prosodic structure

3	3	3	citation tone
	3	3	first cycle
	2	3	second cycle (3TS)

| *3 | 2 | 3 | output (incorrect TS form) |

As can be seen from the earlier discussion, whether Wrap (IP, PP) gets added into the constraint ranking or not, neither Align theory nor Wrap theory can derive the correct TS 2–2–3 for (27a).

The three sentences given in (27) share the same syntactic structure. Both Align theory and Wrap theory are the interface theories driven by syntax, and they predict that the same syntactic structures should have the same prosodic structures. However, as can be seen from the aforementioned analyses, if the three sentences in (27) share the same prosodic structure, they will not produce the correct output form. Likewise, Match theory cannot predict the TS patterns of the sentences in (27) by means of direct matching between syntactic phrase and phonological phrase.

Therefore, the interface theory of syntax-phonology under OT's framework cannot correctly predict or explain the TS patterns in Mandarin.

4.2.4 New solution: Revisit prosodic approach to Mandarin TS

I have discussed some of the domain studies of Mandarin 3TS rule application. And as can be seen from that discussion, no agreement has so far been reached. What I am going to try in the following is to solve the problem with the framework of prosodic phonology.

One of the issues in prosodic phonology is to study the units in the prosodic hierarchy of human languages. These prosodic units directly concern the domains of phonological rule application, the mode of rule application, the ordering of rule application, etc. As for the prosodic units in Mandarin, they include, at least, syllable, prosodic word, clitic group, phonological phrase, intonational phrase, and utterance. Mandarin 3TS happens only to prosodic word, clitic group, phonological phrase, and intonational phrase, but never to utterance. There are two modes of 3TS rule application in Mandarin. One is the cyclic mode and the other is the iterative mode of left to right. The former applies to prosodic word, clitic group, and phonological phrase, while the latter to intonational phrase. There are two phonological rules related to the TS in Mandarin. One concerns 3TS and the other neutral TS. Neutral TS refers to the citation tone, which changes to the neutral tone at the sandhi level. When the 3TS rule meets with the neutral TS rule, its order of rule application differs from that of the latter in the different prosodic domains. At the prosodic word level, the neutral TS rule applies before the 3TS rule, but after it in other prosodic units such as clitic group, phonological phrase, and intonational phrase. These are illustrated as (34)–(38).

(34) Prosodic word
   a. zhang-lan guan
   展　　览　馆
   exhibition hall
   'exhibition hall'

3	3	3	citation tone
2	3		first cycle (3TS)
	2	3	second cycle (3TS)
2	2	3	output (correct TS form)

122 *Some issues in Mandarin interface studies*

b. jie jie
姐 姐
sister sister
'elder sister'

3	3	citation tone
3	0	first step (morphological reduplication, neutral TS)
3		second step (3TS is not applicable)
3	0	output (correct TS form)

(35) Clitic group

a. da ni
打 你
hit you
'to hit you'

3	3	citation tone
2	3	first step (3TS)
2	0	second step (cliticization, neutral TS)
2	0	output (correct TS form)

b. zou zou
走 走
walk walk
'to take a walk'

3	3	citation tone
2	3	first step (3TS)
2	0	second step (syntactic reduplication, neutral TS)
2	0	output (correct TS form)

(36) Phonological phrase

da gou
打 狗
hit dog
'to beat a dog'

3	3	citation tone
2	3	3TS
2	3	output (correct TS form)

(37) Intonational phrase

a.　lao li da xiao gou
　　老 李 打 小　狗
　　old li hit small dog
　　'Old Li beats a puppy.'

3	3	3	3	3	citation tone
2	2	2	2	3	3TS (iteratively left to right)

2	2	2	2	3	output (correct TS form)

b. wo hen xiang da-dao ni
　我 很　想　打倒　你。
　I very want down with you
　'I really want to knock you down.'

3	3	3	3	3	3	citation tone
2	2	2	2	2	3	first step (3TS, iteratively left to right)
			0			second step (cliticization, neutral TS)

2	2	2	2	2	0	output (correct TS form)

(38) Utterance

a. ni wo hen xiang da-dao.
　你, 我 很　想　打倒。
　you, I very want down with
　'You, I really want to knock down.'

3 / 3	3	3	3	3	citation tone
2　3					3TS (problematic step)
	2	2	2	2	3	3TS (iteratively left to right)

| *2 | 2 | 2 | 2 | 2 | 3 | incorrect output |

| **3** #2 | 2 | 2 | 2 | 3 | correct output |

b. Feng you leng, yu you meng, wo you mei you che.
　风 又 冷, 雨 又　猛, 我 又 没 有 车。
　wind and cold rain and violent I and not have car
　'The wind is cold, the rain is heavy, and I don't have a car.'

1	4	**3 / 3**	4	**3 / 3**	4	2	3	1	citation tone
		2　3		**2　3**					3TS

| *1 | 4 | 2 | 3 | 4 | 2 | 3 | 4 | 2 | 3 | 1 | incorrect output |

| 1 | 4 | **3** #3 | 4 | **3** # 3 | 4 | 2 | 3 | 1 | correct output |

124 *Some issues in Mandarin interface studies*

Zhan-lan guan 'exhibition hall' in (34a) is marked with the diacritic [+w], and, therefore, it is identified as a prosodic word. As for *jie jie* 'elder sister' in (34b), it is also identified as a prosodic word by its morphological property, i.e., reduplication of kinship term. Prosodic word constitutes the lowest units in prosodic hierarchy constructed on the basis of mapping rules that make use of non-phonological notions. As can be seen from the cases in (34), the mode of 3TS rule application in Mandarin is cyclic at the prosodic word level, and the rule ordering is that the neutral TS rule applies before the 3TS rule. And this accounts for why *jie jie* in (34b) produces the wrong output form of *T2-T0*, instead of the correct one of *T3-T0*.

Both *da ni* 'to hit you' in (35a) and *zou zou* 'to take a walk' in (35b) are clitic groups, a prosodic unit located between prosodic word and phonological phrase in prosodic hierarchy and formed by a clitic element with the lexical hood, which is its host. Prosodically, a clitic group consists of a prosodic word plus a clitic, and cliticization is one of its phonological processes. For the clitic element of Mandarin, to choose its hood as host on its left is determined by the syntactic properties in cliticization. At the level of clitic group in Mandarin, the mode of 3TS rule application is cyclic. The rule ordering is that the neutral TS rule applies after the application of the 3TS rule. If not, *da ni* in (35a) and *zou zou* in (35b) would have produced the wrong reading, *T3-T0*, instead of the correct one, *T2-T0*.

Da gou 'to beat a dog' in (36) consists of two prosodic words, and, therefore, it is a phonological phrase (PPh). A PPh is a prosodic unit higher than the prosodic word and clitic group in the prosodic hierarchy. It is a unit that is established on the basis of mapping rules that make reference to syntactic concepts, and it includes all the constituents from prosodic words up to the heads of syntactic phrases. As long as the constituents are proposed on the basis of the X-bar principle, they can be employed to analyze the structures of phonological phrases. In Mandarin, at the level of PPh, the mode of 3TS rule application is also cyclic. The rule ordering is also that the neutral TS rule applies after the application of the 3TS rule. However, the major difference between clitic group and phonological phrase in Mandarin lies in their different metricalization, which I will discuss in Section 5.3.3 of Chapter 5.

The case given in (37) is an intonational phrase (IPh), which constitutes the domain of a coherent intonational contour. The semantic and pragmatic information affect the segmentation of an IPh. Certain types of structures, including parenthetical expressions, nonrestrictive relative clauses, and tag questions form IPh domains on their own. Also, focus will influence the segmentation of intonational phrases. So the parameter for forming an IPh is semantic, and it is a prosodic unit, which is sensitive to information structure. In Mandarin, at the IPh level, the mode of 3TS rule application is not cyclic, but iterative (left to right) instead. The rule ordering is also that the neutral TS rule applies after the application of the 3TS rule. If not, (37a) will be unable to produce the correct reading of *T2-T2-T2-T2-T3*, nor will (37b) produce the correct reading of *T2-T2-T2-T2-T2-T0*; instead, they will produce the same wrong phonetic representation of *T2-T2-T2-T2-T3-T0*.

Some issues in Mandarin interface studies 125

The case presented in (38) is that of utterance (Utt), which is the highest or the maximal unit in prosodic hierarchy and subject to the maximum span in applying phonological rules. The prosodic utterance resorts to syntactic information for its definition, though it is not necessarily isomorphic to any syntactic constituent. The only syntactic information used in defining Utt is the left and right boundary of X^n. If a linguistic form has pauses both at the beginning and at the end with a comparatively full meaning, then its intonation contour is an utterance. Therefore, discourse information will influence the segmentation of Utt, which is pragmatic in nature. In Mandarin, the maximal domain of the 3TS rule application is an intonational phrase, rather than an utterance. Nevertheless, the liaison takes Utt as the domain of applying phonological rules. In Mandarin, the linguistic unit that works as an utterance can range in size from a syllable to a clause group illustrated in (38b). As for (38a), we need to compare it with (37b).

(39)=(37b) Intonational phrase

wo hen xiang da-dao ni.
我 很　想　打倒 你。
I very want down with you
'I really want to knock you down.'

3	3	3	3 3 3	citation tone
2	2	2	2 2 3	first step (3TS)
2	2	2	2 2 0	second step (neutral TS)

| 2 | 2 | 2 | 2 2 0 | output (correct TS form) |

(40)=(38a) Utterance

ni wo hen xiang da-dao.
你，我 很　想　打倒。
you, I very want down with
'You, I really want to knock down.'

3 / 3	3	3	3 3	citation tone
2	**3**			first step (3TS)
	2	2	2 2 3	second step (3TS)

| *2 | 2 | 2 | 2 2 3 | output (incorrect TS form) |

As we can, (40) is derived from (39). The TS of (39) is based on information structure (i.e., focusing), while that of (40) is based on topicalization (i.e., discourse parameter). Since (39) is an intonational phrase, there is no problem applying the 3TS rule, and the mode of rule application is iteratively from left to right. But (40) is an utterance, for which the 3TS rule cannot apply.

Now let us revisit the case *Lao Li mai hao jiu*, 'Old Li has bought good wine,' which has been discussed over the past several decades, but still not solved and repeated here in (41).

126 *Some issues in Mandarin interface studies*

(41) Lao Li mai hao jiu
老 李 买 好 酒
Old Li buy good wine
'Old Li has bought good wine.'

	3	3	3	3	3	citation tone
(a)	2	3	3	2	3	slow speed (TS-1)
(b)	2	2	3	2	3	slightly faster (TS-2)
(c)	2	3	2	2	3	faster speed (TS-3)
(d)	2	2	2	2	3	even faster speed (TS-4)
(e)	2	1	1	1	3	fast speed with conversational casualness (TS-5)

The five different TSs in (41) are, in fact, the phonetic representations of five different prosodic domains. The TS-1 takes prosodic word and phonological phrase as the domains of rule application (cyclic mode). The TS-2 and TS-3 all take prosodic word and intonational phrase as the application domains. The TS-4 takes intonational phrase as the application domain (iterative application from left to right). And the TS-5 only takes utterance as the application domain (direct mapping). Thus (42) is a sum-up.

(42) Citation tone: [3–3–3–3–3]

TS-1: [2-3]ω [[3]ω [2-3]ω]φ   (cyclically apply)
TS-2: [2-2-3]ι [2-3]ω   (i. iteratively apply L-to-R; ii. cyclically apply)
TS-3: [2-3]ω [2-2-3]ι   (i. cyclically apply; ii. iteratively apply L-to-R)
TS-4: [2-2-2-2-3]ι   (iteratively apply from-L-to-R)
TS-5: [2-1-1-1-3]υ   (direct mapping)

Therefore, the conclusion is that different TS can be attributed to different domains of rule application, and the domain issue of TS rule application in Mandarin can be addressed within the framework of prosodic phonology.

4.3 Some issues on word-length preferences in Mandarin

4.3.1 *Linguistic facts*

It has long been noticed that some of the left- and right-branching structures of Mandarin tri-syllabic units seem to correspond, respectively, to different Morphosyntactic constructions, to different linguistic units (i.e., word vs. phrase), and to different parts of speech (i.e., noun vs. verb), as shown in (43).

(43) a. *zong3-tong3 fu3* (= modifier-head construction, word, and noun)

总 统 府
president palace
'the presidential palace'

b. *xuan3 zong3-tong3* (= verb-object construction, phrase, and verbal phrase)

选　总　统
elect president
'to elect the president'

With its tree structure being two syllable plus one syllable (i.e., [2+1]), the tri-syllabic *zong-tong fu* in (43a) is a noun and a modifier-head construction. However, the tri-syllabic *xuan zong-tong*, of which the tree structure is one syllable plus two syllable (i.e., [1+2]), is a verb phrase and a verb-object construction. For this observation, Feng (2005: 4–8) proposes the following rules, as shown in (44).

(44) a. Tri-syllabic structures of [2+1] form words, while those of [1+2] form phrases.
　　 b. Being rightward forms words, while being leftward forms phrases.
　　 c. Compound words are composed of rightward foot, while verb-object constructions are composed of leftward foot.
　　 d. Feet that form words are constructed from left to right, while those that form phrases are from right to left.

Some problems exist in the aforementioned rules by Feng. First, if a foot is a prosodic unit, it should be the domain of some rules' application. What are the rules that take the foot in (44) as their domain? Second, Lü (1963: 11–23) has already discussed the distribution of [2+1] and [1+2]. Instead of taking it as a rule such as (44), Lü merely regards it as a tendency. However, rules and tendencies are different. If no distinction is made between them, there may be misunderstandings with regard to linguistic data. Although it is quite easy to differentiate one from the other on a theoretical level, it is difficult to propose a mathematical approach to distinguish the two in practice. Strictly speaking, if it is a linguistic rule, then, although there may be rare exceptions, its accuracy of prediction should at minimum reach 97% (Gravetter & Wallnau 2009). In the case of "A versus non-A," for any set of randomly selected data, the probability for complementary distribution is about 65%. This 65% probability indicates that perhaps there is no applicable rule to ensure the complementary distribution of two patterns. The gap between 97% and 65% clearly illustrates the difference between rules and tendencies. As for the complementary distribution of [2+1] and [1+2] in Mandarin, the differences demonstrated in the preference may be attributed to factors of grammar, lexis, rhetoric, cognition, psychology, language contact, speed of language evolution, etc. The rare exceptions to the rules in a language are often caused by factors that are uncontrollable to speakers. For such rules as 3TS in Mandarin, speakers are sure to know and apply them consciously in their language use. However, speakers are not necessarily aware of such preferences, nor do they produce them consciously. In most cases, we cannot make a correct judgment on linguistic phenomena on the basis of preference since we cannot determine whether such phenomena are intended products of linguistic rules or the secondary effects

128 *Some issues in Mandarin interface studies*

resulting from the pursuit of a completely different aim. Now, let us look at the relevant data to see whether the complementary distribution of [2+1] and [1+2] is a rule or preference.

4.3.2 Preference or rule?

According to the rules in (44), tri-syllabic units of [2+1] should be a noun with modifier-head construction. However, such is not always the case, as shown in (45).[3]

(45) a. [2+1] as noun words with modifier-head construction, such as

qian1-niu2 hua1 牵牛花 'morning glory'
zhong1-xue2 sheng1 中学生 'middle school students'
dian4-shi4 ji1 电视机 'television set'
zong3-tong3 fu3 总统府 'the presidential palace'

b. [2+1] as noun phrases with modifier-head construction such as

chang2-zheng1 lu4 长征路 'the long march road'
jiang1-jun1 cun1 将军村 'general village'
er4-nai3 ming4 二奶命 'the destiny of being a mistress'
ning2-xia4 ren2 宁夏人 'the Ningxia people'

c. [2+1] as verb phrases with verb-object construction such as

re4-ai4 dang3 热爱党 'to love the party'
xin1-teng2 qian3 心疼钱 'to feel sorry for the cost of money'
ku4-ai4 gou3 酷爱狗 'to have strong love of dogs'
zun1-zhong4 ren2 尊重人 'to respect others'

d. [2+1] as noun words with verb-object construction such as

he2-cheng2 nai3 合成奶 'synthetic milk'
tiao2-he2 you2 调和油 'blend oil'
pai2-xie4 wu4 排泄物 'excrement'

e. [2+1] as noun words with subject-predicate construction such as

xian1-ren2 tiao4 仙人跳 'immortal jump [badger game]'
tie3-ban3 shao1 铁板烧 'iron plate burns [the grill cooking]'
xin1-li0 mei3 心里美 'heart (is) good [sweet pink-fleshed radish]'
er4-ren2 zhuan4 二人转 'two people turn [the song-and-dance duet]'

f. [2+1] as verb phrases or clauses with subject-predicate construction such as

ling3-dao3 hao3 领导好 'leaders (are) good'
zhi4-shang1 di1 智商低 'IQ (is) low'
tian3-qi4 huai4 天气坏 'weather (is) bad'

Some issues in Mandarin interface studies   129

For the exceptions of verb-object phrases in (45), Feng (2013: 187) offers the explanation in terms of stress. He argues that the structures of [1+2] comply with the requirements of stress, while those of [2+1] can easily lead to some "trochaic" structures, thus the primary stress is unable to be realized. However, there are still some structures of [2+1] that can hold water. They include *xi3-huan1 qian2* 喜欢钱 'to love money' and *xia4-hu0 ren2* 吓唬人 'to terrify people.' Feng thinks that the reason for this is because the second element of these disyllabic verbs has lost its original tone and the stress, therefore, falls on the first syllable.

However, most of the verb-object phrases in which the second syllable of the verb has not lost its original tone vastly out number those in which the second syllable of the verb lost its original tone, as seen in (46).

(46) *xin1-teng2 qian2* 心疼钱 'to feel sorry for the cost of money'
  kan4-zhong4 qian2 看重钱 'to care about money'
  zun1-zhong4 ren2 尊重人 'to respect others'
  re4-ai4 dang3 热爱党 'to love the party'
  xiang1-xin4 dang3 相信党 'to trust the party'
  yong1-hu4 dang3 拥护党 'to support the party'
  chu1-mai4 dang3 出卖党 'to betray the party'
  ku4-ai4 gou3 酷爱狗 'to love dogs very much'
  chong3-ai4 mao1 宠爱猫 'to pet cats'

Feng goes on to add another example of this type – namely, *hai1-pa4 gui3* 害怕鬼 'to be scared of ghosts,' and proposes that the second syllable is indeed stressed, or the object can only be monosyllabic, such as the word *gui3* 鬼 'ghost' in this case, and never be disyllabic (Feng 2013: 188). If this remedy is acceptable, then the following in (47) are the counter examples.

(47) a.   hai-pa pang→hai-pa fei-pang→pa fei-pang→pa pang→pa fei→pa fei-pang
  害 怕 胖　 害 怕 肥 胖 　 怕 肥 胖 　 怕 胖 　 怕 肥 　怕 肥 胖
  fear obesity fear obesity fear obesity fear obesity fear obesity fear obesity
  'to worry about obesity'

  b.   hai-pa gui → hai-pa gui-guai → hai-pa mo-gui → hai-pa gui-shen → pa gui
  害 怕 鬼　 害 怕 鬼 怪 　 害 怕 魔 鬼 　 害 怕 鬼 神 　 怕 鬼
  fear ghost　 fear ghost　　 fear ghost　 fear spirits　 fear ghosts
  'to be scared of ghosts'

  c.   hai-pa ba → hai-pa lao-ba → pa lao-ba → pa ba
  害 怕 爸　 害 怕 老 爸 　 怕 老 爸 　 怕 爸
  fear daddy fear daddy fear daddy fear daddy
  'to be afraid of daddy'

130 *Some issues in Mandarin interface studies*

d. xiang-xin dang→xiang-xin wo dang/xiang-xin gongdang/xiang-xin zhengdang

相 信 党 相 信 我 党 相 信 共 党　　相 信 政 党
trust party   trust our party / trust Communist party / trust political party
'to trust the party'

e. zun-zhong ren → zun-zhong ren-quan / zun-zhong ren-min

尊 重 人 尊 重 人 权 尊 重 人 民
respect people respect human right / respect people
'to respect others/human rights/people'

f. xin-teng qian → xin-teng qian-cai / xin-teng qian-bao

心 疼 钱　　心 疼 钱 财 心 疼 钱 包
heart ache money heart ache money / heart ache purse
'to feel sorry for the cost of money'

g. ku-ai mao → ku-ai mao-mi

酷 爱 猫　　酷 爱 猫 咪
very love cat very love catty
'to love cat very much'

Thus, it can be seen, the remedy proposed by Feng seems unable to offer a real solution to his problem.

As for tri-syllabic units of [1+2], according to the rules in (44), it should be verb phrases with verb-object construction. However, it may be so in some cases, but not in others, as shown in (48).

(48) a. [1+2] as verb-object verb phrases such as

zu1 qi4-che1 租汽车 'to rent a car'
xie3 wen2-zhang1 写文章 'to write an article'
kan4 dian4-ying3 看电影 'to watch a movie'

b. [1+2] as verb-object verb words such as
tuo1 you2-ping2 拖油瓶 'to be a drag on somebody' [metaphor: a woman's children by a previous marriage]
po4 tian1-huang1 破天荒 'to be unprecedented'

c. [1+2] as modifier-head noun words such as

zhi3 lao3-hu3 纸老虎 'paper tiger'
lao3 bai3-xing4 老百姓 'ordinary people'
tang2 hu2-lu0 糖葫芦 'sugar-coated berry'

re4 chu3-li3 热处理 'heat treatment'
niu2 pi2-qi0 牛脾气 'pigheadedness'
er2 huang2-di4 儿皇帝 'a puppet emperor'

d. [1+2] as modifier-head noun phrases such as

xiao3 yu3-san3 小雨伞 'a little umbrella'
duo1 min2-zu2 多民族 'multi-ethnic groups'
gao1 zhi4-shang1 高智商 'high IQ'
pang4 shi1-fu0 胖师傅 'fat chef'
xin1 kuan3-shi4 新款式 'new fashion'
da4 di4-zhen4 大地震 'big earthquake'

e. [1+2] as subject-predicate phrases such as

gui3 hua4-fu2 鬼画符 'ghost draws magic figures [hypocritical talk]'
wei4 qie1-chu2 胃切除 'stomach (gets) cut [the excision of the stomach]'

For exceptions of modifier-head phrases, Feng (2013: 53–64) argues that the adjective-noun structures of [1+2] should not be phrases, of which a typical example is *xiao yu-san* 小雨伞 'little umbrella.' If they are phrases, as he maintains, then how can one account for such ill-formed structures as *hen xiao yu-san 很小雨伞 'very little umbrella' and **fei-chang wei-da ren-wu* 非常伟大人物 'very great figures'? Therefore, Feng concludes that the ungrammaticality of *hen xiao yu-san* proves that it is not a phrase, or at least not a regular phrase, and both *xiao yu-san* and *wei-da ren-wu* are syntactic words. However, if this is true, then how can we exclude such structures as *xin kuan-shi* 新款式 'a new fashion,' *duo min-zu* 多民族 'multi-ethnical,' and *gao zhi-shang* 高智商 'high IQ'? The truth is that when modified by adverbs of degree, they all turn into structures akin to *zui xin kuan-shi* 最新款式 'the latest fashion,' *hen duo min-zu* 很多民族 'a great number of ethnical groups,' and *ji gao zhi-shang* 极高智商 'a very high IQ.' These structures are naturally regarded as real syntactic phrases. Therefore, the adjective-noun phrases of [1+2] still pose a challenge for "rules" in (44) proposed by Feng.

If the aforementioned examples are still subject to debate, then homographic patterns will serve as systematical counter examples for (44). For instance, such ambiguous [1+2] structures as *chao mi-fen* 炒米粉 'fried rice noodles versus to cook rice noodles,' *kao bai-shu* 烤白薯 'toasted sweet potato versus to toast sweet potato,' and *zheng ji-dan* 蒸鸡蛋 'steamed eggs versus to steam eggs' can either be verb-object (VO) phrases or modifier-head (MH) compound nouns. Data generated from a large-scale survey show that there is no phonetic difference between the verb-object phrase *kao bai-shu* and the modifier-head compound noun *kao bai-shu* in the following two sentences in (49).

132 *Some issues in Mandarin interface studies*

(49) a. Wo3 zai4 kao3 bai2-shu3. (*kao bai-shu*: to roast sweet potato, VO)

我　在　烤　白　薯
I progressive adverb marker roast potato
'I am roasting sweet potato.'

b. Wo3 chi1 kao3 bai2-shu3. (*kao bai-shu*: roasted sweet potato, MH)

我　吃　烤　白　薯
I eat roast potato
'I'll eat the roasted sweet potato.'

Furthermore, such [2+1] structures as *chu1-kou3 yan1* 出口烟 'exported cigarettes versus to export cigarettes,' *jin4-kou3 jiu3* 进口酒 'imported wine versus to import wine,' *ling3-dao3 ren2* 领导人 'leaders versus to lead people,' and *chu1-zu1 che1* 出租车 'taxi versus to rent out a car' can also be either the modifier-head compound nouns or the verb-object phrases.

Moreover, structures such as *dao1-xiao1-mian4* 刀削面 'knife cuts noodle versus the shaved noodles,' *cai4-pao4-fan4* 菜泡饭 'vegetable soaks rice versus the rice soaked in vegetable soup,' and *shen4-yi2-zhi2* 肾移植 'kidney gets transplanted versus transplant of kidney' can be either the subject-predicate (SP) phrases/clauses or the MH compound words.

Homographic patterns such as the aforementioned are in abundance and, above all, they are systematical in Chinese; therefore, they provide enough evidence against the "rules" proposed by Feng in (44).

4.3.3 Evidence from 3TS

Now let us investigate the distribution of [2+1] and [1+2] with regards to the domain of 3TS rule application. Examples in (50) are syntactic phrases. However, the domain of 3TS rule application can sometimes be three syllables or two syllables in other circumstances.

(50) The domain of the 3TS rule in syntactic phrases

xuan3 zong3-tong3 选总统 (to elect president, 1+2, VO phrase)=323=two domains
ling3-dao3 dang3 领导党 (to lead the party, 2+1, VO phrase)=223=one domain
dang3 ling3-dao3 党领导 (the party leads, 1+2, SP clause)=323=two domains
ling3-dao3 hao3 领导好 (leader is good, 2+1, SP clause)=223=one domain
li3 zong3-tong3 李总统 (President Li, 1+2, MH phrase)=323=two domains
qu3-shui3 kou3 取水口 (intake, 2+1, MH phrase)=223=one domain
chao3 mi3-fen3 炒米粉 (to cook rice noodles, 1+2, VO phrase)=323=two domains

Different from examples in (50), those in (51) are syntactic words. However, they have one thing in common: the application domain of 3TS can sometimes be three syllables or two syllables at other times.

Some issues in Mandarin interface studies 133

(51) The domain of the third tone sandhi rule in syntactic words

zong3-tong3 fu3 总统府 (the presidential palace, 2+1, MH)=223=one domain
zhi3 lao3-hu3 纸老虎 (paper tiger, 1+2, MH)=323=two domains
xin1-li3 mei3 心里美 (sweet pink-fleshed radish, 2+1, SP)=123=one domain
chao3 mi3-fen3 炒米粉 (fried rice noodle, 1+2, MH)=323=two domains

Thus it can be seen that the complementary distribution of [2+1] and [1+2] in Mandarin is a case of preference instead of a linguistic rule.

4.4 Summary

The domain of the TS rule application in Mandarin is of great importance to the study of interface theories of syntax-phonology. How to determine the domain of the 3TS rule has always been a hot topic. Should the application of the 3TS rule in Mandarin refer to syntactic information, or prosodic information, or both? I have discussed these issues in this chapter, and reanalyzed the domain of 3TS rule application in Mandarin within the framework of prosodic phonology. The following is my conclusion.

First, in Mandarin, the difference between the domain of the 3TS rule application and other factors such as speed and focus lead to various TS forms for the same sentence. This indicates that the domain of 3TS rule application in Mandarin is related to a prosodic unit, which is a typical case of the Indirect Reference Approach.

Second, given that the domain of 3TS rule application in Mandarin concerns prosodic units, which level of the prosodic hierarchy these prosodic units correspond to turns out to be a question. Most people consider that it is a foot. However, if the domain of 3TS rule application in Mandarin is defined as a foot, it will cause a confusion of terms. In metrical phonology, foot is normally adopted for the analyzing of stress, and one foot is usually a binary branching structure with one strong syllable plus one weak syllable. And, moreover, due to the fact that Chinese is a language in which a so-called foot is a syllable bearing a tone as well as the fact that the condition for the application of 3TS requires two 3Ts, it is inappropriate to define the domain of 3TS rule application in Mandarin as a foot.

Third, the 3TS in Mandarin indicates that the Strict Layer Hypothesis, one of the important principles for Indirect Reference Approach, can be violated. This is because the cyclicity of the 3TS rule application leads to the recursivity of the domain of 3TS.

Fourth, in Mandarin, the differences in such factors as syntactic structures, speed, and focus affect the domain of TS rule application and produce different TS forms at the phonetic representation level. These different TS forms are caused, in fact, by the different modes of rule application in different prosodic units.

Fifth, the difference between left- and right-branching structures is equivalent to the Morphosyntactic difference held between them. This is merely a preference, rather than a rule. Therefore, taking preference as a rule is a misjudgment of linguistic facts.

Notes

1 Although Chen (2000: 409) has discussed this problem imbedded in L. Cheng's proposal, the examples used in his discussion were not natural.
2 In the analyses here after, the square brackets [] are used to indicate syntactic structure and the round brackets indicate prosodic structure.
3 The Arabic numerals 1, 2, 3, 4, and 0 represent, respectively, the first tone, second tone, third tone, fourth tone, and neutral tone in Mandarin.

5 Function words and rhythmic effect

5.1 Introduction

Aiming at accounting for the TS phenomena at the phrase level in Chinese languages, I devoted the previous chapters to the problem of how TS is accessible to syntactic information, including functional relations (such as argument, adjunct, head), m-command, c-command, prosodic units, and so on. In this chapter, I will discuss the TS of function words and the rhythmic phenomenon in the quadrisyllabic TS of Chinese languages.

It has been widely observed that the phonological behavior of function words is different from that of lexical words and phrases. Nespor and Vogel (1986), Hayes (1989), and some others, motivated by the prosodic constituent considerations, combine function words with lexical items to form prosodic units, which they call clitic groups. They suggest that the function word must c-command the lexical item with which it is grouped. But some others such as Selkirk (1984, 1986) and Selkirk and Shen (1990), address the combination of function words and lexical items as prosodic words and claim that a function word is not required to c-command the lexical item within a prosodic word, nor is a lexical item required to c-command its companion function word within a prosodic word. According to Selkirk, the sandhi behavior of those prosodic words, which contain function words, is wholly decided by the edge of X^o or X^{max}, i.e., the edge condition.

What I am trying to do in this chapter is to show that the TS of function words is not so simple as to be accounted for by a single principle. Taking Chinese dialects for example, in some dialects, the different TS behaviors between function words and lexical words or phrases are represented by the different formations of tonal domains, but in some others, they are embodied in either different types of TS rules or different modes of TS rule application.

The other problem that I am going to discuss in this chapter is the rhythmic effect in quadrisyllabic TS, a fairly popular phenomenon in Chinese dialects, with the purpose of finding some possible accounts for some exceptional TS cases in Chinese languages.

136 *Function words and rhythmic effect*

5.2 Function words in Shanghai Chinese

As discussed in Section 3.6, I have proposed a principle for the formation of the Shanghai TS domain, repeated here in (1) for convenience's sake.

(1) TS condition in Shanghai
     The TS rule will be applied iff
     the adjunct is c-commanded by its head.

The principle in (1) is not applicable to the TS of function words, because in the cases of a verb plus a pronoun or preposition, the function word will form a TS domain with its preceding verb in TS. In (2), we see examples of the pronoun case in (2a) and (2d) of the preposition case in (2b) and (2c).

(2) a.

	tɕʰiŋ	noŋ	tɕia	tɕia
	请	侬	姐	姐
	invite	you	sister	
	'to invite your sister'			
BT	MH	LH	MH	MH

*	MH # L = H = L	by (1)
ok	M = H # M = H	by (?)

b.

	zɿ	ləʔ	zã — hɛ
	住	勒	上 海
	live	in	Shanghai
	'to live in Shanghai'		
BT	LH	LH	LH	MH

*	LH # LH # L = H	by (1)
ok	L = H # L = H	by (?)

c.

	sʏ — piɔ	ŋo	fã	ləʔ	zã	lã
	手 表	我	放	勒	床	浪
	watch	I	put	on	bed	over
	'Watch. I put (it) on the bed.'					
BT	MH MH	LH	MH	LH	LH	LH

*	M = H # LH # MH # LH # L = H	by (1)
ok	M = H # LH # M = H # L = H	by (?)

d.

	pa	–	pa	huø	–	ɕi		ŋo
	爸		爸	欢		喜		我
	father			like				I

'Father likes me.'

| BT | MH | MH | HL | MH | LH |

| * | M = H # H = L # LH | by (1) |
| ok | M = H # H = M = L | by (?) |

According to the principle in (1), the adjunct *noŋ* 'you' in (2a) should form a TS domain with the following lexical head *tɕia-tɕia* 'sister,' but this does not happen as expected. Instead, it forms a TS domain with the preceding verb *tɕʰiŋ* 'invite.' In (2b) and (2c), likewise, the adjunct-head relation does not exist between the preposition *laʔ* and the preceding verb *zɿ* 'live' and *fã* 'put,' but the TS rule still applies between *zɿ* and *laʔ*, and *fã* and *laʔ*, respectively. Likewise, in (2d) the TS rule still applies between the verb *huø-ɕi* 'like' and the pronoun *ŋo* 'me,' although the relation between them is not that of adjunct-head. Obviously, in the Shanghai dialect, the TS of function words does not conform to the principle in (1).

Thus the hypothesis proposed by Selkirk and Shen (1990) seems to be particularly fit for the TS case of function words in the Shanghai dialect. According to Selkirk and Shen, a prosodic word will extend from the left edge of one lexical item to the left edge of the next, incorporating the function word that lies between. And the function word necessarily loses its base tone and receives the sandhi tone either from the preceding lexical item, or by default tone insertion. The analysis by Selkirk and Shen seems able to explain the TS phenomena of function words in (2). In (2a), the first prosodic word starts from the left edge of *tɕʰiŋ* 'invite,' a lexical word; leaps over *noŋ* 'you,' a function word; and then extends till right before the left edge of *tɕia-tɕia* 'sister,' another lexical word. Accordingly, (2a) should have two TS domains for *tɕʰiŋ noŋ* and *tɕia-tɕia*, respectively. In the same way, an answer can be given to the question why in (2b) *zɿ* 'live' forms a TS domain with *laʔ* 'in,' while in (2c) *fã* 'put' and *laʔ* 'on' also form one TS domain. As for (2d), it seems to be the supporting evidence to the hypothesis proposed by Selkirk and Shen too. But as a matter of fact, the *edge condition*, proposed by Selkirk and Shen, cannot really account for the Shanghai TS, including the TS of function words. For instance, in (2c) the function word *ŋo* 'I' lies between the lexical compound *sɿ-piɔ* 'watch' and the lexical word *fã* 'put.' According to the edge condition, it seems that *ŋo* should form a TS domain with the preceding *piɔ*. But the fact is that they belong to two different domains. In (3) are some more examples that serve as strong counterevidence to the hypothesis proposed by Selkirk and Shen.

138 *Function words and rhythmic effect*

(3) a. (compare with (2a))

io — tɕʰiŋ noŋ tɕia — tɕia
邀　請　儂　姐　姐
　invite　　you　　sister
'to invite your sister'

BT		HL		MH		LH		MH		MH		
*		H	=	M	=	L	#	M	=	H		(by Selkirk and Shen)
*		H	=	L	#	L	=	H	=	L		(by Duanmu)
ok		H	=	L	#	LH	#	M	=	H		(by ?)

b. (compare with (2b))

huø — ɕi lɔʔ zã — hɛ zʅ
欢　喜　勒　上　海　住
　like　　in　Shanghai　live
'to like to live in Shanghai'

BT		HL		MH		LH		LH		MH		LH	
*		H	=	M	=	L	#	L	=	H	#	LH	(by Selkirk and Shen)
*		H	=	L	#	L	=	H	=	L	=	L	(by Duanmu)
ok		H	=	L	#	LH	#	L	=	H	#	LH	(by ?)

c. (compare with (2c))

sʏ — piɔ ŋo kʰø — tɕi lɔʔ zã lã
于　表　我　看　见　勒　床　浪
　watch　I　see　　on　bed　over
'Watch, I saw (it) on the bed.'

BT		MH		MH		LH		MH		MH		LH		LH		LH		
*		M	=	H	#	LH	#	M	=	H	=	L	#	L	=	H		(by Selkirk and Shen)
*		M	=	H	=	M	=	M	=	L	#	L	=	L	=	LM	(by Duanmu)
ok		M	=	H	#	LH	#	M	=	H	#	LH	#	L	=	H		(by ?)

d. (compare with (2d))

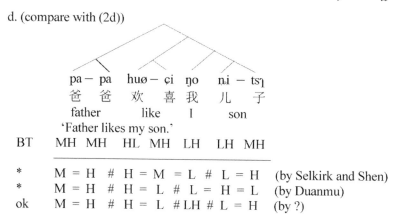

*	M = H	#	H = M	=	L #	L	= H	(by Selkirk and Shen)
*	M = H	#	H = L	#	L = H	=	L	(by Duanmu)
ok	M = H	#	H = L	# LH #	L = H			(by ?)

According to Selkirk and Shen, a sequence of a lexical item plus function word(s) only forms a single domain. But in (3a)–(3d), every function word, either pronoun or preposition, forms a tonal domain all by itself instead of joining its preceding lexical item or compound in forming a TS domain. Therefore, the edge condition is ineffective not only in the TS of phrase structure, discussed in the previous chapter, but also in the TS of function words in Shanghai.

As seen from (2) and (3), the metrical approach, proposed by Duanmu, also has some problems when applied to Shanghai TS. Without differentiating the TS at phrasal level from that of function words, Duanmu tries to account for all of the Shanghai TS with his metrical principles. If the metrical principles are strictly applied, there will be only one association domain in (2a) and (2b) because by the Stress Clash Rule (i.e., remove the stress column next to a higher column). All of the uniform right-branching structures will end up with only one stress, as shown in (4).

(4) = (2a) and (2b)

a. By stress equalization convention

```
       *
       *         *
       *         *          *
     ( X1 )    ( X2 )    ( X3  -  X4 )
```

b. By stress clash rule

```
       *
       *
       *
     ( X1 )     X2        X3  -  X4 )
```

140 *Function words and rhythmic effect*

c. By association domain formation

```
  *
  *
  *
( X1   =   X2   =   X3 = X4 )      output
  |_____|           one domain
```

   As seen from (4), there should be only one TS domain in uniform right-branching structures. But the fact is that there are two TS domains in both (2a) and (2b).
As for (2c), it would have two TS domains by the metrical analysis, but in fact it
has four TS domains. As for the wrong predictions, which result from the application of the metrical approach to the TS of function words, they are already given
in (3a)–(3c). In each case of (3a)–(3c), the first wrong prediction is produced with
the application of the edge condition of Selkirk and Shen, the second wrong prediction results from the application of the metrical approach of Duanmu, and only the
third prediction is the correct output form of TS.
   It seems that neither the edge condition nor the metrical approach can get the correct output forms for the TS of function words in the Shanghai dialect. In (5), I offer
the principle that I propose for the TS formation of function words in Shanghai.

(5)   Principle of TS formation of function words in Shanghai

      The TS rule will be applied iff

         (a) the function word is at the right edge of XP; or
         (b) it is c-commanded by its preceding syllable.

   It should be noted that TS formation at the phrasal level differs from that at the
function word level. As can be seen in (5a), in the Shanghai dialect, the function
word at the final position of an XP will form a TS domain with the preceding lexical item, as shown in (2d). On the other hand, as can be seen in (5b), the TS at the
function word level is sensitive to syllables instead of to lexical items. Now let us
use the principle in (5) to reanalyze the cases in (2) and (3).
   In (2a), since the function word *noŋ* 'you' is c-commanded by its preceding
syllable *tcʰiŋ* 'invite,' the TS rule is applied, and *tcʰiŋ* and *noŋ* together form one
TS domain. In the same way, we can find out why *zŋ* 'live' with *laʔ* 'in' in (2b)
and *fã* 'put' with *laʔ* 'on' in (2c) will each form one TS domain of its own. As for
(2d), the pronoun *ŋo* 'I' forms one TS domain with the preceding verb *huo-ci*
'like' simply because it is at the final position of the IP. Now let us consider the
cases in (3). As for (3a), the pronoun *noŋ* 'you' is not c-commanded by its preceding syllable *tcʰiŋ*, so the TS rule cannot be applied, and *tcʰiŋ* and *noŋ* belong to
different tonal domains. In (3b), the preposition *laʔ* 'in' is not c-commanded by
its preceding syllable *ci*, thus bringing *ci* and *laʔ* into different TS domains. In
(3c), since neither the pronoun *ŋo* 'I' nor the preposition *laʔ* 'on' is c-commanded
by their preceding syllables, *piɔ* and *tci*, respectively, the TS rule cannot be applied,

and *piɔ* and *ŋo* as well as *laʔ* and *tɕi* have to go into different TS domains. As for (3d), it is same as (3a). So far, I have explained the TS phenomena of function words in Shanghai with the principle in (5). It should be emphasized that, although Shanghai dialect is a word-sensitive language, the TS of its function words is sensitive to syllables instead of lexical items, as exemplified by the comparison between the cases in (2a) and (3a). If the TS of function words in question is sensitive to lexical items, *iɔ-tɕʰiŋ* 'invite' in (3a) as a lexical item will c-command the following pronoun *noŋ* 'you' and form a TS domain with it, which is a wrong TS form, as seen in (6a). Since the fact is that the TS of function words is sensitive only to syllables, *tɕʰiŋ* in (3a) as a syllable does not c-command the following *noŋ*, but leaves it to form a TS domain all by itself, thus producing the correct output form, as seen in (6b).

(6) a. Lexical item sensitive

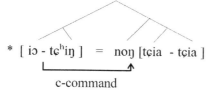

* [iɔ - tɕʰiŋ]   =   noŋ [tɕia - tɕia]

c-command

b. Syllable sensitive

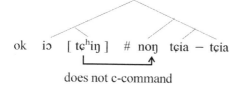

ok   iɔ   [tɕʰiŋ]   # noŋ   tɕia — tɕia

does not c-command

Recall the discussion about clitic groups by Nespor and Vogel (1986) or Hayes (1989), for whom the function word (read "clitic") must c-command the lexical item with which it is grouped. But in the Shanghai dialect, although c-command works as an important condition in the TS of function words, the function word needs neither to c-command nor to be c-commanded by the lexical item with which it is grouped. In fact, in Shanghai, the function word that undergoes TS only needs to be c-commanded by its preceding syllable.

5.3 Function words in Xiamen Chinese

As discussed previously in Chapter 2, a well-known TS rule in Xiamen Chinese is as follows in (7).

(7)   Xiamen TS rule
      T ⟶ T′/ ____ T]α

142 *Function words and rhythmic effect*

This rule refers to the kind of phenomenon that given two adjacent tones, the first becomes a sandhi tone with the second remaining as its citation form. It has been observed that the TS rule operates in the domain of the tone group (Shih 1986; Chen 1987, 1992c; Hsiao 1991; Zhang 1992). Previously, in Chapter 2, I proposed a re-revised TG formation principle for Xiamen TS, repeated in (8).

(8) TG formation in Xiamen

Mark the right edge of every XP with #, except where XP is an adjunct m-commanding its head on the right, except Infl.

However, the TG formation in (8) is applicable only to TS at the phrase structure level, not to that of function elements. Please compare (9a) with (9b) given in (9).

(9) a. 'Lazy boy'

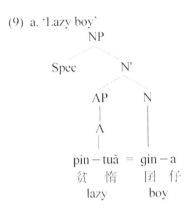

b. 'Lazy boy' (e = subordinator)

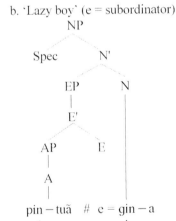

Although in both (9a) and (9b), the adjunct *pin-tuah* 'lazy' c-commands the following *gin-a* 'boy' and *e* 'subordinator,' respectively, it forms a TG only with *gin-a* in (9a) while in (9b) *pin-tuã* and *e* belong to different TGs. One of the

Function words and rhythmic effect 143

possible causes for the two tonal domains in (9b) is the rhythmic effect. In (9b), there are five syllables and the tonal pattern might be a rhythmic pattern [XX#XXX]. The rhythmic effect on Xiamen TS has been widely discussed (Hsiao 1991; Chen 1992c; Hsu 1992), and I too will cover it in my discussion later on. However, further analysis proves that the tonal phenomenon in (9b) has nothing to do with the rhythmic effect, despite the fact that such a rhythmic pattern as [XX#XXX] does exist in Xiamen, as seen in (10a) and (10b).

(10) a. 'new video movie'

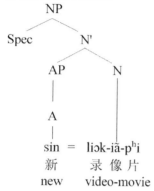

b. 'new video movie'

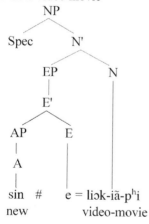

Like (9a) and (9b), (10a) and (10b) have four and five syllables, respectively, but the tonal pattern of (10b) is not like that of (9b), i.e., [XX#XXX], instead it is [X#XXXX]. Obviously, the factor determining the tonal pattern for (9b) and (10b) is not the rhythmic effect but the position of the genitive marker *e*. This proves that TS for function markers in Xiamen is very peculiar, and it differs not only from TS at the phrase structure level, discussed in Chapter 2 but also from the TS resulting from the rhythmic effect.

144 *Function words and rhythmic effect*

The other supporting evidence for the difference in TS between function words and phrase structures in Xiamen is the case of neutral tone. Located in the final position of a sentence, the function word in Xiamen often receives a neutral tone instead of a citation tone, as seen in (11). But according to (7), the syllable at the final position of a tonal domain should remain its citation tone, as shown in (12).

(11) Neutral tone case

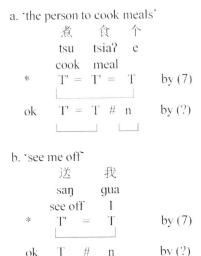

a. 'the person to cook meals'
　　　煮　　食　　个
　　　tsu　tsiaʔ　e
　　　cook　meal
*　　　T' = T' = T　　by (7)

ok　　T' = T # n　　by (?)

b. 'see me off'
　　　送　　我
　　　saŋ　gua
　　　see off　I
*　　　T' = T　　by (7)

ok　　T # n　　by (?)

(12) Citation tone case: 'send book'
　　　送　　冊
　　　saŋ　tsʰeʔ
　　　send　book
ok　　T' = T　　by (7)

Another piece of evidence is the pronoun TS in Xiamen. The pronoun in the SP structures receives sandhi tone instead of keeping its citation tone when it is the subject, as seen in (13). According to the TG formation in (8), the right edge of NP should be marked with #, as shown in (14).

(13) Case of pronoun as subject
'I came.'

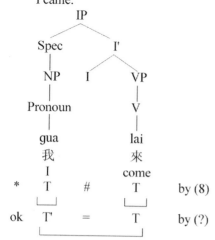

(14) Case of noun as subject
'Miss Ting came.'

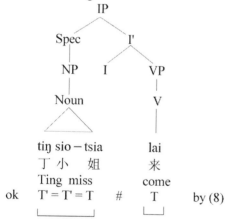

As seen in the previous examples, the TS of function words in Xiamen is unique, and the TS rule for it can be summed up in (15).

(15) TS rule for function words (FW) in Xiamen
    a. FW ⟶ T' / _____ T ...]α
    b. FW ⟶ n/T _____ #

As seen in (15), the function word, if in the non-final position of the TS domain, will have its citation tone changed into a sandhi tone, as stated by (15a), but if in the final position of a sentence, it will have its citation tone changed into a neutral tone, as given by (15b).

Now let us see how the TS rules in (15) operate within the TS domain, which I marked off with the boundary symbol # as a notational device, as seen in the earlier cases. I discussed in Chapter 2 the tonal domain at the phrase structure level, i.e., the tone group (TG), in Xiamen and reproduced the TG formation principle in (8) in this section. As can be seen from (8), the tonal domain at the phrasal level is determined by three factors: (1) the edge condition, (2) functional relations, and (3) syntactic conditions (i.e., the c-command condition). But the examples in (9)–(14) prove that the TG formation in (8) is not workable for the TS of function words because there is a #, the tonal domain boundary symbol, right before the function word, as seen in (9b), (10b), (11a), and (11b). Based on this fact, I propose a TS formation principle for function words, as given in (16).

(16) TG formation for function words (preliminary)

Mark the left edge of a function word with #.

Although the principle in (16) can be used to account for the examples in (9)–(11), it fails in the cases in (17)–(18).

(17) 'send me the book'

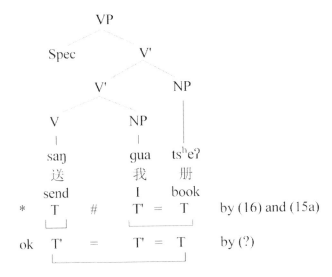

(18) 'train ... to be both red and expert'

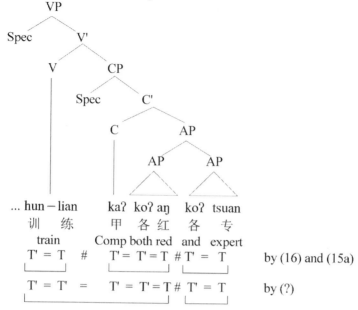

According to the principle in (16), a tonal boundary symbol '#' should be put before both the pronoun *gua* 'I' in (17) and the complementizer *ka?* in (18). However, the fact is that the symbol '=,' indicating the application of the TS rule, takes the place of '#' in both cases. Since an X° instead of an XP is put before the function word in both (17) and (18), the TS rule is blocked. All this shows that the principle in (16) is problematic, and so I have revised the principle for the TG formation of function words accordingly, as seen in (19).

(19) TG formation of function words (revised)
  Mark with # the right edge of an XP located before a function word.

The revised principle in (19) can explain why in (17) and (18) the symbol '=' is placed in front of the function word, while in (9b), (10b), and (11a) it is replaced by the symbol '#.' That is because in the former, the function word is preceded by an X°, while in the latter, it is preceded by an XP. But the principle in (19) still needs further revision. Consider (11b) again. According to the principle in (19), the pronoun *gua* 'I' in (11b) cannot be preceded by the symbol '#' because *gua* does not follow an XP, as seen in (20).

148 *Function words and rhythmic effect*

(20) = (11b) 'see me off'

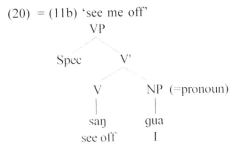

As shown by the previous structure, *gua* is preceded by an X° instead of an XP. According to the principle in (19), *gua* should be preceded by the symbol '=.' But as a matter of fact, it is preceded by the symbol '#.' Thus the principle in (19) needs to be revised again. The re-revised principle for TG formation of function words is given in (21).

(21) TG formation of function words (re-revised)

Mark with # the right edge of both the XP located before a function word and the X° located before a neutral tone.

As can be seen from (21), if the function word is preceded by an XP, it should be marked with '#,' otherwise, the TS rule will be applied to the elements preceding the function word, as exemplified by (9b), (10b), (17), and (18). Then, if the function word is in the final position of the sentence, its base tone will be changed to a neutral tone. Moreover, the lexical syllable preceding the function word will keep its tone unchanged and keep its citation form, as exemplified by (11a) and (11b). To test the aforementioned analysis, more examples (23)–(28) are provided.

(22) Subordinator marker 'e' case

    a. 'Zhang-zhou's narcissus'
       漳　州　个　水　仙　花
       tsiaŋ – tsiu　e　tsui – sian – hua
       zhang-zhou　　　narcissus
       T' = T # T' = T' = T' = T

    b. 'Black (thing?)'
       乌　个
       ɔ　e
       black
       T # n

Function words and rhythmic effect   149

(23) Co-ordinate marker 'kaq' case

'Water is incompatible with fire.'

水	甲	火	不	相	容
tsui	kaq	he	bue	siɔng –	iɔng
water	and	fire	not	compatible	

T # T' = T # T' = T' = T

(24) Aspect marker 'tio/' case

a. 'to think of friends'   (ASP = aspect)

想	着	朋	友
siũ	tioʔ	piŋ –	iu
think	ASP	friend	

T' = T' = T' = T

b. 'to have thought of'

想	着
siũ	tioʔ
think	ASP

T # n

(25) Reduplicated verb marker 'tse' case

'to have a look'   (RED = reduplicated)

看	下
kʰuã	tse
look	RED

T # n

(26) Interrogative marker 'm' case

'Do you want to come?'   (INT = interrogative)

你	要	来	不
li	beʔ	lai	m
you	want	come	INT

T' = T' = T # n

150   *Function words and rhythmic effect*

(27) Mood marker 'la' case

'He is the boss.'   (MOD = mood)

伊	就	是	头	家	啦
i	tsiu	si	tʰau − ke		la
he	just	be	boss		MOD
T'	= T' =	T' =	T' =	T	# n

(28) Personal pronoun case

a. 'I am a student.'

我	是	学	生
gua	si	hak − siŋ	
I	be	student	
T'	= T' =	T' =	T

b. 'to see you off'

送	恁
saŋ	lin
see off	you
T #	n

As can be seen from the examples, in Xiamen Chinese, the TS behavior of function words differs greatly from that at the phrasal level. By comparing the TG formation of function words in (21) with the TG formation of lexical words in (8), we see that the former is only sensitive to the edge condition, while the latter is sensitive to 1) the edge condition, 2) functional relations, and 3) syntactic conditions. In the framework proposed by Nespor and Vogel (1986), Hayes (1989), and others, the TS of function words is taken as TS at the level, which is called a clitic group. Generally speaking, prepositions, pronouns, aspect markers, complementizers, indefinite determiners, articles, and classifiers are all function words, which, with only primarily grammatical import, have less semantic content (Selkirk 1984, 1986; Selkirk & Shen 1990). But it should be pointed out that in Xiamen Chinese, not all of the aforementioned function words have unique TS behavior. As a matter of fact, the unique ones are only such function words as the subordinator marker *e*, the co-ordinate marker *kaʔ*, the aspect marker *tioʔ*, the reduplicated verb marker *tse*, the interrogative marker *m*, the mood marker *la*, and personal pronouns, which are regarded as *xu-ci* 'empty word' or 'bleaching word' by Chinese linguists. However, the TS of some other function words is identical to that of content words belonging to the TS at the phrasal level. For instance, prepositions are usually considered as function words, but their TS behavior is the same as that of content words, as shown in (29).

(29) Preposition TS case

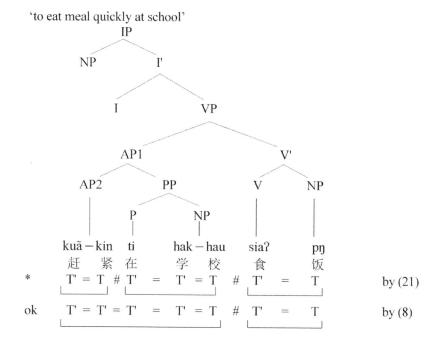

If the TS behavior of the preposition belongs to that of function words, the symbol '#' should be inserted between the function word and its preceding XP by the principle in (21). But the fact is that the symbol '=' is placed there instead, conforming to the principle in (8). Thus it can be seen that in Xiamen not all of those items considered as function words will have unique TS behaviors. Moreover, although the TS of function words is unique in many dialects, its manifestation may not be the same in different dialects. For instance, the TS of the preposition belongs to the TS type of function words in Shanghai, as discussed in Section 5.2, but is identical to the TS of content words in Xiamen.

5.4 Clitic groups in Chongming Chinese

In the literature, the domain of rule application for the clitic group (CG) is either determined by the edge of XP or X° (Selkirk 1984, 1986) or by the c-command condition (Nespor & Vogel 1986; Hayes 1989). However, the real situation is not that simple. So far, I have discussed the effect of the c-command condition on the formation of CG TS domain in the Shanghai dialect (cf. Section 5.2) and the sensitiveness of CG TS to the edge condition in Xiamen dialect (cf. Section 5.3). In this section, I will discuss another type of CG TS in the Chongming dialect, which distinguishes itself not only by being sensitive to syntactic categories but also by differing from lexical TS in choosing a different mode of rule application.

152 *Function words and rhythmic effect*

5.4.1 Basics of Chongming tone and tone sandhi

Chongming is a northern Wu dialect spoken by some 900,000 inhabitants on the namesake island located in the Yangzi delta, north of Shanghai city.[1] Before going on to reveal and discuss the CG TS phenomenon, I shall first provide some background information concerning the tonal system of Chongming.

The four Middle Chinese (ca. sixth century AD) tones have evolved into a symmetrical eight-tone system in Chongming, neatly partitioned into two registers corresponding to the voicing contrast of the initial consonants, as shown in table (30).

(30) The citation tones in Chongming

Middle Chinese Categories		*ping*	*shang*	*qu*	*ru*
		even	*oblique*		*even*
Chongming tones	High register	1H	3HMH	5M	7Hq
	Low register	2LM	4LML	6MLM	8Lq

Given the uncertain nature of the exact phonetic values of the Middle Chinese tonal categories, I follow the custom of referring to them by their traditional terms: *ping*, *shang*, *qu*, and *ru*, which translate roughly as level, ascending, departing, and entering tones, respectively. The Chongming tones are numbered sequentially from one to eight, with their pitch contours indicated by a combination of *H, M, L* (high, mid, low). The symbol *q* stands for a glottal stop, a Chongming residue reflecting the Middle Chinese stop endings [p, t, k]. As will become obvious from the account to follow, Chongming TS behavior cannot be described without constant reference to the dichotomy between 'even' and 'oblique' tones (henceforth abbreviated as *E* and *O*, respectively). Synchronic data strongly suggest that the original E/O distinction must have been rooted in the relative complexity of the tonal structure: *O* tones tend to exhibit complex pitch movements (HMH, LML, and MLM), while *E* tones appear to represent, for the most part, steady-state pitches (H, Hq, and Lq). This otherwise clearly phonetically based partition must have been obscured by intervening historical changes: thus the dynamic tone 2 (*LM*) is classified as *E*, while the level tone 5 (*M*) behaves like an *O* tone.[2]

Now let us turn back to TS. One of the pervasive features in Chongming is the distinction between lexical and post-lexical TS. Generally speaking, the former operates within lexical compounds or syntactic words, while the latter affects larger units such as syntactic phrases and clitic groups.

The following table in (31) summarizes the correspondences between the citation tones and their sandhi forms generated by lexical TS (LTS) applying to a disyllabic compound.[3]

Function words and rhythmic effect   153

(31) The disyllabic LTS in Chongming

1st \ 2nd		even (E)				oblique (O)			
		H	LM	Hq	Lq	HMH	LML	H	MLM
E	H							$-n	
	LM			$-H					
	Hq								
	Lq							$-M	
O	H	HMH		HMH-H					
	R	M						$-n	
	L	LML		MLM-H					
	R	MLM						$-M	

The citation tones of the first and the second syllable of a disyllabic compound are indicated in the left column and in the top row, respectively. The sandhi tones of such combinations are given in the cells where the two citation tones intersect. Thus, for instance, a sequence of *M-LM* (or tone 5 + tone 2) shows up as *HMH-H* in lexical compounds, while *H-MLM* (or tone 1 + tone 6) surfaces as *H-n* (unchanged citation tone $ (= *H*) plus a neutral tone *n*). Some generalizations readily emerge from (31). Apart from the *O-E* combination, the first syllable keeps its base tone unchanged in a disyllabic compound. Where the first tone does undergo change, it surfaces uniformly as a high or low fall-rise (i.e., "dipping") tone, depending on its underlying high/low register (HR/LR) contrast. Based on (31), the rules for disyllabic LTS are proposed in (32).

(32) Disyllabic LTS rules in Chongming

(a)
$$O \; - \; E$$
$$HR \quad LR$$
$$\downarrow \quad \downarrow$$
$$HMH \quad MLM$$

(b)
$$E \; - \; E$$
$$\downarrow \quad \downarrow$$
$$\$ \quad H$$

(c)
$$T \; - \; O$$
$$\downarrow \quad \downarrow$$
$$\$ \quad M, \quad \text{if } T = Hq, Lq, HMH \text{ or } MLM;$$
$$\quad \quad n, \quad \text{elsewhere.}$$

Put in another way, as shown in (32), disyllabic LTS maintains the register contrast, but reduces all tone melodies to a dipping (i.e., fall-rise) contour. However, the clitic group seems to constitute a particular domain for the post-lexical level, which refers to the clitic group TS (hereafter, CTS).

154 *Function words and rhythmic effect*

5.4.2 *Morphosyntactic-based rule selection of CTS in Chongming*

Phonologically speaking, CTS in Chongming is more complicated than LTS in that the diverse phonetic outputs of CTS rules are determined by the register and melody contrasts not only of the input tone but also of those of the neighboring syllables. Moreover, CTS is sensitive to specific types of Morphosyntactic structures (such as number-classifier, verb-pronoun, verb-directional complement). In (33), the tables of disyllabic CTS in Old Chongming dialect are shown.[4]

(33) The Disyllabic CTS in Chongming

CTS type			CTS-A		CTS-B		CTS-C		CTS-D	
Morphosyntactic structure			NM, VR		MR		VPr		VD	
1st syll.		2nd syll.	E	O	E	O	E	O	E	O
E		H	S-H	S-n	S-H	S-n	S-H		S-H	
		LM								
		Hq		S-M		S-M				
		Lq								
O	H R	M		S-H	HMH-M				HMH-H	
		HMH	S-M				S-M			
	L R	LML			LML-n				LML-H	
		MLM								

It is worthwhile to pay attention to the structure-sensitivity of CTS in (33), which offers not only a different set of CTS rules distinct from LTS, but indeed several sets of CTS rules for different types of Morphosyntactic structures within a clitic group.

CTS-A applies to two different structures, i.e., number-measure (NM) and verb-resultative complement (VR), as illustrated in (34).

(34) CTS-A case

    a. Number-measure

        四　　　頓

        sๅ　−　təŋ

        four　　meal

        'four meals'

    BT   M　-　M

         O　-　O

      *　 M　-　n　　(by LTS)

      ok　 M　-　H　　(by CTS-A)

Function words and rhythmic effect 155

b. Verb-resultative

做　　完
tsu — va
do　finish
'to have done'
BT　M　-　LM
　　O　-　E

　*　　HMH -　H　　(by LTS)
　ok　　M　-　H　　(by CTS-A)

From the example we can see that (34a) is a number-measure structure. Since the second tone is oblique, it is subject to the CTS-A rule. Since the first tone is M, the TS form is MH. It should be noted that application of the LTS rule would lead to an ungrammatical result. Example (34b) shows a verb-resultative complement, to which the CTS-A rule applies, since the tone of the second syllable is even.

Disyllabic CTS-B is applicable only to reduplicated measure words (MR). The example for this type is interpreted in the same manner given in (35).

(35) CTS-B case: Reduplicated measure

次　　　次
tsʰ⌐ — tsʰ⌐
time　　time
'every time'
BT　　M　-　M
　　　O　-　O
　　　HR　-　HR

　*　　　M　-　n　　(by LTS)
　*　　　M　-　H　　(by CTS-A)
　ok　　HMH　-　M　　(by CTS-B)

The Morphosyntactic structure that undergoes CTS-C is the verb-pronoun (VPr), and it is exemplified by (36).

(36) CTS-C case: Verb-pronoun

帮　　你
pã — n
help　you
'to help you'
BT　H　-　LML
　　E　-　O

　*　　H　-　n　　(by LTS, by CTS-A, by CTS-B)
　ok　　H　-　H　　(by CTS-C)

156   *Function words and rhythmic effect*

Disyllabic CTS-D is applicable only to the structure of verb plus directional complement (VD), as shown in (37).

(37) CTS-D case: Verb-directional

```
         进      上
       tçiŋ  —  kʰi
       enter   DIR
       'to enter'
BT     M   -   M
       O   -   O
       HR  -   HR
─────────────────────────────
 *     M   -   n     (by LTS)
 *     M   -   H     (by CTS-A, by CTS-C)
 *    HMH  -   M     (by CTS-B)
ok    HMH  -   H     (by CTS-D)
```

Needless to say, clitic groups with different internal Morphosyntactic structures do not contrast in all phonological contexts. Thus all of the clitic groups with underlying *E-E* tones show up as *$-H*. In other words, they retain the citation tone of the first syllable while changing the second tone to *H*. However, despite such partial convergences, the systematic asymmetries made evident by (33) make it impossible to collapse the four types of CTS rules.

The Chongming disyllabic CTS sheds interesting new light on the issue of how phonological rules may interact with morphosyntax. It has been shown that under certain syntactic conditions, CTS rules may or may not apply. The problem posed by the Chongming dialect is not whether or not CTS rules apply, but which CTS rule is selected. The same tonal input forms undergo different CTS rules, depending on their syntactic status. For instance, in Chongming disyllabic CTS, an input form consisting of two *M* tones may have as many as three output forms based on different Morphosyntactic conditions, as shown in (38).

(38)

	Base form	Sandhi form

M-M ⟶
| M - H / in number-measure and verb-resultative structures |
| HMH - M / in a reduplicated measure structure |
| HMH - H / in a verb-directional structure |

It can be seen from (38) that although the citation tone form is *M-M*, the sandhi form for the number-measure structure will be *M-H* ('four meals' in (34a)); for the reduplicated-measure structure, it will be *HMH-M* ('every time' in (35)); and for the verb-directional structure, it will be *HMH-H* ('enter' in (37)). Therefore, in spite of having the same underlying phonological representation, we have different phonological outputs depending on the clitic status.

Now let us turn to tri-syllabic TS, which is much more complicated than disyllabic TS because it involves syntactic branching structures. In Chongming, the mode of rule application for tri-syllabic LTS is direct mapping (DM) no matter if it is a left-branching structure or right-branching structure,[5] as seen in (39) and (40), respectively.

(39) The tri-syllabic LTS in Chongming

1st syll.	3rd yll. 2nd syll.		Even (E)			Oblique (O)		
		1 M	2 LM	7 Hq	8 Lq	3 HMH	4 LML	5 M	6 MLM
E	E		$-H-H				$-H-n	
	O		$-M-H				$-M-n	
O	High register	E		HMH-H-H				HMH-H-n	
		O		HMH-M-H				HMH-M-n	
	Low register	E		MLM-H-H				MLM-H-n	
		O		MLM-M-H				MLM-M-n	

(40) Tri-syllabic LTS rule

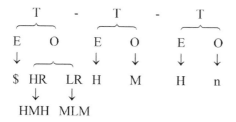

As seen in (40), the subrules of tri-syllabic LTS apply simultaneously. In other words, they directly map the base tones into their corresponding sandhi forms. We can see that (40) is context-free because it predicts the value of the sandhi tones solely from the underlying contrasts of E/O (and HR/LR in some cases) without regard to preceding or following tones.

As for the tri-syllabic CTS, it is sensitive to both syntactic categories and branching structures. The tri-syllabic CTS rule applies simultaneously in right-branching structures, while in left-branching structures it obeys the cycle.

Let us take a look at the CTS of right-branching structures first. Evidence indicates that right-branching CTS (CTS-R) calls for three conditioned subrules as given in (41).

(41) Rules for right-branching tri-syllabic CTS (CTS-R)

a.   T1   -   T2   -   T3   (for CTS-R-A: number + noun)
                     E   O
                     ↓   ↓
                     H   n

158 *Function words and rhythmic effect*

b. T1   -   T2   -   T3   (for CTS-R-B: verb + number + CL)

$\downarrow$

n, if initial T = H or LM

H, elsewhere

c. T1   -   T2   -   T3   (for CTS-R-C: verb + directional complement)

$\downarrow$

H

d. T1   -   T2   -   T3   (for all constructions)

E   O

$\downarrow$ $\downarrow$

$ H   M

Characteristically, the first syllable of a tri-syllabic clitic group keeps its base tone unaltered. The second tone is realized as either an *H* or an *M* depending on whether it is underlyingly an even (E) or an oblique (O) tone, respectively, regardless of the structure type instantiated by the clitic group. The final syllable undergoes one or the other of the CTS-R rules as dictated by the Morphosyntactic structure in question. This structure-selective application of CTS-R is illustrated by the examples given in (42)–(44).

(42) Example for CTS-R-A (only for the number-noun structure)

四   面   盆

[sɿ [mie - bɔŋ]]

four   basin

'four basins'

BT   M - MLM - LM

      O - O - E

---

*   HMH - M - H   (by tri-syllabic LTS)

ok   M - M - H   (by tri-syllabic CTS-R-A)

(43) Example for CTS-R-B (verb followed by number-measure)

唱   ·   首

[tsʰã̃ [iəʔ   sə]]

sing   one song

'to sing a song'

BT   M - Hq - HMH

       O - E - O

---

*   HMH - H - n   (by tri-syllabic LTS)

*   M - H - n   (by tri-syllabic CTS-R-A)

ok   M - H - H   (by tri-syllabic CTS-R-B)

(44) Examples for CTS-R-C (verb-directional complement)

a. 搬 出 去
[bɔ [tsʰə? - kʰi]]
carry out DIR
'to carry (it) out'
BT LML - Hq - M
  O - E - O

*	MLM - H - n	(by tri-syllabic LTS)
*	LML - H - n	(by tri-syllabic CTS-R-A)
ok	LML - H - H	(by tri-syllabic CTS-R-C)

b. 抬 进 来
[dɛ [tɕiŋ - lɛ]]
lift enter DIR
'to carry (it) in'
BT LM - M - LM
  E - O - E

*	LM - M - n	(by tri-syllabic CTS-R-B)
ok	LM - M - H	(by tri-syllabic CTS-R-C)

Chongming tri-syllabic CTS is sensitive not only to Morphosyntactic categories but also to tree structures. In Old Chongming, the phonological process for left-branching structures is cyclic, as schematized in (45). The rule is formulated as given in (46).

(45)

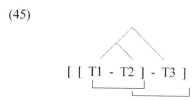

[[T1 - T2] - T3]

(46) Rule for left-branching tri-syllabic CTS (CTS-L)

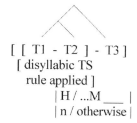

[[T1 - T2] - T3]
[disyllabic TS
 rule applied]
  | H / ...M___ |
  | n / otherwise |

The disyllabic TS rules first apply to the first and second syllables, i.e., to the constituent on the left branch of the structure. The TS form of the third syllable depends on the output form of this operation: if the output form of the second

160 *Function words and rhythmic effect*

syllable is *M*, the third syllable changes into *H*; otherwise, the third syllable carries a neutral tone. Sample derivations are given in (47).

(47) Examples for CTS-L (cyclic)

a.

看　　好　　伊
[[kʰø – hɔ] ji]
take care of　　he
'to take care of him'

BT　M - HMH - LM
　　O -　O　- E
　　HR - HR - LR

*	HMH -	M - H	(by tri-syllabic LTS; direct mapping)
*	M -	M - H	(by tri-syllabic CTS-R: direct mapping)
	[M -	H]	(by disyllabic CTS-A)
		[H - n]	(by tri-syllabic CTS-L)
ok	M -	H - n	(cyclic)

b.

两　　碗　　饭
[[liã – ʋie] va]
two　　bowl　rice
'two bowls of rice'

BT　LML - HMH - MLM
　　O -　O　- O
　　LR - HR - LR

*	MLM -	M - n	(by tri-syllabic LTS; direct mapping)
	[LML -	M]	(by disyllabic CTS-A)
		[M - H]	(by tri-syllabic CTS-L)
ok	LML -	M - H	(cyclic)

c.

赞　　成　　伊
[[tsø – dzəŋ] ji]
　　praise　　he
'to agree with him'

BT　M - LM - LM
　　O - E - E
　　HR - LR - LR

*	HMH -	H - H	(by tri-syllabic LTS; direct mapping)
	[HMH -	H]	(by disyllabic LTS)
		[H - n]	(by tri-syllabic CTS)
ok	HMH -	H - n	(cyclic)

Function words and rhythmic effect 161

The description of tri-syllabic TS reveals a more complicated picture of the syntax-phonology interface. A cyclic process can account for some of the facts. Specifically, the surface tone of the third syllable in certain left-branching, tri-syllabic structures (i.e., those containing a clitic group) is determined on the basis of the output form derived by applying the appropriate disyllabic TS rule to the initial disyllable as shown in (48).

(48)　　　　　看　　好　　伊
　　　　[[kʰø － hɔ] ji]
　　　　　see　　good　　he
　　　　'to take good care of him'
　　BT　　M - HMH - LM
　　――――――――――――――――
　　　　　[M - H]　　　　(by disyllabic CTS-A)
　　　　　　　　[H - n]　　(by tri-syllabic CTS-L)
　　ok　　M - H - n　　(cyclic)

But cyclic application fails in right-branching cases such as in (49).

(49)　　　　　买　　五　　磅
　　　　[mɑ [n － pã]]
　　　　　buy　five　pound
　　　　'to buy five pounds'
　　BT　LML - LML - M
　　――――――――――――――――
　　　　　　　[LML - M]　　(by disyllabic CTS-A)
　　　　[LML - n]　　　　(by disyllabic LTS)
　　*　　LML - n - M　　(cyclic)
　　ok　LML - M - H　　(by tri-syllabic CTS-R-B; direct mapping)

Based on the contrast between (48) and (49), we can conclude that Old Chongming tri-syllabic clitic TS has two modes of application: (i) cyclic, for left-branching structures, and (ii) direct mapping, for right-branching structures. For lexical items, on the other hand, direct mapping is the only mode of application, regardless of the direction of branching.

It is clear that there is the distinction between lexical sandhi and clitic sandhi. As shown earlier, a lexical item undergoes lexical TS (LTS), which exclusively selects the direct mapping mode of application; clitic groups, on the other hand, undergo clitic TS (CTS), which adopts different modes of application depending on tree geometry and on syntactic categories, as seen in (50).

(50) a.　Left-branching: Cyclic (e.g., 47)
　　　b.　Right-branching: Direct mapping (DM)

　　DM ⟶　｜ CTS-A, if a number-noun (e.g. 42)
　　　　　　｜ CTS-B, if a verb-number-measure (e.g. 43)
　　　　　　｜ CTS-C, if a verb-directional complement (e.g. 44)

162   *Function words and rhythmic effect*

Although the prosodic theory is the most constrained of the competing theories, the Chongming facts suggest that it is untenable in its strongest form. It is clear that Old Chongming CTS cannot be syntax-blind. On the contrary, it is syntax-sensitive in two ways: (i) tree structure determines the mode of rule application (CTS applies cyclically to left-branching structures, while the direct mapping of CTS prevails in right-branching structures) and (ii) regardless of whether direct mapping or cyclical application is used, different syntactic categories select different subrules of CTS. Its characteristic is that syntactic structures directly exert an influence within prosodic domains.

Thus it can be seen that the TS behavior of the clitic groups is far more complex than imagined, and its manifestations in various languages can hardly be completely covered by any one of the approaches, including the edge condition and the c-command hypothesis.

5.4.3 Neutralization: Historical perspective

The relationship between LTS and CTS in the Old Chongming, in fact, shows us the trace of sound change. Diachronically, CTS in nature is a new sandhi form, which resulted from the merging and simplification of TS. This merging and simplification can be called neutralization, which refers to the fact that there are T^n possible tonal combinations for an n-syllable sequence if T tonal categories are given. Thus, for disyllabic compounds, there are 64 (= 8 × 8) possible tonal sequences in the Old Chongming dialect. TS can be seen in this context as a redundancy reduction mechanism: when we survey one Chinese dialect after another, where TS operates, it invariably has the effect of reducing the combinatorial possibilities of tonal strings. Not surprisingly, for the eight underlying tonal combinations of disyllabic sequences in Old Chongming chosen for investigation, only two LTS patterns occur, as seen in (51).

(51) The merging case of LTS

Input Form					Output Form
1st syll.	2nd syll.				1st syll. + 2nd syll.
HMH	E	H	1	H	HMH-H
		R	7	Hq	
		L	2	LM	
		R	8	Lq	
	O	H	3	HMH	HMH-M
		R	5	M	
		L	4	LML	
		R	6	MLM	

As seen in the table, in Chongming LTS, merging and simplification occur at the second syllable. And at the sandhi level, there is only a contrast between even

Function words and rhythmic effect   163

(E) and oblique (O) in tones, instead of that between high and low register. Thus in LTS with the tone of the first syllable as *HMH*, only two sandhi forms, i.e., *HMH-H* and *HMH-M*, will be produced.

If we compare the LTS and CTS, whose first syllables' tones are both *HMH*, we will see that the merging in sound change is more fully completed in CTS. As can be seen from a survey of all the types of CTS, the tone of the second syllable involves neither a contrast between high and low register nor a conflict between even and oblique tone at the sandhi level. In other words, each type of CTS will get only one sandhi form if the tone of its first syllable is *HMH*, as seen in (52).

(52) Comparison between LTS and CTS merging cases

TS Types	2nd / 1st	E				O			
		HR		LR		HR		LR	
		H	Hq	LM	Lq	HMH	M	LML	MLM
LTS	HMH	HMH-H				HMH-M			
CTS-A		HMH-M							
CTS-B		HMH-M							
CTS-C		HMH-M							
CTS-D		HMH-M							

In (52), CTS, compared with LTS, is a newer change, a more thorough merging, and a complete neutralization. Thus LTS can only be considered a partial merging and an incomplete neutralization.

It should be noted that like the partial merging in LTS of the Old Chongming, the LTS in the old Shanghai also has a differentiation between even and oblique tone instead of between high and low register. The LTS in the new Shanghai is just like the CTS in the Old Chongming in that it has a complete and thorough neutralization, i.e., there is no contrast between high and low register nor between even and oblique (B. Xu et al. 1981, 1988). So if we consider the merging in question as a certain kind of sandhi change, we may think that the LTS in the Old Chongming represents an old sandhi phenomenon while the CTS in the Old Chongming represents a new one. The new form replacing the old one is completed through Morphosyntactic diffusion (Zhang 1989; Zhang & Chen 1995; Zhang 2008a).

5.5 The rhythmic effect in Chinese dialects

5.5.1 The rhythmic effect in Xiamen

In this section, I will discuss the rhythmic effect in the TS of Chinese dialects, for which general TS rules or principles fail to account. Let us look at the Xiamen case first seen in (53).

164   *Function words and rhythmic effect*

(53) 'China television news'

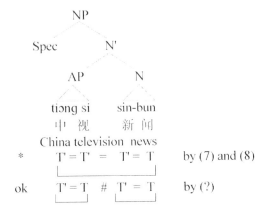

As seen in (53), *tiɔag si* 'China television' is the adjunct of *sin-bun* 'news' and m-commands its head *sin-bun*. According to the principle in (8), the TS rule should be applied to *si*, but, in fact, *si* retains its citation form instead of the sandhi form. Moreover, without the function word, the TS of case (53) is not that of a clitic group. So *tiɔag=si # sin=bun* is an exceptional reading that is irregular. Therefore, we may ask what causes such irregular readings. I believe that it is a rhythmic effect, which has been discussed by Chen (1984, 1992c), Hsiao (1991), and Hsu (1992). Hsiao centers on the rhythm of idioms, Hsu's discussion is mainly concerned with the rhythm of set-pattern phrases and proper names, while Chen provides us with a thorough study of the rhythmic effect on locative phrases, numerals, morphosyntax, and so on. All of these discussions reveal only one fact, i.e., in Xiamen dialect, sometimes the quadrisyllabic and pentasyllabic TS domains are determined by the pre-set rhythmic patterns given in (54), instead of by the principles in (8) or (21).

(54) Pre-set rhythmic patterns

a. [X - X - X - X]
     T' = T # T' = T

b. [X - X - X - X - X]
     T' = T # T' = T' = T

c. [X - X - X - X - X]
     T' = T' = T # T' = T

The patterns in (54) are in fact the basic patterns for the metrical structures in classic Chinese poetry. The primary pattern for classic poetry in Chinese is to have four syllables for every line. And its rhythm is that every two syllables form a meter and every two meters make up a line, very similar to (54a). This metrical characteristic, i.e., a pause after the second syllable, has been kept till this day

Function words and rhythmic effect 165

embodied, in particular, in the readings of four-syllable idioms in Chinese. And, moreover, the disyllabification from ancient Chinese to modern Chinese is also related to this metrical property. After the poetry with the pattern of four syllables composing a line, there came into being poems in which each line is made up of five syllables and the two meters are constituted, respectively. Based on the preceding two and the remaining three syllables, it is very similar to (54b), or based on the first three syllables and the remaining two, very similar to (54c). However, the pattern in (54b) is more popular and more frequently used than that in (54c), thus becoming the main metrical pattern for the poems with five syllables in each line. Chen (1979, 1980, 1984), who has made some linguistic analyses of Chinese poetry and provided us with the metrical patterns as seen in (54), probes into such problems as the relationship as well as the interplay between metrical patterns and syntactic structures. Interestingly, the rhythmic patterns in (54), which were derived from poetry, exert a great influence on the phonological structures, especially TS, in modern Chinese. In fact, many so-called irregular and exceptional cases are the results of the rhythmic effect. In (55), I provide some examples of the quadrisyllabic TS in Xiamen dialect.

(55) Examples of Xiamen quadrisyllabic TS

a. 'Jin-lan soy sauce'
金　兰　豆　油
kim－lan　tau－iu
brand name soy-sauce
*　T' = T' = T' = T　　　　　by (8)

ok　T' = T　#　T' = T　　　　by (54a)

b. 'Jin-men district'
金　门　地　区
kim－bun　te－k^{h}u
place name district
*　T' = T' = T'= T　　　　　by (8)

ok　T' = T　#　T'= T　　　　by (54a)

As seen in the previous example, *kim-lan* 'brand name' in (55a) and *kim-bun* 'place name' in (55b) are both adjuncts m-commanding the lexical heads *tau-iu* 'soy sauce' and *te-k^{h}u* 'district,' respectively. According to the principle in (8), *kim-lan* and *tau-iu* will form one tone group and so will *kim-bun* and *te-k^{h}u*, but actually there are two tone groups in each of these two cases. It is the rhythmic effect that gives rise to such irregular readings whose tonal pattern is exactly the same as the rhythmic pattern in (54a). Now let us take a look at cases of pentasyllabic TS in Xiamen in (56).

(56) Examples of Xiamen pentasyllabic TS

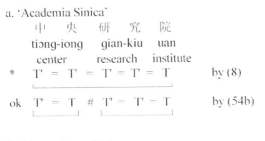

In (56a), *tiɔng-iɔng* 'center' is the adjunct of NP and m-commands its head *gian-kiu-uan* 'research institute.' By the principle in (8), they should form one tonal domain, but in fact, each of them belongs to its own domain because a rhythmic pattern is involved, as in (54b). As for (56b), it also has a rhythmic pattern in accordance with (54c). Although the adjunct in (56b), i.e., *kue-bin-sing* 'allergic,' m-commands its head *pʰe-iam* 'dermatitis,' it does not form a tone group with it. Thus it can be seen that in Xiamen, such so-called irregular TS cases as mentioned earlier are in fact the results of rhythmic effect.

5.5.2 The rhythmic effect in Shanghai

Since the rhythmic effect, which affects TS behaviors, is relevant to the metrical structures of classic Chinese poetry, it cannot be an ad hoc phenomenon for a particular Chinese dialect and must be a common phenomenon in almost all of the Chinese dialects. In (57), I provide examples from Shanghai dialect.

(57) Rhythmic effect in Shanghai

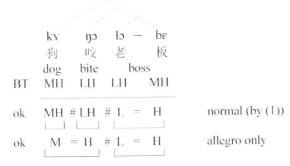

Function words and rhythmic effect 167

b. 'the critical moment'

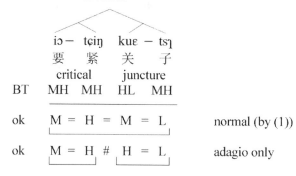

c. 'The cat is smaller than the dog.'

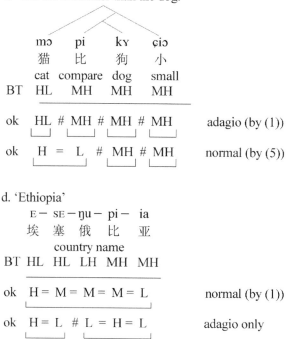

d. 'Ethiopia'
```
      E – SE – ŋu – pi – ia
      埃   塞   俄   比   亚
            country name
BT   HL   HL   LH   MH   MH
```

ok   H = M = M = M = L   normal (by (1))

ok   H = L # L = H = L   adagio only

Whichever of the TS cases in (57) it is, quadrisyllabic or pentasyllabic, the example will have two reading forms, one of which must result from the rhythmic effect. For instance, in (57a), *kɤ* 'dog' is the external argument of the sentence, thus violating the condition for TS rule application in Shanghai given in (1). But in allegro speech (i.e., casual style), *kɤ* and *ŋɔ* form one TS domain, the TS pattern of which is just a rhythmic pattern. Another example is (57b), in which *kuɛ-tsʅ* 'juncture', the head of NP, c-commands *iɔ-tɕiŋ* 'critical', the adjunct of *kuɛ-tsʅ*, so *iɔ-tɕiŋ* and *kuɛ-tsʅ* form one TS domain in normal speech, but split into two TS domains in adagio speech (i.e., deliberate style) in accordance with the

168   *Function words and rhythmic effect*

rhythmic principle. As for (57c), its TS domain in normal speech seems to be obtained only from the rhythmic effect. The most convincing case for the rhythmic effect on Shanghai dialect is the case in (57d), which is a transliteration without the internal branching structure. With only one morpheme, it naturally has only one TS domain in normal speech. But in adagio speech, this five-syllable morpheme is read as having two TS domains, the formation of which follows the pattern given in (58d) instead of (58a)–(58c).

(58) Possible formation patterns for (57d)

    a. *   X # X = X = X = X

    b. *   X = X = X = X # X

    c. *   X = X = X # X = X

    d. ok   X = X # X = X = X

As mentioned already, *ɛ-sɛ-ŋu-pi-ia* is a morpheme without internal structure. So, logically speaking, the TS patterns in (58a)–(58c) are all possible. But only (58d) is chosen, while all of the other three possible patterns are ruled out in the Shanghai dialect. This fact shows us that (58d) is a competing TS pattern, which chances to be the main rhythmic pattern for the pentasyllables in Chinese. All this proves that many so-called irregular or exceptional TS cases in Chinese dialects are, in fact, the results of the rhythmic effect.

5.5.3 The rhythmic effect in Mandarin

The phenomenon of the rhythmic effect is also found in standard Mandarin. As mentioned in Chapter 4, Mandarin Chinese has four citation tones that are repeated in (59).

(59) The citation tones in Mandarin

Tonal Categories		T1	T2	T3	T4
Tonal contour		even	rising	dipping	falling
Tonal value	High register	H	MH		HL
	Low register			MLM	

At the phonological level, Mandarin has a third TS (3TS) rule, which is that its dipping tone (MLM, T3) changes into a rising tone (MH, T2), as shown in (60).

Function words and rhythmic effect 169

(60) 3TS rule in Mandarin
MLM (T3) ⟶ MH (T2) / ___ MLM (T3)

While studying the conditions for the TS rule application in Mandarin, many people (Shih 1986, 1997; Hung 1987; Hsiao 1991; and others) consider the rule in (60) as applied obligatorily within a prosodic unit called the foot and optionally across feet. Owing to the limitation of space, I am not going to probe deeply into the problem of how the Foot Formation Rules for Mandarin work out in this chapter. What I want to do is to try to prove the popularity of the rhythmic patterns given in (54) in the TS of Chinese dialects with the analyses of some Mandarin TS data, which are relevant to the rhythmic phenomenon. So consider (61) first.

(61) Rhythmic effect on Mandarin

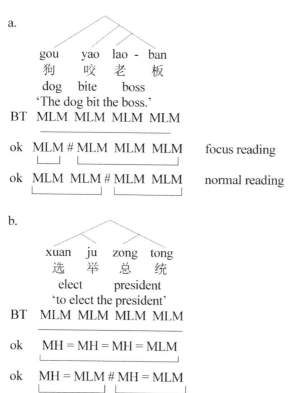

170 *Function words and rhythmic effect*

c.

```
        gou      bi        ma   xiao
        狗       比        马    小
        dog  compare   horse small
        'The dog is smaller than the horse.'
BT   MLM  MLM  MLM  MLM

ok    MLM # MH = MH = MLM
      └────┘  └────────┘

ok    MH = MLM # MH = MLM
      └────────┘ └────────┘
```

d.

```
        huo    nu     lu    lu    dao
        火     努     鲁    鲁    岛
               place name          island
               'Honolulu Island'
BT   MLM MLM MLM MLM MLM

ok   MH = MH = MH = MH = MLM
     └────────────────────┘

ok   MH = MLM # MH = MH = MLM
     └────────┘ └──────────────┘
```

The examples in (61) show us that if a phrase has two reading forms, one of them is usually produced as a result of the rhythmic effect and its TS pattern is more often than not the metrical pattern of either [XX#XX] or [XX#XXX].

If such a rhythmic effect in Mandarin reflects a kind of metricalization, then such metricalization mainly manifests in the quadrisyllabic unit. However, not all of the quadrisyllabic units in Mandarin will undergo metricalization. For instance, if a Mandarin quadrisyllabic unit is a clitic group with its third syllable being a clitic element, then it cannot be metricalized as [σσ # σσ]. Please compare the cases given in (62).

(62) a.= (61c) Phonological phrase   b. Clitic group

```
                    狗  比  马  小                         我  比     你    小
                    gou bi ma xiao                        wo  bi    ni  xiao
Citation tone:       3   3   3   3                        3   3     3    3
Metricalized TS: ok  2   3 # 2   3                       *2   3  #  2    3
                    dog compare horse small               I compare you small
                    'Dogs are smaller than horses.'      'I am younger than you.'
```

Although (62a) and (62b) share the same syntactic tree, they belong to different prosodic units. The former is a phonological phrase and the latter a clitic group. As can be seen from the earlier example, (62a) can be metricalized and will have a metricalized TS (i.e., σσ # σσ), but (62b) cannot be metricalized and will not have a metricalized TS. The example in (63) is another case of a Mandarin quadrisyllabic unit, which is a clitic group and cannot be metricalized.

(63)

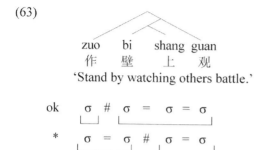

Thus it can be seen that, in Mandarin, the metricalization rule applies only to some specific prosodic domains, such as phonological phrase, and whether or not it applies is decided by prosodic structure. This proves that the clitic group does exist in Mandarin as one of the prosodic units – namely, the one that exists between prosodic word and phonological phrase, though its existence has been questioned by many people (Zec 1988, 1993; Inkelas 1989; Booij 1996; Selkirk 1996; among others).

5.5.4 Metricalization: A case of Morphosyntactic diffusion

As presented in the earlier discussion, the rhythmic effect in Mandarin manifests mainly in a quadrisyllabic unit, and it reflects a kind of metricalization. Thus we may ask such questions as why these metrical patterns, originally used in poetry, would affect TS as well as evolve themselves into TS patterns and how this development is completed.

I believe that the reason of the rhythmic effect in Chinese dialects is relevant to language change in Chinese, i.e., disyllabification. It is well known that Chinese is a disyllabic-word language derived from a monosyllabic-word language (L. Wang 1980). In old Chinese, the word-bearing unit is one Chinese character, i.e., one syllable. However, modern Chinese is usually made up of disyllabic words. In other words, the word-bearing unit in modern Chinese is mostly two Chinese characters, i.e., two syllables. There are many factors responsible for the disyllabification, but one of them could be the impact of the metrical structures of Chinese poetry. The poetic foot, especially the first one, in a Chinese poem is usually made up of two syllables. And such a unit form in poetry easily influences the Chinese morphology by bestowing its metrical property upon the morphological unit, thus turning Chinese into a disyllabic-word language. Attention should be paid to the fact that this language change is not confined to morphology, and what has happened to morphology will surely happen to phonology and syntax. Also because of this language change, Chinese has gradually changed from a syllable-tone language into a word-tone language (Chen 1986a; Shih 1986; Z. Zhang 1988; Zhang &

172 *Function words and rhythmic effect*

Chen 1995; Zhang 2008a). But it is the redividing of Morphosyntactic and phonological units that is most relevant to this language change. Taking morphosyntax, for example, in old Chinese, one syllable is one syntactic word and two syllables form a syntactic phrase, as seen in (64a). However, in modern Chinese, the exact same two syllables form only one syntactic word, as seen in (64b).

(64) a. Old Chinese (phrase)

   xuan yan

   宣   言

   declare speech

   'to make a declaration'

  b. Modern Chinese (word)

   xuan yan

   宣   言

   declare speech

   'declaration'

Since this disyllabification is still underway, in many cases, it is difficult to ascertain whether a disyllable is a syntactic word or a syntactic phrase, and such exceptional cases, the so-called potentialized lexicon (Thompson 1973), actually represent the variant stage in progress. For the same reason, the mismatch naturally appears in phonology. For instance, in Chinese dialects, some rhythmic pattern may be adopted as the pattern for TS. When two monosyllabic words are adjacent and influenced by disyllabification, they will phonologically be taken as one unit to form one TS domain identical to the rhythmic pattern, even though syntactically they are two units.

If we consider those irregular and exceptional TS cases, resulting from the rhythmic effect, to be a kind of TS phenomenon, i.e., metricalization or disyllabification, we may suggest that the completion of such a sound change, just like the sound change due to neutralization discussed in the previous section, is obtained through Morphosyntactic diffusion. In other words, under the same phonological environments, the timing of metricalization is different within different Morphosyntactic structures, and the sound change happened from one structure to another and finally to all of the Morphosyntactic structures, which conform to the conditions of change. The process of Morphosyntactic structure diffusion in a particular dialect is presented in (65).

(65)

Morphosyntactic Structures	*Unchanged Stage*	*Variant Stage*	*Changed Stage*
Structure 1	+	−	−
Structure 2	+	+	+
Structure 3	−	−	+

Function words and rhythmic effect **173**

Now let us take metricalization in TS of the Xiamen dialect for example. As mentioned previously, some so-called irregular quadrisyllabic TS in Xiamen is the result of the rhythmic effect. What I want to point out here is that the rhythmic effect on TS, in fact, reflects the trace of sound change. Diachronically, the disyllabic foot is a new form resulting from the metricalization of TS, while the non-disyllabic foot is an old form, the TS of which occurs according to the principles in (8) or (21). In Xiamen, metricalization has been completed in the locative structure and time expressions. In other words, the TS forms of all of the quadrisyllabic locative words and time words are the new ones, as seen in (66) and (67).

(66) Quadrisyllabic TS of locative structure

    a. 'behind the gate'

        大   门   后   壁

        tua − mŋ au − piaʔ

        gate   behind

  *   T' = T' = T' = T   by (8)

  ok   T' = T # T' = T   metricalization

    b. 'inside the leather box'

        皮   箱   里   面

        pʰe siũ lai − bin

        leather box   inside

  *   T' = T' = T' = T   by (8)

  ok T' = T # T' = T   metricalization

(67) Quadrisyllabic TS of time expression

    a. 'five years ago'

        五   年   以   前

        gɔ   ni   i − tsiŋ

        five year before

  *   T' = T' = T' = T   by (8)

  ok T' = T # T' = T   metricalization

    b. 'three days later'

        三   天   以   后

        sam tʰian i − au

        three day   after

  *   T' = T' = T' = T   by (8)

  ok T' = T # T' = T   metricalization

174 *Function words and rhythmic effect*

As seen from (66) and (67), all of the quadrisyllabic locative words and time words must undergo metricalization, but none of the quadrisyllabic clitic groups can undergo metricalization,[6] as seen in 68.

(68) Quadrisyllabic TS of function words

a. 'the new television'
新　个　电　视
sin　e　tian－si
new GEN television

*　T' = T # T' = T　　　　metricalization

ok　T # T' = T' = T　　　　by (21)

b. 'send me the television'
送　我　电　视
saŋ　gua　tian－si
send me television

*　T' = T # T' = T　　　　metricalization

ok　T' = T' = T' = T　　　　by (21)

c. 'the dog and the pony'
狗　甲　小　马
kau　ka?　sio　be
dog and little horse

*　T' = T # T' = T　　　　metricalization

ok　T # T' = T' = T　　　　by (21)

d. 'The fame is well-supported.'
名　不　虚　传
biŋ　put　hu　tʰuan
fame no false spread

*　T' = T # T' = T　　　　metricalization

ok　T # T' = T' = T　　　　by (21)

In the previous example, the quadrisyllabic clitic groups, including the idioms like (68d), cannot undergo metricalization. As for the structures such as modifier-head (MH) and verb-object (VO), they have both old and new readings. In other

Function words and rhythmic effect 175

words, some of these structures have already undergone metricalization, some have not, and some others have two reading forms. Let us take a look at the MH structure first in (70)–(71).

(69) Metricalization of MH

    a. 'China television news'

       中　視　新　聞

       tiɔng　si　sin — bun

       center television news

    *   T' = T' = T' = T   by (8)

    ok T' = T # T' = T   metricalization

    b. 'Jin-lan soy sauce'

       金　兰　豆　油

       kim — lan tau — iu

       brand name soy sauce

    *   T' = T' = T' = T   by (8)

    ok T' = T # T' = T   metricalization

    c. 'Jin-men district'

       金　门　地　区

       kim — bun te — kʰu

       place name district

    *   T' = T' = T' = T   by (8)

    ok T' = T # T' = T   metricalization

    d. 'wolf in a sheep's skin'

       衣　冠　禽　兽

       i kuan kʰim-siu

       cloth hat   beast

    *   T' = T' = T' = T   by (8)

    ok T' = T # T' = T   metricalization

176   *Function words and rhythmic effect*

(70) Non-metricalization of MH

a. 'China Times'

中　国　时　报

tiɔng-kɔk　si　po

China　time newspaper

*　T' = T # T' = T　　　metricalization

ok　T' = T' = T' = T　　　by (8)

b. 'Taiwan University'

台　湾　大　学

tai-uan　tua-oʔ

place name　university

*　T' = T # T' = T　　　metricalization

ok　T' = T' = T' = T　　　by (8)

c. 'Taizhong district'

台　中　地　区

tai − tiɔng te − kʰu

place name　district

*　T' = T # T' = T　　　metricalization

ok　T' = T' = T' = T　　　by (8)

d. 'a young lady of a rich family'

千　金　小　姐

tsʰian-kim sio-tsia

rich　　miss

*　T' = T # T' = T　　　metricalization

ok　T' = T' = T' = T　　　by (8)

Function words and rhythmic effect   177

(71) MH with two readings

a. 'color television'

彩　色　　电　视

tsʰai-sik　tian-si

color　television

ok　T' = T # T' = T   metricalization

ok　T' = T' = T' = T   by (8)

b. 'white roses'

白　色　　玫　瑰

peʔ-sik　muĩ-kui

white　rose

ok　T' = T # T' = T   metricalization

ok　T' = T' = T' = T   by (8)

We might be puzzled if we compare some of the examples in (69) with those in (70). For instance, although *tiɔŋ si sin bun* 'China television news' in (69a) and *tiɔŋ-kɔk si po* 'China Times' in (70a) are both MH structures, the former undergoes metricalization, while the latter does not. The most puzzling pair are *kim-bun te-kʰu* 'Jin-men district' in (69c) and *tai-tiɔŋ te-kʰu* 'Taizhong district' in (70c), because the former's reading form is [X=X#X=X], while the latter's is [X=X=X=X], although both are place names. As for (69d) and (70d), they are both idioms. But the former, i.e., *i kuan kʰim-siu* 'wolf in a sheep's skin,' undergoes metricalization, while the latter, i.e., *tsʰian-kim sio-tsia* 'a young lady of a rich family,' does not. This puzzling problem can be solved with the lexical diffusion hypothesis (W. Wang 1969; Chen & W. Wang 1975; Zhang & Chen 1995; Zhang 2008a). Suppose that metricalization is a kind of sound change occurring in quadrisyllabic TS. Under the same syntactic and phonological circumstances, this change has already been completed in some of the quadrisyllables, such as the MH cases in (69), but has not started yet in some other quadrisyllables, such as the MH cases in (70). Certainly, there are still quadrisyllables that are in the process of change, such as the MH cases in (71). At this middle stage of change, the quadrisyllables, such as *tsʰai-sik tian-si* 'color television' and *peʔ-sik muĩ-kui* 'white roses,' will accept both readings [X=X#X=X] and [X=X=X=X]. And this middle stage is just the "variant stage" in the lexical diffusion hypothesis. Therefore, metricalization in the MH structure is a typical lexical diffusion case, summed up in (72).[7]

178   *Function words and rhythmic effect*

(72) Lexical diffusion

Stages	Changed Stage	Variant Stage	Unchanged Stage
Status	M	M-NM	NM
Examples	(67)	(69)	(68)

The case of verb-object (VO) structure is just like that of MH with part of its quadrisyllables having undergone the metricalization and part not yet metricalized, as seen in (73a) and (73b), respectively.

(73) Quadrisyllabic TS of VO structure

> a. Example of metricalization
> 'to fight it out'
> ·· 决   雌   雄
> it kuat tsʰu hiɔŋ
> one fight female male
> *   T' = T' = T' = T   by (8)
>   └_____┘
>
> ok T' = T # T' = T   metricalization
>   └_____┘ └_____┘
>
> b. Example of non-metricalization
> 'to have no conscience'
> 丧   尽   天   良
> sɔŋ-tsin   tʰian-liɔŋ
> lose out conscience
> *   T' = T # T' = T   metricalization
>   └_____┘ └_____┘
> ok T' = T' = T' = T   by (8)
>   └_____┘

As for the subject-predicate (SP) structure, metricalization has just occurred in it, but not to a large scale. So most of the SP quadrisyllables, including idioms, get their TS forms in accordance with the TG formation in (8), as seen in (74).[8]

(74) Quadrisyllabic TS of SP structure

> a. 'The dog bit the pony.'
> 狗   咬   小   马
> kau ka sio be
> dog bite little horse
> *   T' = T # T' = T   metricalization
>   └_____┘ └_____┘
> ok T # T' = T' = T   by (8)
>   └┘ └_____┘

Function words and rhythmic effect 179

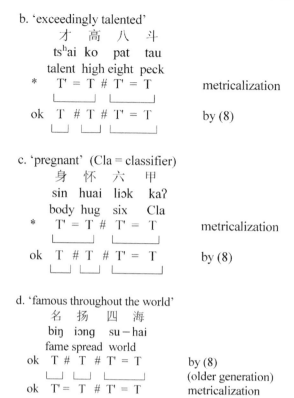

Attention should be paid to the change in VO and SP structures. Basically, metricalization is just happening to the quadrisyllabic idioms with VO structure, as seen in (71a), but has not yet occurred in the non-idiomatic quadrisyllables with VO structure, as seen in (74a). Generally speaking, quadrisyllabic SP structures, including idioms, are not yet in the process of metricalization, as shown by (74a)–(74c). But the example in (74d) shows us that metricalization is now occurring in SP structure. In (74d), two reading forms coexist and both are acceptable. It should be noted that the reading form due to metricalization is accepted by the younger generation, while the other reading form, which does not undergo metricalization, is normally chosen by the older generation. This fact strongly supports the hypothesis, previously mentioned, that the tonal pattern with metricalization is a new form, while that without metricalization is an old form. It is also proved by the comparison among the cases of MH, VO, and SP structures that the change of replacing the old with the new is completed by means of lexical diffusion. If we further compare the cases with such structures as the locative structure, time expressions, clitic groups (CG), MH, VO, and SP, we will find that the process of such a sound change is in fact a process of Morphosyntactic diffusion, as shown in (75).[9]

180   *Function words and rhythmic effect*

(75) Morphosyntactic diffusion

Structures	Changed Stage	Variant Stage	Unchanged Stage
LS and TE	+	−	−
MH	+	+	+
VO and SP	?	+	+
CG	−	−	+

In (75), we see that the sound change due to metricalization has been completed in LS and TE structures, but has not yet started in all of the CGs. As for MH, VO, and SP, they are all undergoing this change and MH seems to be taking the lead.

It should be noted that Morphosyntactic diffusion differs from lexical diffusion in the point that some sound change is completed not only by the lexicon but also by diffusion within Morphosyntactic structures. More precisely, phonological change globally diffuses from one Morphosyntactic context to another, and the change locally diffuses from one specific lexical or phrasal expression to another within a Morphosyntactic type.

In this section, I have tried to account for some so-called exceptional TS cases in Chinese dialects such as Xiamen from the angle of metricalization and to explain, from a historical perspective, the occurrence of the metricalization in TS and the mechanism whereby metricalization evolves.

Notes

1 The corpus of this analysis consists of two published reports (H-Y. Zhang 1979, 1980) and the data I collected in 1987. The informant was in her 40s at the time of elicitation. I refer to the variety of Chongming investigated here as Old Chongming. For a detailed report on New Chongming, see Chen and Zhang 1997.
2 In appropriating the labels *E* and *O*, I am taking a certain terminological license. Traditionally *E* stands for 'ping', while *O* refers to the other three tonal categories. Instead of coining new terms, I have decided to redefine old ones to suit my purpose here.
3 $ = citation tone form is kept in TS, n = neutral tone, HR = high register, and LR = low register.
4 CTS-A stands for clitic tone sandhi type A and similarly for CTS-B, CTS-C, and CTS-D.
5 Here the DM mode refers to the cases where the set of phonological rules is applied directly to the underlying representation to give as output the corresponding phonetic representation. It is often referred to as simultaneous application of the rules.
6 It should be noted that things are different in the Mandarin and Shanghai dialects in which the quadrisyllabic clitic groups are able to undergo metricalization, as exemplified by (55c) and (59c).
7 'M' stands for undergoing metricalization, 'NM' for not undergoing metricalization, and 'M~NM' means that both readings are acceptable.
8 The reading form in (72d) is from Hsu (1992). As for the case in (72d), different forms have been offered by Hsiao (1991) and Chen (1992c). I checked with native speakers in Taiwan. The result is that the reading form acceptable to most of these informants is the same as that of Hsu. So here I adopt Hsu's reading form.
9 *LS* stands for locative structure, *TE* for time expression, and *VO* and *SP*, respectively, for the quadrisyllabic verb-object structure and the subject-predicate structure.

6 Theoretical discussions

6.1 Mapping between syntax and phonology

The nature of the syntax-phonology interface is of crucial importance to prosodic phonology and it involves two fundamental problems: a) how accessible is syntactic information to phonological processes and b) what grammatical properties are relevant to phonology? Looking back at the history of syntax-phonology interface study, we have seen it divided into two phases: the phase before OT and the phase after OT. Before OT came into being, the interface study was conducted within the framework of rule-based derivational phonology. With the rise of OT in the 1990s, the interface study seems to have taken a new direction with an aim to explain the interaction between phonology and other grammatical components from constraint-based perspectives.

The core issues of the syntax-phonology interface are what phonology must know about syntax and what makes the phonological behavior of one syntactic unit different from that of another. To be more precise, we want to know which specific syntactic properties affect the application of phonological rules and how these syntactic properties are incorporated into phonology. In response to these questions, the two most influential but competing theories are proposed. One is proposed by Kaisse, who claims that phonological rules are subject to conditions that are stated directly in terms of syntactic domains. Kaisse distinguishes two types of post-lexical rules (Kaisse 1985: 193) – namely, external sandhi rules (P1 rules) and fast-speech rules (P2 rules). Kaisse thinks that the P1 rules have direct access to the information contained in the labeled bracketing of syntactic structure and apply only under the specific syntactic conditions. What is the type of syntactic information that the P1 rules have access to? According to Kaisse, it is neither the syntactic categories such as NP, VP, AP, or PP, nor the syntactic units such as morpheme, word, or phrase. Instead, it is the syntactic relation, i.e., the domain c-command condition. According to Kaisse, the syntactic information needed to delimit sandhi rules at the P1 level is only determined in terms of the m-command condition, which is defined by Chomsky (1986a). Following Hyman et al. (1987), this syntax-sensitive approach is termed as the Direct Reference Approach (hereafter DRA). The other theory is proposed by Selkirk (1984, 1986), Nespor and Vogel (1986), and some others, according to whom the surface syntactic structure

182 *Theoretical discussions*

is first mapped onto a prosodic structure consisting of prosodic constituents. These prosodic constituents are the domains of phonological rules applying above the level of the word. According to Selkirk and others, the prosodic structure, located between syntactic structure and phonetic representation, consists of different types of domains, including the prosodic word (ω), the clitic group (CG), the phonological phrase (φ), the intonational phrase (ι), and the utterance (υ). These domains are hierarchically organized in a number of layers. Thus a well-formed prosodic representation looks (1).

```
(1)   ( ------------------------------------------ ) υ
      ( ------------------------------ ) ( ---- ) ι
      ( ---- ) ( ------------------------ ) ( ---- ) φ
      ( ---- ) ( ---------------- ) ( ----- ) ( ---- ) CG
      ( ---- ) ( ------ ) ( ------ ) ( ----- ) ( ---- ) ω
```

According to this theory, phonological rules are sensitive to prosodic domains, which are defined based on edge conditions, i.e., the end-based principle. In particular, the end-based hypothesis refers to the notion that prosodic domains are only marked at the right or left edge of an X^{max} or X^{head}. It was defined as the syntax-insensitive approach (Hyman et al. 1987) and named the Indirect Reference Approach (hereafter IRA).

In the competition between DRA and IRA, IRA seems to gain the upper hand. Most of the scholars in the field have accepted IRA, with the thought that between syntax and phonology, there are hierarchical prosodic categories, which form the domain of phonological rule application. The syntax-phonology interface study within the IRA framework has, thus, become part of prosodic phonology study with its focus switched to what is the syntactic information that has built up the prosodic categories and how the mapping between syntax and prosody gets done. For a phonological phrase, one of the prosodic units, for example, there are three different views: (i) end-based mapping (Selkirk 1986; Chen 1987), (ii) relation-based mapping (Nespor & Vogel 1986), and (iii) arboreal mapping (Inkelas & Zec 1990). Basically speaking, the syntactic information that End-Based theory refers to is X-bar structure and the edge of syntactic categories defined by X-bar. There are two parameters for X-bar structure: X^{max} (maximal projection=XP) and X^{head} (head of XP=X^0). There are two parameters for the edge, too: left edge and right edge. According to End-Based theory, the X for mapping is a lexical word, thus excluding the functional word. Different languages have different parameters. Take the Shanghai dialect, for example. The mapping of its phonological phrase refers to the left edge of X^{max} (Selkirk & Shen 1990). While in the case of Xiamen, the TS domain of the phonological phrase references the right edge of X^{max} (Chen 1987). The syntactic information that relation-based theory refers to are head and complement. Therefore, in some languages (such as Chimwiini), head and complement are put together to form a phonological phrase, but in some others (such as French), head and complement each form a phonological phrase, respectively. The syntactic information that arboreal mapping theory refers to is the branchingness of syntactic trees, by which the sister nodes in a syntactic tree map into a phonological phrase, and if the complement is branching, it gets mapped into a phonological phrase; otherwise, it needs to be grouped with its head to form a phonological phrase. The support for arboreal mapping theory is basically from the discussion of English and Hausa.

The aforementioned examples are about the interface studies done before OT. In spite of fundamentally different views regarding the nature of the syntax-phonology interface, both DRA and IRA still belong to the paradigm of rule-based derivational phonology. This is because OT has completely abandoned derivational rules (McCarthy & Prince 1993; Prince & Smolensky 1993) and adopted the paradigm of constraint-based phonology. Under the OT framework, the interface study allows the violation of constraints, which is considered language universal, with the differences of various languages explained by various specific rankings. The mapping between syntactic structure and prosodic structure is defined as a different functional ranking of constraints, which leads to the different prosodic structure in different languages and by which the prosodic structure type in a language gets predicted. The constraints in OT are divided into two categories: (i) mapping constraints of syntax-phonology, also called faithfulness constraints, and (ii) prosodic constraints, also called markedness constraints.

Therefore, the syntax-phonology interface study under the OT framework has no derivations by ordered rules, but only well-formedness constraints, which evaluate possible output representations. These constraints, although with different functions, all keep OT's principles of strict domination and minimal violation.

The typical OT constraints for the mapping between syntax and phonology include alignment constraint, wrap constraint, and Match theory. Alignment theory is developed from End-Based theory (Selkirk 1986), by which the determination of prosodic units refers only to the edge of such syntactic units as morpheme, word, and phrase, with no distinction between syntactic categories such as NP, VP, AP, and PP, but with an agreement between the edge of prosodic units and that of syntactic structures. Alignment constraint is formulated as shown in (2) (McCarthy & Prince 1993).

(2) Generalized alignment
$\qquad$ Align(Cat1, Edge1, Cat2, Edge2) $=_{def}$
$\qquad\qquad \forall$ Cat1 $\exists$ Cat2 such that Edge1 of Cat1 and Edge2 of Cat2 coincide,

$\quad$ where

$\qquad\qquad$ Cat1, Cat2 $\in$ ProsCat $\cup$ GramCat
$\qquad\qquad$ Edge1, Edge2 $\in$ {Right, Left}.

ProsCat consists of prosodic categories (i.e., mora, syllable, foot, prosodic word, phonological phrase), while GramCat consists of morphological categories (i.e., word, stem, affix, root).

Alignment constraint is not a single constraint, but a set of constraints involving various levels of a prosodic hierarchy. At the phrasal level of this hierarchy, there

184   *Theoretical discussions*

are two alignment constraints controlling the mapping between syntax and prosody. One is Align-R (XP, φ), which requires that the right edge of a syntactic phrase XP agree with that of a phonological phrase φ. And the other is Align-L (XP, φ), which asks that the left edge of a syntactical phrase XP agree with the left edge of a phonological phrase φ. The two constraints are stated in (3) (Truckenbrodt 1995, 1999; Selkirk 2000).

(3)   a.   Align-XP, R: Align (XP, R; φ, R)
           Align right edge of XP to right edge of φ.
      b.   Align-XP, L: Align (XP, L; φ, L)
           Align left edge of XP to left edge of φ.

Truckenbrodt (1999) considers that alignment constraints are not enough to explain the mapping between syntax and phonology. Therefore, he proposes wrap constraint, at the phrasal level wrap (XP, PP), for instance, by which each syntactic phrase is wrapped within a phonological phrase, as seen in (4) (Truckenbrodt 1995, 1999: 228).

(4)   Wrap-XP:

      Each XP is contained in a phonological phrase.

The main reason for wrap constraint is that the major syntactical phrases in some languages (such as Chichewa) have the integrity kept instead of being split into various phonological phrases, while Wrap-XP requires the integrity of XP, which suppresses Align-XP when matched with a phonological phrase. The theory that determines the prosodic units through the interaction between the two constraints of alignment and wrap is called the Wrap XP-plus-Align XP theory (Wrap-Align theory).

For the purpose of explaining why some languages need to refer to the features of syntactic information in their phonological process, Selkirk (2011: 435–484) proposes a new theoretical framework of syntax-phonology interface, i.e., Match theory, the constraints of which are seen in (5).

(5)   a.   Match (α, π) [= S-P faithfulness]

           The left and right edges of a constituent of type α in the input syntactic representation must correspond to the left and right edges of a constituent of type π in the output phonological representation.

      b.   Match (π, α) [= P-S faithfulness]

           The left and right edges of a constituent of type π in the output phonological representation must correspond to the left and right edges of a constituent of type α in the input syntactic representation.

Match theory is, as a matter of fact, developed from Selkirk's own End-Based theory (Selkirk 1986, 1996). Match (α, π) can be construed as a constraint

Theoretical discussions   185

requiring simply that both the right and left edges of a syntactic constituent α (such as word, phrase, clause) of a designated type α correspond, respectively, to the right and left edges of a prosodic constituent π (such as prosodic word, phonological phrase, intonational phrase). Match constraint requires the syntactic input corresponds to phonological output, which means that a syntactic word corresponds to a prosodic word, syntactic phrase to phonological phrase, and syntactic clause to intonational phrase. Match constraint requires that the syntactic category and prosodic category are homogeneous. However, in some languages, in reality, such as Xiamen, syntactic category and prosodic category are not homogeneous, thus violating the Match constraint.

With the birth of OT phonology, the phonological study seems to split into two opposing paradigms, i.e., rule-based phonology versus constraint-based phonology. Likewise, the interface study of syntax-phonology also gets split into two opposing paradigms, i.e., the DRA and the IRA. But these two oppositions are not the same in nature. The former is caused by the different understanding of the ontology, i.e., how to interpret the nature of phonology. In other words, the question here is whether the phonological process is a derivational process or constraint-ranking process. As for the latter, it reflects the controversy over such issues as if syntactic information is accessible to phonological processes, what syntactic properties are relevant to phonology, phonological rule application refers to syntactic information directly or indirectly, and syntax is sensitive or insensitive/blind in determining the domain of phonological rule application. The interface studies (including Alignment theory, Wrap theory, Match theory) under the OT framework belong essentially to IRA, although, in the later stage, they did try to incorporate syntactic information into phonological process. Match theory even tried to establish a kind of direct correspondence between syntactic input and phonological output. But such efforts have not changed the fact that DRA and IRA are opposing each other essentially. Strictly speaking, DRA and IRA are not very appropriate as technical terms because they can be misleading due to the fact that the essential difference of these two approaches is not whether the phonological process is directly or indirectly sensitive to the syntactic information. Both of them, as a matter of fact, need to have the phonological process directly sensitive to the syntactic information. The major difference between them actually lies in (i) if a prosodic structure is required and (ii) what syntactic information is needed during the phonological rule application. Syntactic information needs to include at least such things as syntactic units (i.e., morpheme, affix, stem, word, phrase), syntactic categories (i.e., NP, VP, AP, PP), and syntactic relations (i.e., c-command, m-command, binding), but IRA actually cares about only such syntactic information as syntactic units and syntactic categories, while DRA minds syntactic relations. This choice of different kinds of information is what really and most importantly contrasts DRA from IRA.

As for the interface study under the OT framework, it is very much like IRA by caring only about syntactic units and syntactic categories while ignoring syntactic relations. Therefore, the issues that IRA is faced with are exactly the same issues that interface studies conducted under the OT framework are unable to solve. Take

186 *Theoretical discussions*

the cases of Xiamen and Pingyao, for example. The data of Xiamen TS can only help define the right edge of phonological phrases, which means if a monosyllabic word keeps the form of its citation tone unchanged in TS, the right edge of this word will be the right edge of the phonological phrase. However, Xiamen TS cannot define the left edge of phonological phrases. But the Match theory requires that the phonological phrase and syntactic phrase correspond to each other on both right and left edges. For instance, *yi yi-king tsau* 'he has already left' [[yi]$_{DP}$ [[yi-king] $_{VP}$ = tsau]$_{VP}$ = a]$_{IP}$ is predicted by the Wrapping-Align theory as one prosodic unit, i.e., (yi yi-king tsau)$_{\varphi}$, which is a phonological phrase. But the same structure gets analyzed by the Match theory into two phonological phrases "yi ((yi-king)$_{\varphi}$ tsau)$_{\varphi}$," with one of them dominating the other, which is a recursive prosodic structure. Moreover, the pronoun *yi* is not considered within the domain of any phonological phrases. Thus it can be seen that the domain of Xiamen TS is a phonological phrase – the defining of which needs to refer to the right edge of the syntactic phrase plus m-command condition. Both the Wrap-Align theory and the Match theory need to rank Wrap-XP before Align-R as well as place restrictions on the types of XPs in the constraint of Wrap-XP/(XP; φ). However, such XPs cannot be functional phrases, nor empty category, nor the syntactic phrases embedded with the functional phrases. As discussed in Section 2.2.5, whether TS should apply is not decided by the distinction between functional words and lexical words, but by the difference between empty and non-empty categories.

The OT approach also fails in the Pingyao case. As we know, Pingyao has two TS rule types based on the difference in Morphosyntactic constructions: type A (TSA) and type B (TSB). In tri-tonal sequence, the TS domain (TSD) in Pingyao undergoes the restructuring. Let us use OT constraints to delimitate the sandhi domain and account for the modes of rule application first (i.e., cyclical mode versus iterative mode). Under OT constraints, the three syllables will be parsed as either (σσ)σ or σ(σσ), and in order to prevent those unparsed structures from being chosen, a constraint that demands every syllable in the input be parsed into a sandhi domain is needed. Chen (2000) discussed the directionality of TS rules for type A and type B constructions: TS scans construction A right to left and scans construction B left to right. If we redefine that constructions A and B correspond to a phonological phrase and prosodic word, respectively, the directionality of TS in Pingyao can be rewritten because the TS rule scans phonological phrase from right to left and scans prosodic word from left to right. Following Ito and Mester (2009), the larger structure of a tri-syllabic string could be termed as the maximal prosodic category. However, it should be noted that the alignment constraints in Pingyao are not dominated in the prosodic hierarchy, and, consequently, the ranking of constraints for the tri-tonal sandhi in Pingyao is [Align (TSD, ω')L/Align (TSD, φ')R >> Parse σ >> Binary]. The two alignments make different decisions on parsing the sandhi domain. If the input of tri-syllabic TS is a prosodic word, the sandhi domain will be ((σ σ) σ); however, if the tri-syllabic TS input is a phonological phrase, the sandhi domain will be (σ (σ σ)). A tri-syllabic string will form two TSDs. If the internal TSD formed by two syllables is congruent with the intermediate prosodic category, it is the prosodic category that determines what type of TS rule will be chosen (i.e., phonological phrase or prosodic word). Otherwise, it is a maximal prosodic category. Although the constraints and recursive prosodic structures can predict the sandhi domains so as to account for all TS patterns in Pingyao through restructuring, two problems still remain in this OT analysis. The first problem is the property of the alignment. Generally speaking, the term alignment refers to the correspondence of different domains, i.e., the correspondence between the Morphosyntactic category and prosodic category. But if the Align-L (i.e., the sandhi domain, maximal prosodic word) adopted in the analyses considers the domain of TS a prosodic unit, the alignment constraint here will have a correspondence between prosodic units only, rather than between Morphosyntactic units and prosodic units. Another problem is the different TS behaviors of the embedded disyllabic units in tri-syllables. Of all the tri-syllabic patterns in Pingyao, the performance of the embedded disyllabic TS in tri-syllables presents different properties. Some have it made up by a prosodic word with the application of TSB; some get it consisting of a phonological phrase with the application of TSA, and others contain no prosodic unit, and, therefore, have their application of TS rule decided by the property of outer maximal prosodic units. This situation leads to the difficulty in defining the domain of the embedded disyllabic units in tri-syllables as a consistent unit in prosodic hierarchy. Thus the OT approach fails to capture the TS patterns in the Pingyao case by brutal force or ad hoc constraints.

Another problem that the prosodic phonology under the OT framework still faces is its inability in accounting for the non-uniqueness of prosodic segmenting. In other words, the same one syntactic unit can be prosodically segmented in different ways. Take the case *Lao Li mai hao jiu* 'Old Li has bought good wine' in Mandarin Chinese, which has been discussed in Chapter 4 and is repeated here in (6), for example.[1]

(6) Lao Li mai hao jiu
老 李 买 好 酒
Old Li buy good wine
'Old Li has bought good wine.'

	3	3	3	3	3	citation tone
(a)	2	3	3	2	3	slow speed (TS-1)
(b)	2	2	3	2	3	slightly faster (TS-2)
(c)	2	3	2	2	3	faster speed (TS-3)
(d)	2	2	2	2	3	even faster speed (TS-4)
(e)	2	1	1	1	3	fast speed with conversational casualness (TS-5)

The five different TSs in (6) are the phonetic representations of five prosodic domains. The TS-1 takes prosodic word and phonological phrase as the domains of rule application (cyclic mode). The TS-2 and TS-3 all take prosodic word and intonational phrase as the application domains. The TS-4 takes intonational phrase as the application domain (iterative application from left to right). And the TS-5

188 *Theoretical discussions*

only takes utterance as the application domain (direct mapping). Example (7) is a sum-up.

(7) Citation tone: [3–3–3–3–3]
    TS-1: [2–3]ω [[3]ω [2–3]ω]φ   (cyclically apply)
    TS-2: [2–2–3]l [2–3]ω   (i. iteratively apply L-to-R; ii. cyclically apply)
    TS-3: [2–3]ω [2–2–3]l   (i. cyclically apply; ii. iteratively apply L-to-R)
    TT-4: [2–2–2–2–3]l   (iteratively apply from L-to-R)
    TS-5: [2–1–1–1–3]υ   (direct mapping)

In (7), we see that one sentence can have at least five different ways of prosodic segmenting, which is another problem that the prosodic phonology under the OT framework is confronted with.

However, this book, based on the study of TS in Chinese dialects, shows that the phonological process needs to refer to various syntactic information, including both syntactic units and syntactic categories, as well syntactic relations. Those dialects, the phonological process of which involves syntactic relations, will serve as the counterevidence against both IRA and the approaches under the framework of OT. Those other dialects, the phonological process of which involves syntactic units and syntactic categories, will provide counterevidence against DRA. The evidence obtained from Chinese dialects both for and against DRA and IRA proves that the application of TS rules needs both the prosodic information and the syntactic information. For instance, there are at least three prosodic domains in the Old Chongming dialect: (i) the prosodic word, which includes all of the syntactic words and part of the syntactic phrases and which undergoes lexical TS; (ii) the clitic group, which covers all of the structures consisting of a lexical hood plus some cliticized particles or functional words and which undergoes clitic TS (CTS); and (iii) the phonological phrase, which includes part of the syntactic phrases, such as SP, VO, and adverbial MH, and which undergoes phrasal TS (PTS). But in the case of Xiamen TS, syntactic words and function words belong to different prosodic domains, and the TS of each follow individual rules of tone group (TG) formation. Thus it can be seen that prosodic structures are needed, which goes against DRA. However, on the other hand, syntactic relations cannot be ignored either. As can be seen in the discussions of previous chapters, syntactic relations determine both the TS domain and how the TS rule is to be applied. But it needs to be pointed out that the syntactic condition, which determines TS behavior, is not confined to what Kaisse claims in terms of the m-command relation only, nor is what determines prosodic domain limited to what Selkirk maintains in terms of the end points of X^{max} or X^{head}. According to the discussions in this book, what is accessible to phonology includes, at least, functional relations (i.e., argument/ adjunct dichotomy), left/right branching, immediate constituency, c/m-command, directionality, adjacency, syntactic units, and syntactic categories. The parameters set for some major Chinese dialects covered by the discussion of this book are presented in (8).

Theoretical discussions 189

(8)

Chinese Dialects	Parameters Setting
Xiamen	right edge, adjunct, m-command
Fuzhou	directionality, adjunct/argument, c-command
Old Chongming	syntactic units (word-hood), syntactic categories
Ruicheng	c-command, adjacency
Danyang	c-command
Pingyao	argument structures, c-command, directionality
Shanghai	adjunct, c-command, syntactic units

As can be seen from the table, many Chinese dialects need more than one parameter for setting value. For example, in Xiamen Chinese, the information for determining prosodic domain includes not only syntactic relations (i.e., m-command) but also syntactic categories (edge information such as $[X^{max}]$ #) and functional information (adjunct vs. argument). Moreover, if there are several prosodic domains within one language, the syntactic information for one domain is often different from that for the other. In Xiamen, for instance, three parameters are needed in the φ domain, as seen in (9a), while only one parameter is needed in the CG domain, as shown in (9b).

(9)   Xiamen case

    a.   Domain: φ
        Parameter: X^{max}]; adjunct; m-command
        Function: insert '#'
        Target condition: lexical syllable
    b.   Domain: CG
        Parameter: right edge of both XP and X°
        Function: insert '#' and neutral tone
        Target condition: functor syllable

A similar example is found in Shanghai, which has at least three prosodic domains: ω, CG, and φ. The parameter set for each is given in (10).

(10) Shanghai case

    a.   Domain: ω
        Parameter: c-command; adjunct
        Function: insert '='
        Target condition: lexical word
    b.   Domain: CG
        Parameter: c-command; right edge of XP
        Function: insert '='
        Target condition: lexical syllable; functional word

c. Domain: φ
   Parameter: c-command; argument
   Function: insert '#'
   Target condition: lexical word

Therefore, not even one of the approaches can successfully account for the sandhi phenomena of even one single language. For example, in Xiamen, the edge condition by Selkirk may be able to account for the TS of the CG level, but in the case of TS at the φ level, the m-command condition will be effective. Hence, although we agree that there is a prosodic structure between syntax and phonology, the prosodic domains of a prosodic structure are still determined by syntactic information, including functional relations, c/m-command condition, empty categories, syntactic units, and grammatical categories. As for end/edge, it is one of the parameters instead of the only parameter. Moreover, each specific prosodic hierarchy within a particular language will ask for some ad hoc parameters for setting value, as exemplified by the Xiamen TS and Shanghai TS. Therefore, the model I propose here for the mapping between syntax and phonology differs not only from Kaisse's DRA, as shown in (11), but also from Selkirk's IRA, as shown in (12). In sum, neither prosody nor syntax should be ignored, and the process of syntactic accessibility to phonology is just a process during which the prosodic structure is coded by syntactic conditions. Since syntactic conditions are effective within prosodic domains, this model can be thus named the prosodically syntax-sensitive approach (hereafter PSA), as given in (13).[2]

(11) DRA by kaisse

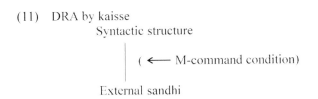

(12) IRA by selkirk

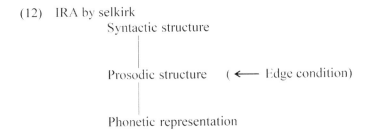

(13) PSA by zhang
    a. Mapping between syntax and phonology
        Syntactic structure
           |
        Prosodic structure (⟵ Coded by syntactic conditions including
           | units, categories, and relations of syntax)
        Phonetic representation

    b. Syntax-based prosodic hierarchy
        PPh (⟵ Syntactic condition A, a, ...)
         |
        CG   (⟵ Syntactic condition B, b, ...)
         |
        PW   (⟵ Syntactic condition C, c, ...)

Cross-linguistically, all languages should possess the mapping relationship depicted in (13a) as well as the morphosyntax-based prosodic hierarchy seen in (13b). But, language specifically, the syntactic conditions needed by each of the prosodic domains within various particular languages will be different. Take the domain of clitic groups, for example. In the Shanghai dialect, it needs the c-command condition; in Xiamen, it needs the parameter of edge setting; in Chongming, it needs syntactic categories, as seen in (14).

(14) Clitic groups domain

Dialects	Parameters
Shanghai	c-command, right edge c-command
Xiamen	right edge
Chongming	syntactic categories

In sum, the complex mapping from syntax to phonology is determined by number of conditions, some of which, such as c-command, m-command, argument/adjunct, edge setting, empty categories, and branchingness, have been widely discussed in this book. Out of a complex array of TS data from Chinese dialects, I have proposed a new approach, which is termed prosody-syntax model, for the interface of syntax-phonology. The key point of this model is that syntactic conditions are accessible within prosodic hierarchies while syntax is mapping phonology.

192   *Theoretical discussions*

6.2 Revisiting the strict layer hypothesis and recursivity

One of the major concerns in prosodic study is the hierarchical nature of prosodic domains. It is generally assumed that a prosodic unit at any given level in a prosodic hierarchy can never be composed of anything but the units at the next lower level. A prosodic constituent of a given level n immediately dominates only constituents of the lower-level $n-1$ and is exhaustively contained in a constituent of the immediately higher-level $n+1$ in the prosodic hierarchy. In other words, recursive prosodic structures are assumed not to occur. Thus comes the Strict Layer Hypothesis (hereafter SLH) proposed by Selkirk (1984, 1986), Nespor and Vogel (1986), Hayes (1989), etc., and provided in (15).[3]

(15)   a.   A given nonterminal unit of the prosodic hierarchy, X^p, is composed of one or more units of the immediately lower category, X^{p-1}.
       b.   A unit of a given level of the hierarchy is exhaustively contained in the super-ordinate unit of which it is a part.

Example (15a) stipulates that each prosodic unit, with the exception of the terminal moras, must directly dominate the unit under it in the tree diagram. Further, example (15b) requires that each prosodic unit must be parsed into its immediate lower-level constituents.

The mapping process between syntactic structure and prosodic structure in early studies is mainly based on X-bar theory. Later research, however, is analyzed on the basis of various constraints (Selkirk 1995, 2011; Truckenbrodt 1995). Within the OT framework, the SLH is interpreted with four constraints as shown in (16).

(16)   Strict layer hypothesis in optimality theory
       (where C^n = some prosodic category)

       a.   Layeredness: no C^i dominates a C^j iff $j > i$ (e.g., no α dominates a Σ)
       b.   Headedness: any C^i must dominate a C^{i-1} (e.g., a ω must dominate a Σ)
       c.   Exhaustivity: no C^i dominates C^j iff $j < i-1$, (e.g., no ω immediately dominates a σ)
       d.   Non-recursivity: no C^i dominates C^j iff $j = i$ (e.g., no Σ dominates a Σ)

The SLH is the well-formedness condition for the tree diagram of prosodic hierarchy. It determines the organization of the hierarchical structure and constrains prosodic constituents, which serve as domains of phonological rules application. The determining of the structural relationship among different prosodic constituents is concerned with the construction principles of prosodic hierarchy. Therefore, the SLH is one of the core principles in prosodic phonology.

However, the SLH is not applicable in many languages (Ladd 1986, 1990; Hyman et al. 1987; Odden 1987; Inkelas 1989; Ito & Mester 2003, 2015; Vogel 2015; and others), and it seems that prosodic recursion is allowed, as shown in (17) (Ito & Mester 2003).

(17) Prosodic recursion

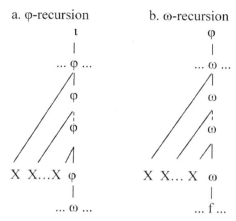

One of such challenges to the SLH has come from Chinese dialects. For instance, there are two different sets of TS rules in old Chongming (Zhang 1989): lexical TS (LTS) and clitic TS at the post-lexical level (CTS). LTS is for phonological words (ω), while CTS is for clitic groups (CG). Of course, there is quite a lot of data conforming to the SLH, and the prosodic domain is a hierarchy of the following order: . . . > φ > CG > ω > . . ., as exemplified by the case in (18). However, there are also many other examples that violate the SLH, which shows that prosodic recursivity is also allowed, as seen in (19).

(18) 'to agree with him'

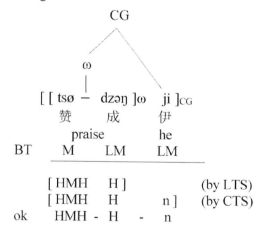

194 *Theoretical discussions*

(19) 'to take good care of him'

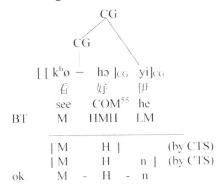

As seen from (18)–(19), the CG in Chongming may dominate both ω (...> CG > ω > ...) and CG (... > CG > CG > ...).

Another violation case is found in Pingyao, which violates not only non-recursivity principle (i.e. no C^i dominates C^j, iff j = i), but also layeredness principle (i.e. no C^i dominates a C^j, iff j > i). As we know, Pingyao also has two types of TS: TS type A (TSA) and TS type B (TSB). As pointed out by Zhang (1992), TSA is for argument structure, while TSB is for non-argument structure. Reproduced in (20) for convenience is the revised principle for the TS rule application in Pingyao.

(20) Edge c-command principle

Within argument structure, TSA applies iteratively right to left if X3 c-commands both X2 and X1, and in non-argument structure where X1 c-commands both X2 and X3, TSB applies iteratively left to right. Otherwise, TSA/B applies cyclically.

According to (20), there are two conditions that determine Pingyao TS. One is the functional relation that determines the TS domain, and the other is the c-command condition that selects the modes of rule application. The one applied by the TSA rule could be considered as the φ domain, and the other applied by the TSB rule might be taken as the ω domain. Moreover, there are two modes for TS rule application: the iterative mode and the cyclic mode. However, in Pingyao, there are at least two prosodic domains, and their hierarchical relation obviously violates the SLH, as seen in (21)–(22), with the former violating layeredness principle while the latter non-recursivity principle.

(21) Violating layeredness in cyclic case

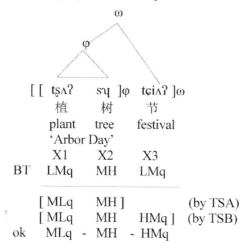

	X1	X2	X3
BT	LMq	MH	LMq

    [MLq   MH]   (by TSA)
    [MLq   MH   HMq]   (by TSB)
ok   MLq - MH - HMq

(22) Prosodic recursivity in iterative case

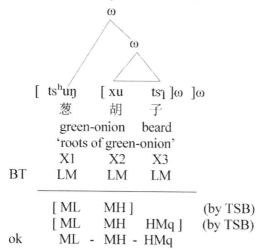

	X1	X2	X3
BT	LM	LM	LM

    [ML   MH]   (by TSB)
    [ML   MH   HMq]   (by TSB)
ok   ML - MH - HMq

As seen from (21), the PW in Pingyao may dominate the prosodic domain, such as PPh, which is at the next higher layer. And (22) shows us that the PW in Pingyao may also dominate the prosodic domain at the same layer. Of course, one may argue with case (21) that the one applied by the TSA rule could be considered as the ω domain instead of the φ domain, and the other applied by the TSB rule might be taken as the φ domain instead of the ω domain. Whichever the case is, hierarchical violation is still an existence as show in (23).

(23) 'move bed-roll'

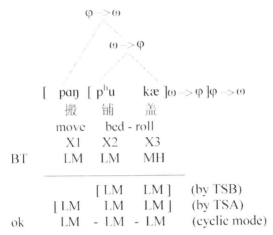

Therefore, some prosodic units can be either recursive or non-layered in Pingyao, and a domain at a given level in the prosodic hierarchy is sometimes composed of categories other than a unit at the next lower level (such as ... > ω > φ > ..., or ... > φ > ω > ..., or ... > ω > ω > ...).

Accordingly, some modified models are proposed among which the most worth mentioning one is from Ito and Mester (2003) and Vogel (2015). The prosodic units in the prosodic hierarchy can be split into two categories depending upon whether they interface with the other grammatical components or not. As for the interface category (i.e., prosodic word and prosodic units above), Ito and Mester (2003), based on their analyses of Japanese data, consider that the prosodic units belonging to the interface category still need to be split into two types: major prosodic category (MaP) and minor prosodic category (MiP). For instance, at the phonological phrase level, Ito and Mester distinguish two interface categories, as shown in (24).

(24)
```
        |
       MaP      major (≈ 'intermediate') phrase
        |           (domain of downstep)
        |
       MiP      minor (≈ 'accentual') phrase
        |           (domains of accent culminativity and initial lowering)
```

They use prosodic phrase as an example to illustrate the relationship between MiP and MaP, as seen in (25).

(25) MiP/MaP versus minimal-φ/maximal-φ

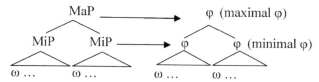

The more complete prosodic structure of MiP/MaP theory can be depicted as seen in (26).

(26)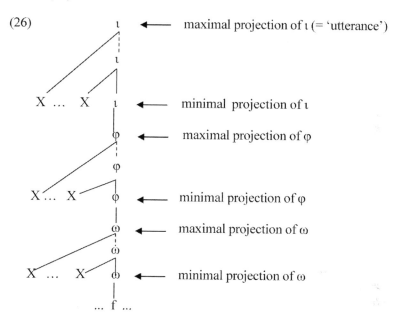

As can be seen in (26), both prosodic word and the prosodic units above it are allowed recursivity, as shown in (27).

(27)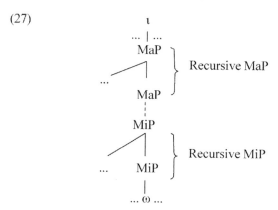

198 *Theoretical discussions*

However, this kind of recursivity as distinguished by MiP/MaP theory is unidirectional, such as one-way traffic, as presented in (28).

(28)

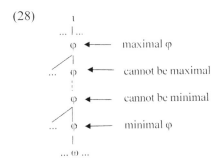

MiP/MaP theory not only accounts for such language phenomena in Japanese as accent culminativity, initial lowering, and downstep but also helps maintain the SLH. However, it still faces the challenge from Pingyao TS. By MiP/MaP theory, the maximal prosodic unit can dominate the minimal prosodic unit, but it cannot dominate the same maximal prosodic unit, nor be dominated by the minimal prosodic unit. And, moreover, the minimal prosodic unit cannot dominate the same minimal prosodic unit either. This is because the domination relationship among prosodic units is one-way traffic, as shown in (29).

(29) K_{MAX} = K not dominated by K
       K_{MIN} = K not dominating K

However, in Pingyao TS, the domination relationship among prosodic units is bidirectional and interactional. Therefore, prosodic unit B can dominate prosodic unit A, as shown in (30a), and prosodic unit A can also dominate prosodic unit B, as shown in (30b).

(30)   a. = (21) 'Arbor Day'

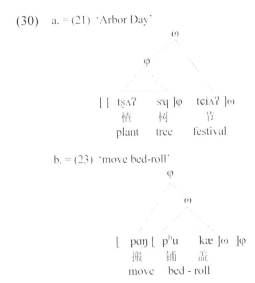

b. = (23) 'move bed-roll'

If TSA's domain of rule application is maximal prosodic unit, TSB's domain of rule application is minimal prosodic unit, then (30a) will serve as the counterevidence against the MiP/MaP theory. On the other hand, if TSA's domain of rule application is minimal prosodic unit and TSB's domain of rule application is maximal prosodic unit, then (30b) will be the counterevidence against the MiP/MaP theory.

The other questions that the MiP/MaP theory is confronted with include what are the prosodic properties of the major prosodic category (MaP) and the minor prosodic category (MiP)? What kind of relationship do they have? And do K_{MAX} and K_{MIN} belong to the same prosodic unit or two different prosodic units? Judged by (25) and (29), K_{MAX} cannot be dominated by either K_{MAX} or K_{MIN}. K_{MAX} can dominate K_{MIN}, and K_{MIN} cannot be dominated by K_{MIN}. If so, the relationship between K_{MAX} and K_{MIN} is obviously like that between the two different prosodic units, such as foot and prosodic word. This means that K_{MAX} and K_{MIN} belong to two different prosodic units too. In that case, recursivity should not happen between K_{MAX} and K_{MIN}. This is because K_{MAX} can be composed of the unit of the immediately lower category, i.e., K_{MIN}. And at a given level of the prosodic hierarchy, K_{MIN} is a unit that is exhaustively contained in the super-ordinate unit (i.e., K_{MAX}) of which it is a part. Therefore, K_{MAX} and K_{MIN} have no chance to violate the SLH.

Vogel (2015) also splits the prosodic units over prosodic word into two categories, which differ from the two categories proposed by Ito and Mester (2003). Instead of major prosodic category and minor prosodic category, Vogel (2015) terms them as outer category and inner category, as seen in (31).

(31)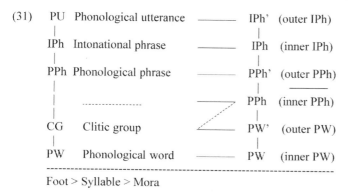

By (31), C_n' is allowed to dominate C_n, as exemplified by (32).

(32)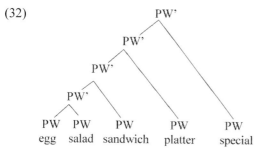

200 *Theoretical discussions*

Vogel's proposal faces the same question: do outer category and inner category belong to the same one prosodic unit or two different prosodic units? As can be seen from (31) and (32), an outer category cannot be dominated by an inner category, an outer category can dominate an inner category, an inner category cannot be dominated by another inner category, but an outer category can dominate another outer category. Therefore, outer category and inner category should belong to two different hierarchical prosodic units, thus not violating the SLH nor involving any recursivity. By Vogel's proposal, recursivity happens only to the outer category. However, recursivity, as a matter of fact, reflects from another perspective the interaction between syntax and phonology, i.e., syntactic recursivity. The so-called recursivity happens only to those prosodic units above prosodic word in the prosodic hierarchy and never to those other prosodic units (such as foot, syllable, and mora) below prosodic word. The so-called interface of syntax-phonology occurs only to those prosodic units above prosodic word and never to those below prosodic word. This proves that only those prosodic units above prosodic word belong to interface categories, thus being able to interface with other components of grammar. In other words, only higher-level units (the prosodic word and units above it) are interface categories whose parsing is regulated by grammatical information on the correspondence between syntactic and phonological constituents. As for foot, syllable, mora, and segments, they are the word-internal units, intrinsically defined in terms of sonority-related phonetic factors and speech rhythm and do not interface with other components of grammar. Prosodic recursivity, thus, in fact, is a mirror image of syntactic recursivity, which is common in syntax. Example (33) displays the cases of recursivity occurring at the syntactic level. In some cases, the recursivity can be unlimited.

(33) Syntactic recursivity

    a. "The dog is brought home by my father who works in a hospital beside which there is a Balzac's statue that was built in 1918 when Lenin was assassinated in Moscow . . ."

    b. $[_{DP} a[_{NP} book[_{CP} that[_{IP} I[_{VP} wrote]]]]]$

    c. $[_{DP} a[_{NP} book[_{PP} about[_{DP} the[_{NP} Chinese women]]]]]$

    d. $[_{PP} about[_{ConjP} [_{DP} a[_{NP} Chinese book]] [_{Conj'} and[_{DP} a[_{NP} Japanese book]]]]]$

Example (33a) is a case that can be infinitely recursive if needed. Example (33b) is a case in which DP can have NP, CP, IP, and VP. In the case in example (33c), NP possesses PP, DP, and NP. Finally, in the case in (33d), PP has CP, DP, and NP. Therefore, it is natural for recursivity to happen only to some specific prosodic units. Such recursivity could be allowed. Moreover, it need be pointed out that some units in both syntactic structure and prosodic structure can be recursive, but only prosodic structure can allow non-layeredness. However, syntactic recursivity is, in some sense, evidence of the direct influence of syntax upon phonology because prosodic recursivity actually reflects syntactic recursivity. Based on such understanding, I would like to propose my revision for the SLH. Before the new proposal is proposed, let us take a look at the prosodic hierarchy first. The prosodic hierarchy can be divided into two parts. The dividing line is usually drawn between the phonological word and the foot. Then the part below the phonological word is considered as the metrical hierarchy, while the other upper part is regarded as the prosodic hierarchy, as seen in (34). On the other hand, if the dividing line is put right beneath the phonological word, the part above it belongs to the prosodic phonology, while the part below it belongs to the prosodic morphology (Ito 1986; McCarthy & Prince 1990; and others) or the prosodic lexical phonology (Inkelas 1989; and others).

(34)

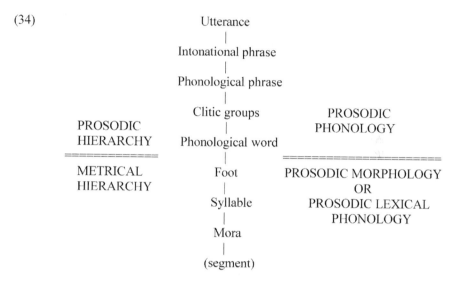

However, I would like to re-divide the hierarchy in (34) into three parts according to the information coded in each. Thus the dividing line for the first part will be drawn between the phonological word and the foot. As for the part below the phonological word, it is the rhythm-based hierarchy because foot, syllable, and mora share the same properties and are all sensitive to sonority features such as strong and weak. The basic structure of the relation among them is schematized in (35).[4]

(35)

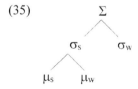

Hence, what the foot, the syllable, and the mora have in common is to be constrained in terms of sonority. And this property is not shared by any of the higher-up prosodic units.

The dividing line splitting the top part from the rest is drawn between the intonational phrase (ι) and the phonological phrase (φ). The prosodic domains below ι but above the foot (Σ) are addressed as the morphosyntax-based hierarchy. The property

202 *Theoretical discussions*

shared by the components of this group is the sensitivity to various types of syntactic information, including functional relations, the c/m-command condition, syntactic units, empty categories, and branchingness. The mapping relationship between syntax and phonology is indicated at the left of this group. As for the two domains above the phonological phrase, they belong to the third part, which we may call the focus-based hierarchy or the speech-rate-based hierarchy. And this part is mainly sensitive to information structure, discourse, pragmatics, etc. (Selkirk 1984; Nespor & Vogel 1986; Zec 1988; and others). The re-divided prosodic hierarchy is given in (36).

(36) Prosodic hierarchies

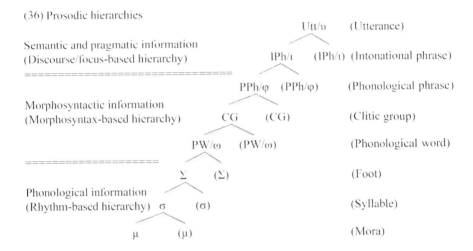

As can be seen in (36), it is the hierarchy in the middle that is most closely, as well as most directly, related to the syntax-phonology interface. And this has been proved by the data discussed in this book. Almost all of the phenomena of the accessibility of syntax to phonology that I have discussed are found in such prosodic domains such as φ, CG, and ω, and in a very few cases they might be seen in some other domains. The chart given in (37) shows which specific prosodic domains in each of the languages, covered in the discussion of this book, are sensitive to syntactic information.

(37)

Languages	Prosodic Domains
Xiamen	CG, φ
Fuzhou	ω, φ
Chongming	ω, CG, φ
Ruicheng	Φ
Danyang	Φ
Pingyao	ω, φ
Shanghai	ω, CG, φ
Mandarin	ω, CG, φ, ι, υ

Theoretical discussions 203

As can be seen from (37), almost all of the prosodic domains sensitive to syntactic conditions belong to the morphosyntax-based hierarchy. Needless to say, it must be certain identical properties that have brought these domains to the same group.

Although the dividing of the prosodic hierarchy into three parts is based on the information coded in the hierarchy, it is supported, in some way, by the SLH. As discussed previously, prosodic recursivity is allowed in many cases. For instance, in some Chinese dialects, such as Chongming and Pingyao, CG may dominate CG, and PW may dominate PPh. This fact, on one hand, indicates that the concept of having the hierarchy divided into three instead of two may be on the right track and that these three different prosodic hierarchies possibly really exist; and on the other hand, it helps us redefine the function of the SLH in prosodic phonology. But it should be pointed out that all the available cases are examples of recursivity occurring among the prosodic units above the rhythm-based hierarchy without crossing the dividing line. Hence it is necessary to add a supplementary principle to the SLH, as given in (38).

(38)   Stipulation of prosodic recursivity

Prosodic recursivity is prohibited between the units of different hierarchies (language-universal), but optionally in the units of the same hierarchy (language-specific).

The principle in (38) indicates that there is no recursivity among prosodic units between different hierarchies. For example, φ cannot dominate ι because the former belongs to the morphosyntax-based hierarchy while the latter belongs to the discourse/focus-based hierarchy, and, therefore, there is no recursive relationship between them. The discussion shows that with the supplementing of the stipulation in (38), the SLH can still serve as an important principle in prosodic studies.

6.3 Prosodic units and Mandarin prosodic hierarchy

One of the major aims for prosodic phonology is to investigate prosodic units of human languages and construct the prosodic hierarchy. Thus come the following questions: in what ways are these prosodic units defined and constructed? How should we define such units as mora, syllable, foot, prosodic word, clitic group, phonological phrase, intonational phrase, and utterance?

As the minimal unit in the tree diagram of prosodic hierarchy in human languages, **mora** acts mainly to determine the weight of syllables in some quantity-sensitive languages. It is defined as the element that makes up the rime of each syllable and is used to measure the weight of each syllable. A heavy syllable consists of two moras, while a light syllable consists of only one mora. A long vowel or two segments that carry two moras can, therefore, form a heavy syllable, while a short vowel without a coda carries only one mora and, thus, forms a light syllable. Moras have played an important role in some quantity-sensitive languages. For instance, the requirement of *śloka* poetic prosody in Sanskrit poetry

204 *Theoretical discussions*

can be achieved by alternation of heavy and light syllables. This can be exemplified in (39) and (40) as follows.

(39)

line 1:	X	X	X	X
line 2:	∨	(—)	(—)	(∨)
line 3:	X	X	X	X
line 4:	∨	—	∨	X
line 5:	X	X	X	X
line 6:	∨	(—)	(—)	(∨)
line 7:	X	X	X	X
line 8:	∨	—	∨	X

(40)

Odd pādā	X	X	X	X	∨	(—)	(—)	(∨)
Even pādā	X	X	X	X	∨	—	∨	X

However, Mair and Mei (1991: 375–470) misinterpret the prosody of *śloka* in Sanskrit poetry as the contrast of short and long syllables, as shown in (41).

(41) "*Śloka* consists of four *pādā*, or quarter verses, of eight syllables each, or two lines of sixteen syllables. Each line allows great liberty except for the 5th, 13th, 14th, and 15th syllable, as in the above schema, where the crosses denote either long or short, the bars long, and the breve signs short."

Due to this misunderstanding, they are unable to explain why short syllables *vat, mos* in (42a) and *ṣot, har* in (42b) can be poetically metricalized. It is apparent, however, that the metrical pattern of *śloka* in Sanskrit poetry is constructed by resorting to the contrast of heavy and light syllables, rather than the contrast of short and long syllables (Mishra 1999: 21–22).

(42)   a.   namaste puruùādhyakùa namaste bhakta **vat** sala |
          namaste'stu hçùākeśa nārāyaõa na **mos** tute ||
          (Quoted from *Adhyātma Rāmāyaõa, 1.5.59.*)
   b.   lokānāü tvaü paro dharmaþ puru **üot** tamaþ |
          śaraõyaü śaraõaü ca tvām āhurdivyāþ ma **har** üayaþ ||
          (Quoted from *Vālmāki Rāmāyaõa, V, CXIX, 14.*)

Likewise, in the field of Chinese linguistics, there are similar assertions that confuse the contrast of heavy and light syllables with that of short and long syllables. For example, some scholars (Feng 2013: 46) claim that in some longer syllables, the nucleus can be bi-syllables (VV) while the coda can be consonant clusters (CC), as shown in (43).

(43) a. Short syllable: V
          Long syllable: V(V)C
          Super long syllable: VVCC(C)

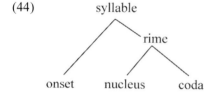

The classification in (43) is incorrect because the third type VC in (43b) is neither a long syllable nor a foot. Instead, it is a short, but heavy, syllable.

Syllable is the minimal structural unit that can be identified naturally in speech and form a foot within words in some stress languages. It has its internal structure and can be decomposed into onset and rime, which is further divided into nucleus and coda, as illustrated in (44).

(44)

```
              syllable
             /      \
          onset     rime
                   /    \
               nucleus  coda
```

In some languages, syllables can be categorized into strong syllables (i.e., stressed syllables) and weak syllables (i.e., unstressed syllables). A metrical foot is formed by a strong syllable plus a weak syllable adjacent to it. Syllable is the minimal hierarchical prosodic unit in Mandarin Chinese, the construction of which must conform to the phonotactic constraints of Mandarin. The erroneous representation of syllables *biao* /piau/ and *bian* /piɛn/ in Mandarin in (45) clearly indicates an incorrect understanding of how to define syllables. The construction of syllables must comply with the sonority sequence principle and, as a result, one syllable can only have one nucleus.

(45)
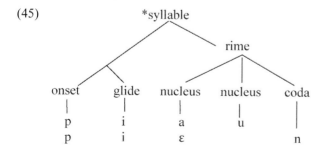

206 *Theoretical discussions*

Foot is a prosodic unit that is higher than a syllable and lower than a prosodic word in the prosodic hierarchy. It works as the domain within which some segmental rules apply. In prosodic phonology, the definition of foot is closely related to that of metrical binary contrast. In stress languages, a foot often consists of a strong syllable and a weak syllable, with the strong syllable carrying the primary stress. Foot can be classified into two different categories – namely, within-word foot and cross-word-boundary foot. The foot in prosodic phonology is within-word foot, which is also referred to as metric-prominent foot. The universal rules can guarantee that only one syllable in a foot is the metrical prominent (i.e., strong, heavy, long, or high pitched). As to which syllable is prominent, it falls into the sphere of certain specific linguistic rules. In particular languages, there are strict constraints for syllables on foot formation. Whether foot as a prosodic unit exists in a language or not is determined by the existence of metrical binary contrast. This contrast is frequently represented by the stress, duration, pitch, or strength of syllables. In Mandarin, however, there is no such metrical binary contrast, thus, denying the existence of foot defined in phonology. A literary review of all available publications indicates that discussions of foot within the Chinese linguistics field are confused and full of misunderstandings, and (46) presents some of that confusion.

(46)   a.   "A prosodic word is also a foot. . . . A prosodic word is equivalent to a foot. . . . The basic foot or standard foot in Mandarin Chinese consists of two standard stresses" (Cao 2001: 177).

   b.   "A foot is a prosodic word. In Chinese a syllable is usually a 'syllabic word,' thus forming a 'two-syllabic-words-combined' unit . . . . In some languages, moras can form foot directly. For example, *cat* [kæt] functions as an independent intonational group and can be a foot in and of itself. In other languages, however, moras are not allowed to form foot" (Feng 2013: 46).

The aforementioned quoted statements are problematic because the definition of foot is not based on the number of syllables, but on the metrical prominence property. They also confuse foot with prosodic word. Foot is not a prosodic word because foot and prosodic word are two different units in a prosodic hierarchy. Example (46a) also goes against the definition of foot since two syllables within the same foot cannot carry two of the same standard stresses. The analysis of *cat* as well as the units lower than foot in (46b) is erroneous because *cat* is just a syllable, not a foot. The phonological structures in Mandarin are lacking in metrical binary contrast. Therefore, there is no foot in the prosodic hierarchy of Mandarin Chinese because Mandarin is a syllable-based tonal language without prominent metrical contrast between two adjacent syllables.

Prosodic word is the minimal prosodic unit that is higher than foot in prosodic hierarchy and directly dominates foot. When the words defined in morphosyntax cannot correspond to those defined in phonology, the concept of prosodic word becomes extremely essential. Prosodic word constitutes the lowest units in prosodic hierarchy constructed on the basis of mapping rules that make use of non-phonological notions. Prosodic word represents the interaction between the

Theoretical discussions 207

phonological and morphological components. The domain of prosodic word should be the terminal constituents in syntax trees. The domain of prosodic words consists of (i) a stem, (ii) any element identified by specific phonological and/or morphological criteria, (iii) any element marked with the diacritic [+w] or any attached elements within the terminal constituents of a syntactic tree that forms part of the adjacent prosodic word closest to the stem, and (iv) if no such prosodic word exists, then the independent elements form a prosodic word on their own (Nespor & Vogel 1986: 141). Although the concept of prosodic word is not new, it seems to have not yet been truly understood in the Chinese linguistics field. In (47), some quotations from various published works in China on prosodic word and foot, which exhibit nothing but the misunderstanding of the concept, are presented.

(47) a. "'Prosodic word,' from the perspective of prosody, can be defined as 'the smallest language unit that can be used freely.' In prosody, 'language unit' means 'prosodic unit' and, therefore, prosodic words are based upon the prosodic units in languages" (Feng 2009: 1).

   b. "The smallest unit that can be used freely is foot" (Feng 2009: 1).

   c. "In prosodic morphology, the smallest prosodic unit that can be used is 'foot.' Therefore, a prosodic word must contain at least one foot. And if a foot consists of two syllables, then a prosodic word naturally must contain at least two syllables . . . Regardless of the relations between the elements forming foot, so long as they fulfill the basic requirements of foot, prosodic words can still hold water" (Feng 2009: 2).

As we have seen, (47a) claims that prosodic word is "the smallest prosodic unit that can be used freely." But then in (47b) and (47c), foot is "the smallest prosodic unit that can be used freely," thus, confusing prosodic word with foot. From earlier discussions, it can be concluded that prosodic word and foot are two kinds of completely different prosodic hierarchical units. Foot is determined on the basis of phonological notions, while prosodic word constitutes the lowest units in prosodic hierarchy constructed on the basis of mapping rules that make use of those notions that represent the interface between phonology and syntax. The TS in Mandarin Chinese can provide evidence for the proposal of prosodic word as a hierarchical unit, but there is no foot as a prosodic unit in Mandarin. So prosodic word in Mandarin should be the smallest prosodic unit higher than syllable in prosodic hierarchy and dominates syllable directly.

Clitic group is the prosodic unit located between prosodic word and prosodic phrase in prosodic hierarchy. It is formed by a clitic element plus the lexical hood, which is its host. **Phonological phrase** is a unit higher than prosodic word or clitic group in the prosodic hierarchy and consists of one or more prosodic words or clitic groups. The phonological phrase is a phonological unit that is established on the basis of mapping rules that make reference to syntactic concepts and it includes all the constituents from prosodic words up to syntactic phrases. Phonological phrases across languages have demonstrated a great similarity, and the minor differences can be accounted for by parameters. As long as they are proposed on the basis of the fundamental principles defined by X-bar theory, they can be employed

208 *Theoretical discussions*

to analyze the structures of phonological phrases. The TS in Chinese provides support for distinguishing the clitic group and phonological phrase as two different prosodic units. This is illustrated in (48a)–(48b).

(48)   a. Clitic group   b. phonological phrase

	我	比	你	小		狗	比	马	小
	wo	bi	ni	xiao		gou	bi	ma	xiao
Citation tone:	3	3	3	3		3	3	3	3
Tone sandhi:	*2	3	2	3		2	3	2	3

          I compare you small   dog compare horse small
         'I am younger than you.'   'Dogs are smaller than horses.'

Both (48a) and (48b) are the same with regard to the tones of each set of syllables as well as their surface structure of syntactic trees. Nevertheless, the TS of (48a) is illegitimate, while that of (48b) is legitimate. This is because (48a) is a clitic group and (48b), however, is a phonological phrase.

Being a prosodic unit defined in terms of intonation, **intonational phrase** constitutes the domain of a coherent intonational contour. The semantic and pragmatic information may affect the segmentation of intonation phrase. There are certain types of constructions (including parenthetical expressions, nonrestrictive relative clauses, tag questions, vocatives, and preceding elements) that seem to form intonational domains on their own. Topics and focus will also influence the segmentation of intonational phrases. Intonational phrase is not a syntactic unit since an utterance connected to pitch contour can never be formed by syntactic structures. It is also not defined by boundary of the sentence. In languages with special pitch contour, intonational phrase constitutes a part of prosodic constituents expressed by phonological rules. It is semantic in nature and a unit of information structure. There are two modes for applying the TS rules in Mandarin Chinese: a cyclic model and an iterative mode going from left to right. The former applies to prosodic words and phonological phrases, while the latter applies to intonational phrases, as illustrated in (49).

(49)   老 李 买 好 酒

	Lao Li	mai	hao	jiu
	Old Li	buy	good	wine

         'Old Li has bought the good wine.'

Citation tone: 3   3   3   3   3

TS-1: |2-3|ω ||3|ω [2-3|ω |φ (cyclic application)
TS-2: |2-2-3| l [2-3|ω   (iterative application from left to right; cyclic application)
TS-3: |2-3|ω |2-2-3| l   (cyclic application; iterative application from left to right)
TS-4: |2-2-2-2-3| l   (cyclic application)

The TS-1 in (49) takes prosodic word and phonological phrase as the application domain (cyclic application). The TS-2 and TS-3 all take prosodic word and intonational phrase as the application domains. And the TS-4 only takes intonational phrase as the application domain.

Utterance is the highest or maximal unit in prosodic hierarchy and also subjects to the maximum span in applying phonological rules. It consists of one or more intonational phrases and can extend the length of the string dominated by the highest node in the syntactic tree, thus being called X^n. However, utterance is not merely the phonological counterpart of X^n since it can incorporate two or more sentences into a unit of a greater level. The difference here provides a strong motivation for the existence of utterance as a prosodic hierarchical unit because the application domain of some phonological phenomena cannot be directly generalized on the basis of syntactic structures.

The phonological utterance makes use of syntactic information in its definition, though it is not necessarily isomorphic to any syntactic constituent. To put it concretely, the only syntactic information that is used in defining utterance is the left and right boundary of X^n. If a linguistic form has pauses both at the beginning and at the end, as well as a comparatively full meaning, then its intonation contour is an utterance. In Chinese, the maximal application domain of the third TS rule is intonational phrase, rather than utterance. Nevertheless, the phenomenon of liaison takes utterance – namely, the overall clause group with complete intonation – as the widest domain of applying phonological rules. In Mandarin Chinese, the linguistic unit that works as an utterance can range in size from a syllable to a group of clauses (Zhu 1982: 21–22), as illustrated in (50).

(50) A clause group with an utterance as the domain

风　又　冷,／雨　又　猛,／我　又　没　有　车。
Feng1 you4 leng3,/ yu3 you4 meng3,/ wo3 you4 mei2 you3 che1.
wind and cold   rain and violent   I and not exist car
'The wind is cold, the rain is heavy, and I don't have a car.'

To sum up the aforementioned points, there is a complete prosodic hierarchy that is condensed in Mandarin Chinese, as shown in (51).

(51) The prosodic hierarchy in Mandarin Chinese

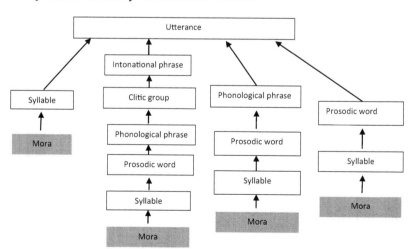

210   *Theoretical discussions*

It is concluded that *foot* as a prosodic unit does not exist in Mandarin Chinese, which is typologically a syllable-based tonal language. This is an issue concerning the existence of a particular prosodic unit in a specific language. It is language universal that any human language can have all of its prosodic units found in the prosodic hierarchy presented in (36), but it is language specific that not all of the human languages need necessarily possess all of the prosodic units included in this hierarchy. Therefore, it does not make much sense to argue about whether a particular prosodic unit, such as clitic group, does exist or not in the prosodic hierarchy of human languages given in (36), because if a particular prosodic unit is not found in one language, it does not mean that it does not exist in other human languages. So this is a language-specific issue in terms of language typology.

Although foot is a widely used term, it must be noted that foot has different definitions and properties in different frameworks. Foot is defined as the main unit for constructing the metrical grid in metrical phonology. However, in prosodic phonology, foot works as one of the prosodic units in the prosodic hierarchy. The term 'foot' is also used in poetic prosody. Sapir (1921: 246) once proposed that Chinese verse has developed along similar lines as French verse. The syllable in Chinese is an even more integral and sonorous unit than that in French, while quantity and stress are too uncertain to form the basis of a metrical system. The alternation of syllables with level tonal category (i.e., *ping* 平) and syllables with inflected tonal category (i.e., *ze* 仄) is peculiar to Chinese. Here the alternation between *ping* (i.e., even tone) and *ze* (i.e., rising, or dipping, or falling tone) syllables is defined as foot in Chinese poetic prosody. However, foot in poetic prosody is not equivalent to that of linguistics. In linguistics, a foot usually contains two syllables with a metric-prominence relation (usually strong versus weak). But in Chinese, poetic foot with a *ping-ze* contrast involves four syllables, which can be reflected in the rules of poetry-writing: one does not need to pay attention to the tone of the first, third, and fifth syllables of a regulated style verse, but should clearly specify the tone of the second, fourth, and sixth syllables. Example (52a) is the typical tonal pattern for a hepta-syllabic quatrain with the metrical prominence underlined, and (52b) is a poem written by the author of the book by strictly following the aforementioned rules.

(52)   a.   ping-***ping***-ze-***ze***-ping-***ping***-ze
            ze-***ze***-ping-***ping***-ze-***ze***-ping
            ze-***ze***-ping-***ping***-ping-***ze***-ze
            ping-***ping***-ze-***ze***-ze-***ping***-ping

       b.   Hepta-syllabic Quatrain – *Fall Rain*
            千   松   千   竹   千   年   寺
            Qiang song   qiang zhu qiang nian   si
            Thousand pines thousand CL thousand year temple
            秋   雨   秋   风   秋   叶   情
            Qu   yu   qiu feng qiu ye   qing
            Fall rain   fall wind fall leave love
            红   树   红   螺   红   峡   谷

Hong	shu	hong	luo	hong	xia-gu
Red	tree	red	snail	red	canyon
绿	山	绿	水	绿	人 生
lü	shan	lü	shui	lü	ren-sheng
green	mountain	green	water	green	life

It can be clearly seen that foot in poetic prosody refers to the beats or units of metrical verse. Whether rhymed or not, it divides the rhythm of a verse as a whole into several units, thus being a cycle of poetic prosody. Therefore, it is inappropriate to lump the various concepts of foot in different frameworks under one head, as they must be distinguished from one another. In a word, foot is the main unit for constructing the metrical grid in metrical phonology, also one of the prosodic units in the prosodic hierarchy of prosodic phonology, and a primary unit for constructing poetic meters in poetic tonal prosody. In other words, the term 'foot' means different things under different circumstances, but maintains its unique property of metrical prominent binary contrast unchanged.

6.4 Summary

This chapter has discussed some major theoretical issues of phonology-syntax interface, including the nature of the interface, the mapping between syntax and phonology, the most influential syntactic information (i.e., structures, categories, relations) that are accessible to phonology, and the nature of prosodic domains, as well as presented some hypotheses/assumptions for the organization of prosodic hierarchy. Also, I have discussed the principles determining the construction of prosodic units and tested them in Mandarin Chinese. With various terminologies in different hierarchical levels of prosodic phonology being clarified, this chapter also makes clear what a prosodic unit is and how a specific prosodic unit is defined. Additionally, this chapter clarifies the issue of language universal versus language specific in prosodic studies. Finally, this chapter reflects on the existing misunderstandings in current Chinese prosodic studies, particularly concerning foot and prosodic word. It is hoped that this study can lay a foundation for the establishment of Chinese prosodic phonology in the real sense.

Notes

1 A similar situation has been observed in English. The sentence "He teaches Chinese" can have two results after prosodic segmentation: "(He teaches) (Chinese)" and "(He teaches Chinese)".
2 'A, a . . .' in (13b) means that the syntactic conditions, needed by a prosodic domain, include condition a besides condition A; and the same for 'B, b . . .' and 'C, c . . .'.
3 The adopted definition here is the interpretation by Nespor and Vogel (1986: 7).
4 S stands for 'strong' and w for 'weak'.

7   Concluding remarks

In this book, I have studied some outstanding issues of phrasal phonology, such as the nature of the syntax-phonology interface, the accessibility of syntactic information to phonology, and the property of prosodic structure. Also, I evaluated several current models of prosodic phonology and proposed some new hypotheses for furthering the understanding of grammar.

I have argued in this book that a number of conditions determine the complex mapping from syntax to phonology, including functional relations, c-command, m-command, Morphosyntactic units, syntactic categories, X-bar information, and the edge condition. One by one, I have revealed how these different conditions affect phonology by using TS data from various Chinese dialects. Based on such discussions, I have inquired further into the organization of prosodic hierarchies, the properties of prosodic structure, and the relationships between different rules at the post-lexical level. With the data from Xiamen, Fuzhou, Wu, and Pingyao, I have discussed how functional relations affect TS. With the analyses of the TS phenomena of Danyang, Ruicheng, Pingyao, and Shanghai, I have summed up four types of c-command condition that influence TS. Moreover, I have introduced and elaborated on some concepts of prosodic phonology, discussed the principles defining prosodic units, and further tested the application of these principles before finally pointing out the misunderstanding existing in Chinese prosodic studies. With various terminologies for different levels of prosodic hierarchy being clarified, I have explained the definitions for prosodic units. In Chapter 5, I discussed some special cases, such as the TS of function words and the rhythmic phenomenon in the quadrisyllabic TS of Chinese dialects. The phonological behavior of function words is different from that of lexical words and phrases in many languages. What I have tried to do is to show that the TS of function words is not so simple. Taking Chinese dialects, for example, the different TS behaviors between function words and lexical words or phrases are represented by the different formations of TS domains in some Chinese dialects, but in others, they are embodied by either different types of TS rules or different modes of rule application. The other issue that I have discussed is the rhythmic effect on quadrisyllabic TS, a fairly popular phenomenon in Chinese dialects, with the purpose of finding some possible accounts for some exceptional TS cases and proposed, from a historical perspective, the Morphosyntactic diffusion hypothesis. Chapter 6 includes some theoretical discussions in which I have presented some new hypotheses and assumptions for the mapping relationship between syntax and phonology, as well as for the organizing of prosodic hierarchy; suggested the possible way to revise the Strict Layer Hypothesis; and pointed out the problems in the OT.

As is well known, two questions have been fundamental in the study of the syntax-phonology interface: (i) which specific syntactic properties affect the application of phonological rules and (ii) how should these syntactic properties be incorporated into phonology? In response to these two questions, two different leading theories have been developed separately. One claims that phonological rules are subject to conditions that are stated directly in terms of syntactic domains (i.e., sandhi rules have direct access to relevant properties of the surface syntactic structure). The other suggests that the surface syntactic structure is first mapped onto a prosodic structure consisting of prosodic constituents, which are the domains of phonological rules applying above the level of the word. According to the former, the syntactic information needed to delimit the sandhi domain is defined by the m-command condition, while by the latter, the prosodic domain is marked at the right or left edge of an X^{head} or X^{max}. In fact, the mapping from syntax to phonology is not so simple, but is rather a complex mapping determined by several different conditions. As I have pointed out, not any single one of the current approaches, neither the m-command condition, nor the edge condition, nor the OT approach, can explain the sandhi phenomena of all the languages. Many languages need more than one parameter for setting value. Based on an extensive observation and discussion of the sandhi phenomena of Chinese dialects, I have proposed a model for the mapping between syntax and phonology, which is called the prosodic-syntax model, as seen in (1a), the prosodic structure of which can be profiled as given in (1b), and the trisected model for prosodic hierarchy as given in (2).

(1) a. Mapping between syntax phonology

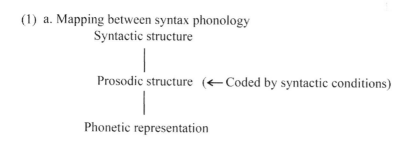

b. Syntax-based prosodic hierarchy
      PPh/φ   (← Syntactic condition A, a, ...)
      |
      CG   (← Syntactic condition B, b, ...)
      |
      PW/ω   (← Syntactic condition C, c, ...)

214   *Concluding remarks*

(2) Prosodic hierarchy

Utt/υ
   | Discourse/focus-based hierarchy
IPh/ι
   | =================================
PPh/φ
   |
CG   Morphosyntax-based hierarchy
   |
PW/ω
   | -----------------------------------
Ft/Σ
   |
σ   Rhythm-based hierarchy
   |
μ

The basic idea of the aforementioned models is that the process of syntactic accessibility to phonology is a process during which the prosodic structure is coded by syntactic information. In other words, syntactic conditions are effective within prosodic domains.

In sum, this book has offered some theoretical discussions, revisited the issue of recursivity, revised the SLH, pointed out the problems of the OT, presented the Mandarin prosodic structure, and proposed some new hypotheses for the mapping relationship of syntax-phonology and for the organization of prosodic hierarchy. Although the study of post-lexical rules sensitive to syntactic or prosodic structure may be still in its infancy, quite a few influential theories and approaches have been proposed in this field. "All models are wrong, but some are useful," and I hope that the conclusions reached in this book on the interface studies of syntax-phonology have made a more distinct picture of the organization of phonological components and will further the understanding of grammar in general.

Bibliography

Abney, S. 1987. *The English Noun Phrase in Its Sentential Aspect*. Ph.D. dissertation, MIT.

Adger, D. 2007. Stress and Phrasal Syntax, *Linguistic Analysis*, vol. 33: 238–266.

Anderson, S. R. 1975. On the Interaction of Phonological Rules of Various Types, *Journal of Linguistics*, vol. 11.

———— 1978. Tone features. In V. Fromkin (ed.), *Tone: A Linguistic Survey*. New York: Academic Press, 133–176.

Aronoff, M. 1976. *Word Formation in Generative Grammar*. Cambridge, MA: MIT Press.

Baker, M. C. 1988. *Incorporation*. Chicago: University of Chicago Press.

Ballard, W. L. 1980. On Some Aspects of Wu Tone Sandhi, *Journal of Asian & African Studies*, vol. 19: 83–163.

Bao, Z.-M. 1990. *On the Nature of Tone*. Ph.D. dissertation, MIT.

———— 1999. *The Structure of Tone*. Oxford: Oxford University Press.

Barrack, C. 1976. Lexical Diffusion and the High German Consonant Shift, *Lingua*, vol. 40: 151–175.

Bauer, R. 1979. Alveolarization in Cantonese: A Case of Lexical Diffusion, *Journal of Chinese Linguistics*, vol. 7: 132–141.

Beckman, M. & Janet Pierrehumbert. 1986. Intonational Structure in Japanese and English, *Phonology Yearbook*, vol. 3: 15–70.

Berendsen, E. 1985. Tracing Case in Phonology, *Natural Language and Linguistics Theory*, vol. 3: 95–106.

Bickmore, L. 1989. *Kinyambo Prosody*. Ph.D. dissertation, UCLA.

———— 1990. Branching nodes and prosodic categories. In S. Inkelas and D. Zec (eds.), *The Phonology-Syntax Connection*. Chicago: The University of Chicago Press, 1–17.

Bloomfield, L. 1933. *Language*. New York: Holt, Rinehert, & Winston.

Bolinger, D. 1975. *Aspect of Language*. Chicago: Harcourt Brace Jovanovich.

Booij, G. 1983. Principles and Parameters in Prosodic Phonology, *Linguistics*, vol. 21: 249–280.

———— 1985a. The interaction of phonology and morphology in prosodic phonology. In Edmund Gussmann (ed.), *Phono-morphology: Studies in the Interaction of Phonology and Morphology*. Lublin: Katolicki Universytet Lubelski, 23–34.

———— 1985b. Coordination reduction in complex words: A case for prosodic phonology. In Harry van der Hulst and Norval Smith (eds.), *Advances in Nonlinear Phonology*. Dordrecht: Foris, 143–160.

———— 1986. Two cases of external sandhi in French: Enchainement and liaison. In Henning Andersen (ed.), *Sandhi Phenomena in the Languages of Europe*. Berlin: Mouton de Gruyter, 93–103.

216 *Bibliography*

———— 1996. Cliticization as Prosodic Integration: The Case of Dutch, *The Linguistic Review*, vol. 13: 219–242.

Bowers, J. 1988. *A Structural Theory of Predication*. MS. Cornell University.

———— 1989. *The Syntax and Semantics of Predication*. MS. Cornell University.

Box, George, J. S. Hunter & Hunter, W. G. 2005. *Statistics for Experimenters* (2nd ed.). Hoboken, NJ: John Wiley & Sons.

Brame, M. 1974. The Cycle in Phonology: Stress in Palestinian, Maltese, and Spanish, *Linguistic Inquiry*, vol. 5.

Bresnan, J. 1971. *Contraction and the Transformational Cycle in English*. Bloomington: Indiana University Linguistics Club.

Calhoun, S. 2006. *Information Structure and the Prosodic Structure of English: A Probabilistic Relationship*. Ph.D. dissertation, Linguistics, University of Edinburgh.

Cao, Jianfen. 2001. The Phonetic and Linguistic Evidence of Chinese Prosodic Phrasing. In *Modern Phonetics of New Century-Collected Papers of 5th National Conference on Modern Phonetics*. Beijing: Tsinghua University Press.

Cao, Wen. 2010. *The Prosodic Realization of Chinese Focus-related Accent*. Beijing: Beijing Language and Culture University Press.

Chan, K. M. 1980. *Syntax and Phonology Interface: The Case of Tone Sandhi in the Fuzhou Dialect of Chinese*. MS. University of Washington.

———— 1985. *Fuzhou Phonology: A Non-Linear Analysis of Tone and Stress*. Ph.D. dissertation, University of Washington.

———— 1989. Contour-Tone Spreading and Tone Sandhi in Danyang Chinese. In *Proceedings of the International Conference on Wu Dialects*, vol. 1. Hong Kong.

———— 1991. Contour-tone Spreading and Tone Sandhi in Danyang Chinese, *Phonology Yearbook*, vol. 8: 237–259.

Chao, Y.-R. 1930. A System of Tone Letters, *Le Meitre Phonetique*, vol. 45: 24–27.

———— 1933. Tone and Intonation Letters, *The Bulletin of the Institute of History and Philology*, vol. 4: 363–397.

———— 1968. *A Grammar of Spoken Chinese*. Berkeley: University of California Press.

Chen, M. 1979. Metrical Structure: Evidence from Chinese Poetry, *Linguistic Inquiry*, vol. 10: 371–420.

———— 1980. The Primacy of Rhythm in Verse: A Linguistic Perspective, *Journal of Chinese Linguistics*, vol. 8: 15–41.

———— 1984. Unfolding Latent Principles of Literary Taste: Poetry as a Window onto Language, *Tsing Hua Journal of Chinese Studies*, vol. 16: 203–240.

———— 1985. *The Syntax of Xiamen Tone Sandhi*. MS. UCSD.

———— 1986a. An Overview of Tone Sandhi Phenomena across Chinese dialects. In *Proceedings of Conference on the Languages and Dialects of China*. Oakland.

———— 1986b. The Paradox of Tianjin Tone Sandhi, *Chicago Linguistics Society*, vol. 22: 98–114.

———— 1987. The Syntax of Xiamen Tone Sandhi, *Phonology Yearbook*, vol. 4: 109–150.

———— 1989. *Wenzou Tone Sandhi*. MS. UCSD.

———— 1990. What Must Phonology Know about Syntax? Paper presented at *The Phonology-Syntax Connection Workshop*. Stanford University. To appear in Inkelas-Zec (1990).

———— 1991a. *From Tone to Intonation: A Case Study on Wenzhou*. MS. UCSD.

———— 1991b. Competing Strategies Toward Tonotatic Targets. Paper presented at *The 3rd North American Conference on Chinese Linguistics*.

———— 1992a. Competing Sound Changes: Evidence from Kam-Tai, Miao-Yao and Tibeto-Burman, *Journal of Chinese Linguistics*, vol. 20: 193–210.

Bibliography 217

———— 1992b. Phonological Diagnostics of Morphological Structure. To appear in *Proceedings of International Symposium on Chinese Languages & Linguistics*, vol. 3. Taiwan.

———— 1992c. *Argument vs. Adjunct: Xiamen Tone Sandhi Revisited*. MS. UCSD.

———— 2000. *Tone Sandhi: Patterns across Chinese Dialects*. Cambridge University Press.

Chen, M. & W. Wang. 1975. Sound Change: Actuation and Implementation, *Language*, vol. 51.2: 255–281.

Chen, M. & H.-M. Zhang. 1997. Lexical and post-lexical Tone Sandhi in Chongming. In *Studies in Chinese Phonology*, vol. 1. Berlin: Mouton de Gruyter Publishers, 13–52.

Chen, Z.-M. 1987. *Nanhui Phonology*. M.A. thesis. Fudan University, Shanghai, China.

Cheng, C.C. 1970. Domains of Phonological Rule Application. In J.M. Sadock and A. L. Vanek (eds.), *Studies Presented to R. B. Lees by His Students*. Edmonton: Linguistic Research, 39–59.

———— 1973. *A Synchronic Phonology of Mandarin Chinese*. The Hague: Mouton.

Cheng, Lisa. 1987a. On the Prosodic Hierarchy and Tone Sandhi in Mandarin. In *Toronto Working Papers in Linguistics* 7: 24–52, Linguistic Graduate Course Union. University of Toronto.

———— 1987b. Derived Domains and Mandarin Third Tone Sandhi. In *Proceedings of the Chicago Linguistics Society*, 16–28.

Cheng, R.-L. 1968. Tone Sandhi in Taiwanese, *Linguistics*, vol. 41: 19–42.

———— 1973. Some Notes on Tone Sandhi in Taiwanese, *Linguistics*, vol. 100.

———— 1991. Interaction, Modularization, and Lexical Diffusion: Tone Sandhi in Taiwanese Verbs. Paper presented at *North America Conference on Chinese Linguistics*, 3. Ithaca: Cornell University Press.

Cho, Y.-M. Y. 1990a. Syntax and phrasing in Korean. In S. Inkelas and D. Zec (eds.), *The Phonology-Syntax Connection*. The University of Chicago Press, 47–62.

———— 1990b. *Parameters of Consonantal Assimilation*. Ph.D. dissertation, Stanford University.

Chomsky, N. 1973. *The Logical Structure of Linguistic Theory*. New York: Plenum.

———— 1981. *Lectures on Government and Binding*. Dordrecht, Holland: Foris.

———— 1986a. *Barrier*. MIT Press.

———— 1986b. *Knowledge of Language, Its Nature, Origin, and Use*. New York: Praeger.

———— 1993. A minimalist program in linguistics theory. In K. Hale and S. J. Keyser (eds.), *The View from Building 20*. Cambridge, MA: MIT Press.

———— 1995. *A Minimalist Program*. Cambridge, MA: MIT Press.

———— 1999. Derivation by phase. In *MIT Occasional Papers in Linguistics, No. 18*. Cambridge, MA: MIT Working Papers in Linguistics. Reprinted in Michael Kenstowicz (ed.), *Ken Hale: A Life in Language*. Cambridge, MA: The MIT Press, 2001, 1–52.

———— 2001. Beyond explanatory adequacy. In *MIT Occasional Papers in Linguistics, No. 20*. Cambridge, MA: MIT Working Papers in Linguistics, 1–28.

Chomsky, N. & M. Halle. 1968. *The Sound Pattern of English*. Harper and Row.

Chomsky, N., M. Halle and F. Lukoff. 1956. On Accent and Juncture in English. In M. Halle, H. G. Lunt, H. McLean and C. H. van Schooneveld, eds. *For Roman Jakobson: Essays on the occasion of his sixtieth birthday*. Hague: Mouton & Co, 65–80.

Chomsky, N. & H. Lasnik. 1977. Filters and Control, *Linguistic Inquiry*, vol. 8: 425–504.

Chung, R.-F. 1987. *Aspects of Ke-jia Phonology*. Ph.D. dissertation, University of Illinois, Urbana-Champaign.

Cinque, G. 1993. A Null Theory of Phrase and Compound Stress, *Linguistic Inquiry*, vol. 24.2: 239–297.

218 Bibliography

Clements, G. N. 1978. Tone and syntax in Ewe. In D. J. Napoli (ed.), *Elements of Tone, Stress, and Intonation*. Washington, DC: Georgetown University Press, 21–99.

Cohn, A. 1989. Stress in Indonesian and Bracketing Paradoxes, *Natural Language and Linguistic Theory*, vol. 7: 167–216.

Condoravdi, C. 1990. Sandhi rules of Greek and prosodic theory. In S. Inkelas and D. Zec (eds.), *The Phonology-Syntax Connection*. Chicago: The University of Chicago Press, 63–84.

Cowper, E. & K. Rice. 1987. Are Phonosyntactic Rules Necessary? *Phonology Yearbook*, vol. 4: 185–194.

Deng, Dan. 2010. *Experimental Study of Chinese Prosodic Words*. Beijing: Beijing Language and Culture University Press.

Dobashi, Y. 2003. *Phonological Phrasing and Syntactic Derivation*. Ph.D. dissertation, Cornell University.

Dong, Xiufang. 2011. *Lexicalization: The Origin and Evolution of Chinese Disyllabic Words*. Beijing: The Commercial Press.

Downing, L. J. 1990. *Problems in Jita Tonology*. Ph.D. dissertation, University of Illinois at Urbana-Champaign.

Duanmu, S. 1990. *A Formal Study of Syllable, Tone, Stress and Domain in Chinese Languages*. Ph.D. dissertation, MIT.

———— 1991. Stress and Syntax-Phonology Mismatches: Tonal Domains in Danyang and Shanghai, *WCCFL*, vol. 10.

———— 1992. End-Based Theory, Cyclic Stress, and Tonal Domains, *Chicago Linguistics Society*, vol. 28.

———— 1999. Metrical Structure and Tone: Evidence from Mandarin and Shanghai, *Journal of East Asian Linguistics*, vol. 8.1: 1–38.

———— 2000a. *The Phonology of Standard Chinese*. Oxford: Oxford University Press.

———— 2000b. The Rhythm of Chinese, *Contemporary Linguistics*, vol. 4: 203–209.

———— 2007. *The Phonology of Standard Chinese* (2nd ed.). Oxford University Press.

———— 2014. Stress Theory and Stress Phenomena in Chinese, *Contemporary Linguistics*, vol. 16.3: 288–302. Beijing, China.

Edkins, J. 1868. A Grammar of Colloquial Chinese: As Exhibited in the Shanghai Dialect (2nd edition). Shanghai: Presbyterian Mission Press.

Ernst, T. 1988. Chinese Postpositions? – Again, *Journal of Chinese Linguistics*, vol. 16: 219–245.

Feng, Shengli. 1997. *Interactions between Morphology, Syntax and Prosody in Chinese*. Beijing: Peking University Press.

———— 2001. Prosodic Words and the Construction of Scientific Theory, *Chinese Teaching in the World*, vol. 1: 53–64.

———— 2005. *Studies on Chinese Prosodic Grammar*. Beijing: Peking University Press.

———— 2009. *Interactions between Morphology, Syntax and Prosody in Chinese* (the revised ed.). Beijing: Peking University Press.

———— 2013. *Prosodic Syntax in Chinese* (enlarged and revised ed.). Beijing: The Commercial Press.

Fox, D. & D. Pesetsky. 2005. Cyclic Linearization of Syntactic Structure, *Theoretical Linguistics*, vol. 31: 1–46.

Frota, S. 2000. *Prosody and Focus in European Portuguese*. New York, NY: Garland.

Ghini, M. 1993. *Phonological Phrase Formation in Italian: A New Proposal*. MS. University of Toronto.

Goldsmith, J. 1976. *Autosegmental Phonology*. Ph.D. dissertation, MIT.

Bibliography 219

———— 1990. *Autosegmental and Metrical Phonology*. Basil Blackwell.

Gravetter, F. & L. Wallnau. 2009. *Statistics for Behavioral Sciences*. Belmont: Wadsworth Cengage Learning.

Gu, Y. 1992. Verbal Measure Phrases and Light Predicate Raising. Paper presented at *The Fourth North American Conference on Chinese Linguistics*. Michigan.

Gussenhoven, Carlos. 2004. *The Phonology of Tone and Intonation*. Cambridge: Cambridge University Press.

Haegeman, L. 1991. *Introduction to Government and Binding Theory*. Basil Blackwell.

Hall, K. & E. Selkirk. 1987. Government and Tonal Phrasing in Papago, *Phonology Yearbook*, vol. 4.

Halle, M. & K. Mohanan. 1985. Segmental Phonology of Modern English, *Linguistic Inquiry*, vol. 16: 57–116.

Halle, M. & J.-R. Vergnaud. 1987. *Stress and the Cycle*. MIT and Tilburg University.

Hammond, M. & M. Noonan, (eds.). 1988. *Theoretical Morphology*. New York: Academic Press.

Hayes, B. 1981. *The Metrical Theory of Stress Rules*. Bloomington: Indiana University Linguistics Club.

———— 1984a. The Phonology of Rhythm in English, *Linguistic Inquiry*, vol. 15: 33–74.

———— 1984b/1989. The prosodic hierarchy in meter. In Paul Kiparsky and Gilbert Youmans (eds.), *Rhythm and Meter*. Orlando, Florida: Academic Press, 201–260.

———— 1990. Precompiled Phrasal Phonology. In S. Inkelas and D. Zec (eds.), *The Phonology-Syntax Connection*. Chicago: The University of Chicago Press, 85–108.

———— 1995. *Metrical Stress Theory: Principles and Case Studies*. Chicago: University of Chicago Press.

Hayes, B. & A. Lahiri. 1991. Bengali Intonational Phonology, *Natural Language and Linguistic Theory*, vol. 9: 47–96.

Hellmuth, S. 2007. The Relation between Prosodic Structure and Pitch Accent Distribution: Evidence from Egyptian Arabic, *The Linguistic Review*, vol. 24: 291–316.

Hetzron, R. 1992. Phonology in Syntax, *Journal of linguistics*, vol. 8: 251–262.

Hou, J.-Y. 1980. Tone Sandhi in Pingyao, *Dialect*, vol. 1: 1–14.

———— 1982. Trisyllabic Tone Sandhi in Pingyao. In *Dialect*, vol. 1: 7–14.

Hsiao, Y.-C. 1991. *Syntax, Rhythm and Tone: A Triangular Relationship*. Ph.D. dissertation, UCSD.

Hsu, H.-C. 1992. Domain of Tone Sandhi in Idioms: A Tug of War between the Foot Formation Rule and the Tone Group Formation. Paper presented at *North America Conference on Chinese Linguistics*, 4. Michigan.

Hu, Y.-S. 1981. *Modern Chinese*. Shanghai: Shanghai Educational Publishing House.

Huang, C. T. James. 1982. *Logical Relations in Chinese and the Theory of Grammar*. Ph.D. dissertation, MIT.

———— 1984. Phrase Structure, Lexical Integrity, and Chinese Compounds, *Journal of Chinese Language Teachers Association*, vol. 4.

———— 1990. Reconstruction, the A/A' Distinction, and the Structure of VP. Paper presented at *The 2nd Northeast Conference on Chinese Linguistics*. Philadelphia.

———— 1991. Verb-movement, (In)Definiteness, and the Thematic Hierarchy. To appear in *Proceedings of International Symposium on Chinese Linguistics and Language*, vol. 2. Taiwan.

———— 1992. On Lexical Structure and Syntactic Projection. To appear in *Proceedings of International Symposium on Chinese Languages & Linguistics*, vol. 3. Taiwan.

Hung, T. 1987. *Syntactic and Semantic Aspects of Chinese Tone Sandhi*. Ph.D. dissertation, UCSD.

220 Bibliography

──── 1990. Syntax-phonology Interaction in Chinese Tone Sandhi: An Overview, *Journal of Chinese Language Teachers Association*, vol. 25, no. 3: 43–60.

Hyman, L. 2006. Word-prosodic Typology, *Phonology*, vol. 23: 225–258.

Hyman, L., F. Katamba & L. Walusimbi. 1987. Luganda and the Strict Layer Hypothesis, *Phonology Yearbook*, vol. 4.

Inkelas, S. 1989. *Prosodic Constituency in the Lexicon.* Ph.D. dissertation, Stanford University. Published by Garland Publishing, New York, 1990.

Inkelas, S. & D. Zec. 1990. *The Phonology-syntax Connection.* Chicago: The University of Chicago Press.

──── 1995. Syntax-phonology interface. In John Goldsmith (ed.), *The Handbook of Phonological Theory.* Cambridge, MA & Oxford: Blackwell Publishers Ltd, 535–549.

Ishihara, S. 2003. *Intonation and Interface Conditions.* Ph.D. dissertation, MIT.

──── 2007. Major Phrase, Focus Intonation, Multiple Spell-out, *The Linguistic Review*, vol. 24: 137–167.

Ito, J. 1986. *Syllable Theory in Prosodic Phonology.* Ph.D. dissertation, University of Massachusetts.

Ito, J. & A. Mester. 1992/2003. Weak layering and word binarity. In Takeru Honma, et al. (eds.), *A New Century of Phonology and Phonological Theory: A Festschrift for Professor Shosuke Haraguchi on the Occasion of His Sixtieth Birthday.* Tokyo: Kaitakusha. 26–65.

──── 2006. Prosodic Adjunction in Japanese Compounds. Paper presented at *Formal Approaches to Japanese Linguistics*, 4. Osaka, Japan.

──── 2007. Categories and Projections in Prosodic Structure. In *OCP4 [Old World Conference in Phonology].* Rhodes, Greece.

──── 2009. Trimming the prosodic hierarchy. In Toni Borowsky, Shigeto Kawahara, Takahito Shinya and Mariko Sugahara (eds.), *Prosody Matters: Essays in Honor of Elisabeth Selkirk.* London: Equinox Publishers.

──── 2015. Match Theory and Prosodic Wellformedness Constraints. Paper presented at *The 1st International Conference on Prosodic Studies.* Tianjin, China.

Jaeggli, O. 1980. Remarks on to Contraction, *Linguistic Inquiry*, vol. 11: 239–246.

Jackendoff, R. 1977. *X' Syntax: A Study of Phrase Structure.* MIT Press.

Jin, S.-D. 1986. Shanghai Morphotonemics. *Indiana University Linguistics Club.*

Jun, Sun-Ah. 1993. *The Phonetics and Phonology of Korean Prosody: Intonational Phonology and Prosodic Structure.* Ph.D. dissertation, Ohio State University.

──── 2005. Prosodic typology. In Sun-Ah Jun (ed.), *Prosodic Typology: The Phonology of Intonation and Phrasing.* Oxford, New York: Oxford University Press, 430–458.

Kabak, B. & Irene Vogel. 2001. The Phonological Word and Stress Assignment in Turkish, *Phonology*, vol. 18: 315–360.

Kager, R. 1993. Alternatives to the Iambic-Trochaic Law, *Natural Language and Linguistic Theory*, vol. 11.2: 381–432.

Kahnemuyipour, A. 2003. Syntactic Categories and Persian Stress, *Natural Language and Linguistic Theory*, vol. 21: 333–379.

──── 2009. *The Syntax of Sentential Stress.* Oxford: Oxford University Press.

Kaisse, E. M. 1985. *Connected Speech: The Interaction of Syntax and Phonology.* New York & San Diego: Academic Press.

──── 1987. Rhythm and the Cycle, *Chicago Linguistics Society*, vol. 23: 199–209.

──── 1990. *Toward a Typology of Post-lexical Rules.* To appear in Inkelas and Zec (1990).

Kaisse, E. & A. M. Zwicky. 1987. Syntactic Influences on Phonological Rules, *Phonology Yearbook*, vol. 4.

Bibliography 221

Kanerva, J. 1989. *Focus and Phrasing in Chichewa Phonology.* Ph.D. dissertation, Stanford University.

——— 1990. Focusing on phonological phrases in Chichewa. In S. Inkelas and D. Zec (eds.), *The Phonology-Syntax Connection.* The University of Chicago Press, 145–161.

Kennedy, G. 1953. Two Tone Patterns in Tangsic, *Language*, vol. 29: 367–373.

Kenstowicz, M. & H.-S. Sohn. 1997. Phrasing and focus in Northern Kyungsang Korean. In P. M. Bertinetto et al. (eds.), *Certamen Phonologicum* III. 137–149.

Kidima, L. 1990. Tone and syntax in Kiyada. In S. Inkelas and D. Zec (eds.), *The Phonology-Syntax Connection.* The University of Chicago Press, 195–216.

Kiparsky, P. 1973. Elsewhere in phonology. In S. Anderson and P. Kiparsky (eds.), *A Festschrift for Morris Halle.* New York, NY: Holt, 93–106.

——— 1982a. From cyclic phonology to lexical phonology. In Harry van der Hulst and Norval Smith (eds.), *The Structure of Phonological Representations*, vol. 1. 131–176.

——— 1982b. Lexical morphology and phonology. In I.-S. Yang (ed.), *Linguistics in the Morning Calm.* Seoul: Hanshin Publishing, 3–91.

——— 1984. On the lexical phonology of Icelandic. In C. Elert, I. Johansson and E. Strangert (eds.), *Nordic Prosody.* Stockholm: Almqvist & Wiksell, 135–162.

——— 1985. Some Consequences of Lexical Phonology, *Phonology Yearbook*, vol. 2: 83–138.

Koopman, H. & D. Sportiche. 1988. *Subjects.* MS. University of California, Los Angeles.

Kratzer, A. & E. Selkirk. 2007. Phase Theory and Prosodic Spellout: The Case of Verbs, *The Linguistic Review*, vol. 24: 93–135.

Kung, H.-Y. A. 1992a. Scope, Specificity and the Mapping Hypothesis. Paper presented at *The Fourth North American Conference on Chinese Linguistics.* Michigan.

——— 1992b. Word Order, Specificity and Object Positions in Mandarin Chinese. To appear in *Proceedings of International Symposium on Chinese Languages & Linguistics*, vol. 3. Taiwan.

Kuroda, S.-Y. 1985. *Whether You Agree Or Not: Rough Ideas about the Comparative Grammar of English and Japanese.* MS. UCSD.

Labov, W. 1981. Resolving the Neogrammarian Controversy, *Language*, vol. 57.

Ladd, D. R. 1986. Intonational Phrasing: The Case for Recursive Prosodic Structure, *Phonology*, vol. 3: 311–340.

——— 1990. *Compound Prosodic Domain.* MS. University of Edinburgh.

——— 1996. *Intonational Phonology.* Cambridge: Cambridge University Press.

Larson, R. 1988. On Double Object Constructions, *Linguistic Inquiry*, vol. 19.

Levergood, B. 1987. *Topics in Arusa Phonology and Morphology.* Ph.D. dissertation, UT Austin.

Li, Aijun. 2008. Prosodic Studies in Chinese – The Academic Idea of Professor Wu Zongji and Its Profound Influence. *Report of Phonetic Research.* Institute of Linguistics, Chinese Academy of Social Sciences, Beijing.

Li, C. & S. Thompson. 1981. *Mandarin Chinese: A Functional Reference Grammar.* University of California Press.

Li, R.-L. 1962. Sandhi Tone and Neutral Tone in Xiamen, *Journal of Xiamen University*, vol. 3: 78–114.

Li, Y.-H. A. 1990. *Order and Constituency in Mandarin Chinese.* Dordrecht: Kluwer Academic Publishers.

Li, Zhuqing. 2002. *Fuzhou Phonology and Grammar.* Hyattsville: Dunwoody Press.

Liberman, M. 1975. *The Intonational System of English.* Ph.D. dissertation, MIT.

Liberman, M. & A. Prince. 1977. On Stress and Linguistic Rhythm, *Linguistic Inquiry*, vol. 8: 249–336.

222 Bibliography

Lin, H.–S. 2012. Construction Sensitivity in Pingyao Tone Sandhi, *Taiwan Journal of Linguistics*, vol. 10.1: 143–210.

Lin, Jo-wang. 1994. Lexical Government and Tone Group Formation in Xiamen Chinese, *Phonology*, vol. 11: 237–275.

Lin, T. 1985. Preliminary experiments in the exploration of the nature of Mandarin neutral tone. In *Working Papers in Experimental Phonetics*. Peking University.

Lü, S.-X. 1963. Monosyllables and Disyllables in Chinese: A Preliminary Study, *Studies of the Chinese Language*, vol. 1: 10–22.

———— 1979. *On Chinese Grammar*. Beijing: The Commercial Press.

Lü, S.-X, et al. 1980. *800 Functional Words in Chinese*. Beijing: The Commercial Press.

Lu, Z.-J. 1987. Shanghai Tones: A Non-Linear Analysis, *Studies in the Linguistics Sciences*, vol. 17: 93–113.

Lü, Z.-J. 1987. Tone Sandhi in Ruicheng. Paper presented at *The Fourth Conference on Chinese Dialects*. Taiyuan, China.

Lu, Z.-W. 1957. *Chinese Morphology*. Beijing: Science Press.

Ma, Zhe. 2015. *"Word Stress" in Chinese*. Ph.D. dissertation, Nankai University, Tianjin, China.

Mahajan, A. K. 1990. *The A/A-bar Distinction and the Movement Theory*. Ph.D. dissertation, MIT.

———— 1991. Operator Movement, Agreement and Referentiality, *MIT Working Papers in Linguistics*, vol. 15: 77–96.

Mair, V. & T.–L. Mei. 1991. The Sanskrit Origins of Recent Style Prosody, *Harvard Journal of Asiatic Studies*, vol. 51.2: 375–470.

Manzini, R. 1983. Syntactic Conditions on Phonological Rules, *MIT Working Papers in Linguistics*, vol. 5: 1–9.

McCarthy, J. & A. Prince. 1990. Prosodic morphology and templatic morphology. In M. Eid and J. McCarthy (eds.), *Perspectives on Arabic Linguistics: Papers from the Second Symposium*. Amsterdam: John Benjamins Publishing Co., 1–54.

———— 1993. Generalized alignment. In Geert Booij and Jaap van Marle (eds.), *Yearbook of Morphology*. Dordrecht: Kuwer, 79–153.

Mester, A. 1994. The Quantitative Trochee in Latin, *Natural Language and Linguistic Theory*, vol. 12.1: 1–61.

Mishra, S. 1999. *Chandovallari: A Handbook of Sanskrit Prosody*. Pondicherry: Sri Aurobindo Society, 21–22.

Mohanan, K. 1982. *Lexical Phonology*. Ph.D. dissertation, MIT.

———— 1986. *The Theory of Lexical Phonology*. Reidel.

Napoli, D. J. & M. Nespor. 1979. The Syntax of Word-initial Consonant Gemination in Italian, *Language*, vol. 55: 812–841.

Neijt, A. 1985. Clitics in arboreal phonology. In Harry van der Hulst and Norval Smith (eds.), *Advances in Nonlinear Phonology*. Dordrecht: Foris, 179–192.

Nespor, M. 1985. The phonological word in Italian. In Harry van der Hulst and Norval Smith (eds.), *Advances in Nonlinear Phonology*. Dordrecht: Foris, 193–204.

———— 1986. The phonological word in Greek and Italian. In Henning Anderson (ed.), *Sandhi Phenomena in the Languages of Europe*. Berlin: Mouton de Gruyter, 65–74.

Nespor, M. & I. Vogel. 1979. Clash Avoidance in Italian, *Linguistic Inquiry*, vol. 10: 476–482.

———— 1982. Prosodic domains of external sandhi rules. In H. van der Hulst and N. Smith (eds.), *The Structure of Phonological Representations Part I*. Dordrecht: Foris, 225–256.

Bibliography 223

———— 1983. Prosodic structure above the word. In Anne Cutler and Robert Ladd (eds.), *Prosody: Models and Measurements*. Berlin: Springer, 123–140.

———— 1986. *Prosodic Phonology*. Foris.

———— 2007. *Prosodic Phonology: With a New Forward*. Berlin: Mouton de Gruyter.

Odden, D. 1987. Kimatuumbi Phrasal Phonology, *Phonology Yearbook*, vol. 4: 13–36.

———— 1990a. C-command or Edges in Makonde, *Phonology Yearbook*, vol. 7: 163–169.

———— 1990b. Syntax, lexical rules and post-lexical rules in Kimatuumbi. In S. Inkelas and D. Zec (eds.), *The Phonology-Syntax Connection*. The University of Chicago Press, 259–277.

———— 1996. *The Phonology and Morphology of Kimatuumbi*. Oxford: Clarendon Press.

Ogura, M. 1987. *Historical English Phonology: Lexical Perspective*. Tokyo: Kenkyusha.

Pak, M. 2008. *The Post-syntactic Derivation and Its Phonological Reflexes*. Ph.D. dissertation, University of Pennsylvania.

Pan, W.-Y. 1988, *Functional Words in Wenzhou*. MS. Shanghai Normal University.

Peperkamp, S. 1997. *Prosodic Words*. Ph.D. dissertation, University of Amsterdam.

Phillips, B. S. 1984. Word Frequency and the Actuation of Sound Change, *Language*, vol. 60: 320–342.

Pierrehumbert, J. & Mary E. Beckman. 1988. *Japanese Tone Structure*. Cambridge, MA: MIT Press.

Pollock, J.-Y. 1989. Verb-movement, Universal Grammar and the Structure of IP, *Linguistic Inquiry*, vol. 20.

Poser, W. 1981. *Some Topics in Non-Linear Phonology*. MS. MIT.

———— 1984. *The Phonetics and Phonology of Tone and Intonation in Japanese*. Ph.D. dissertation, MIT.

———— 1985. There is No Domain Size Parameter, *Glow Newsletter*, vol. 14: 66–67.

Postal, P. & G. K. Pullum. 1982. The Contraction Debate, *Linguistic Inquiry*, vol. 13: 122–138.

Prieto, P. 2005. Syntactic and Eurhythmic Constraints on Phrasing Decisions, *Studia Linguistica*, vol. 59: 194–222.

———— 2006. Phonological phrasing in Spanish. In S. Colina and F. Martinez-Gil (eds.), *Optimality-theoretic Advances in Spanish Phonology*. Amsterdam & Philadelphia: John Benjamins Publishing Co, 39–60.

Prince, A. 1983. Relating to the Grid, *Linguistic Inquiry*, vol. 14: 19–100.

Prince, A. & P. Smolensky. 1993. *Optimality Theory: Constraint Interaction in Generative Grammar*. Cambridge, MA: MIT Press.

Pulleyblank, D. 1986. *Tone in Lexical Phonology*. Dordrecht: Reidel.

Pullum, G. & A. Zwicky. 1991. *The Syntax-Phonology Interface*. New York: Academic Press.

Qian, N.-R. 1981. *Fengxian Phonology*. M.A. thesis, Fudan University, China.

———— 1988. *The Pattern and Derivation of Tonal System in Wu Chinese*. MS. Shanghai University.

Reinhart, T. 1976. *The Syntactic Domain of Anaphora*. Ph.D. dissertation, MIT.

———— 1981. Definite NP Anaphora and C-command, *Linguistic Inquiry*, vol. 12: 605–635.

———— 1983. *Anaphora and Semantic Interpretation*. London: Croom Helm.

———— 2006. *Interface Strategies: Optimal and Costly Computations*. Cambridge, MA: MIT Press.

Rice, K. 1993. The structure of the Slave (Northern Athabaskan) verb. In S. Hargus and E. Kaisse (eds.), *Phonetics and Phonology 4: Studies in Lexical Phonology*. San Diego, CA: Academic Press, 145–171.

224 *Bibliography*

Rizzi, L. & L. Savoia. 1993. Conditions on /u/ propagation in Southern Italian Dialects: A locality parameter for phonosyntactic processes. In A. Belletti (ed.), *Syntactic Theory and the Dialects of Italy*. Torino: Resenberg and Sellier, 252–318.

Rotenberg, J. 1978. *The Syntax of Phonology*. Ph.D. dissertation, MIT.

Sagey, E.C. 1986. *The Representation of Features and Relations in Non-Linear Phonology*. Ph.D. dissertation, MIT.

Samek-Lodovici, V. 2005. Prosody Syntax Interaction in the Expression of Focus, *Natural Language and Linguistic Theory*, vol. 23: 687–755.

Samuels, B. 2009. *The Structure of Phonological Theory*. Ph.D. dissertation, Harvard University.

Sandalo, F. & H. Truckenbrodt. 2002. Some Notes on Phonological Phrasing in Brazilian Portuguese, *MIT Working Papers in Linguistics*, vol. 42: 285–310.

Sapir, E. 1921. *Language: An Introduction to the Study of Speech*. New York, NY: Harcourt, Brace and Company.

Seidl, A. 2001. *Minimal Indirect Reference: A Theory of the Syntax-phonology Interface: Outstanding Dissertations in Linguistics*. London & New York: Routledge.

Selkirk, E. 1972. *The Phrase Phonology of English and French*. Ph.D. dissertation, MIT.

———— 1978. On prosodic structure and its relation to syntactic structure. In T. Fretheim (ed.), *Nordic Prosody II*. Trondheim: TAPIR, 111–140.

———— 1980a. Prosodic domains in phonology: Sanskrit revisited. In Mark Aronoff and Mary-Louise Kean (eds.), *Juncture*. Saratoga: Anma Libri, 107–129.

———— 1980b. The Role of Prosodic Categories in English Word Stress, *Linguistic Inquiry*, vol. 11: 563–605.

———— 1981. The nature of phonological representation. In John Anderson, John Laver and Terry Myers (eds.), *The Cognitive Representation of Speech*. Dordrecht: North Holland Publishing Company, 379–388.

———— 1984. *Phonology and Syntax: The Relation between Sound and Structure*. MIT Press.

———— 1986. On Derived Domain in Sentence Phonology, *Phonology Yearbook*, vol. 3: 371–405.

———— 1995. Sentence prosody: Intonation, stress and phrasing. In John A. Goldsmith (ed.), *The Handbook of Phonological Theory*. Cambridge, MA & Oxford, UK: Blackwell, 550–569.

———— 1996. The prosodic structure of FW. In James L. Morgan and Katherine Demuth (eds.), *Signal to Syntax: Bootstrapping from Speech to Grammar in Early Acquisition*. Mahwah, NJ: Lawrence Erlbaum Associates, 187–214.

———— 2000. The interaction of constraints on prosodic phrasing. In Merle Horne (ed.), *Prosody: Theory and Experiments*. Dordrecht: Kluwer, 231–262.

———— 2006. Strong minimalist spell-out of prosodic phrases. In *GLOW Workshop on Prosodic Phrasing*. Universitat Auònoma Barcelona.

———— 2008. Contrastive Focus, Givenness and the Unmarked Status of "Discourse-new", *Acta Linguistica Hungarica*, vol. 55: 331–346.

———— 2009. *On Clause and Intonational Phrase in Japanese: The Syntactic Grounding of Prosodic Constituent Structure*. Gengo Kenkyu.

———— 2011. The syntax-phonology interface. In John Goldsmith, Jason Riggle and Alan Yu (eds.), *The Handbook of Phonological Theory*. Oxford: Blackwell.

Selkirk, E. & T. Shen. 1990. Prosodic domains in Shanghai Chinese. In S. Inkelas and D. Zec (eds.), *The Phonology-Syntax Connection*. The University of Chicago Press, 313–337.

Bibliography 225

Selkirk, E. & K. Tateishi. 1988. Minor Phrase Formation in Japanese, *Papers from the Annual Regional Meeting of the Chicago Linguistic Society*, vol. 24: 316–336.

Shen, T. 1985. The Underlying Representation of Shanghai Tones, *Yuyan Yanjiu [Language Studies]*, vol. 2: 85–101. Wuhan, China.

Shen, Y. 1988. *A Tentative Hypothesis Regarding Tri-syllabic Tone Sandhi in Pingyao*. MS. UCSD.

Sherard, M. 1972. *Shanghai Phonology*. Ph.D. dissertation, Cornell University.

Shi, R.-J. 1985. *Chuansha Phonology*. M.A. thesis, Fudan University, Shanghai, China.

Shih, C.-L. 1986. *The Prosodic Domain of Tone Sandhi in Chinese*. Ph.D. dissertation, UCSD.

———— 1997. Mandarin third tone sandhi and prosodic structure. In N. Smith and J. Wang (eds.), *Studies in Chinese Phonoüogy*. Foris, Dordrecht.

Steriade, D. 1987. Locality Conditions and Feature Geometry, *NELS*, vol. 17: 595–617.

Tang, J. 1990. *Chinese Phrase Structure and the Extended X'-theory*. Ph.D. dissertation, Cornell University.

Thompson, S. 1973. Resultative Verb Compounds in Mandarin Chinese: A Case for Lexical Rules, *Language*, vol. 49: 361–379.

Ting, P.-H. 1984. Reconstruction of Proto-Wu Tones, *The Bulletin of the Institute of History and Philology*, vol. LV, Part IV: 755–788. Taipei.

Truckenbrodt, H. 1995. *Phonological Phrase: Their Relation to Syntax, Focus and Prominence*. Ph.D. dissertation, MIT, Cambridge, MA.

———— 1999. On the Relation between Syntactic Phrases and Phonological Phrases, *Linguistic Inquiry*, vol. 30: 219–256.

———— 2002. Variation in p-phrasing in Bengali. In P. Pica and J. Rooryck (eds.), *Linguistic Variation Yearbook*, vol. 2. Amsterdam: John Benjamins, 259–303.

———— 2006. The syntax-phonology interface. In Paul de Lacy (ed.), *The Cambridge Handbook of Phonology*. Cambridge University Press, 435–456.

Vogel, I. 1985. On constraining prosodic rules. In Harry van der Hulst and Norval Smith (eds.), *Advances in Nonlinear Phonology*. Dordrecht: Foris, 217–233.

———— 1986. External sandhi rules operating between sentences. In Henning Andersen (ed.), *Sandhi Phenomena in the Languages of Europe*. Berlin: Mouton de Gruyter, 55–64.

———— 2009. The status of the clitic group. In Janet Grijzenhout and Barış Kabak (eds.), *Phonological Domains: Universals and Deviations* (Interface Explorations 16). Berlin: Mouton de Gruyter, 15–46.

———— 2015. Life After the Strict Layer Hypothesis: Prosodic Structure Geometry without the SLH. Paper presented at *The 1st International Conference on Prosodic Studies*. Tianjin, China.

Wagner, M. 2005. *Prosody and Recursion*. Ph.D. dissertation, MIT.

Wang, Hongjun. 1999. *Non-linear Phonology of Chinese*. Beijing: Peking University Press.

———— 2008. *Non-linear Phonology of Chinese* (Enlarged and Revised ed.). Beijing: Peking University Press.

Wang, Li. 1980. *Brief History of Chinese Language*. Beijing: China Book Press.

Wang, W. S.-Y. 1967. Phonological Features of Tones, *IJAL*, vol. 33: 93–105.

———— 1969. Competing Changes as a Cause of Residue, *Language*, vol. 45.

———— 1977. *The Lexicon in Phonological Change*. The Hague: Mouton.

———— 1979. Language Change: A Lexical Perspective, *Annual Review of Anthropology*, vol. 8.

———— 1991. *Explorations in Language*. Taipei: Pyramid Press.

226 *Bibliography*

Wee, Lian-Hee. 2008. Opacity from Constituency, *Language and Linguistics*, vol. 9.1: 127–160. Taipei.

Wright, M. 1983. *A Metrical Approach to Tone Sandhi in Chinese Dialects*. Ph.D. dissertation. University of Massachusetts, Amherst.

Wu, Weishan. 2006. *An Investigation of Chinese Prosodic Syntax*. Shanghai: Xuelin Press.

Xu, Baohua, et al. 1981. Tone Sandhi in New Shanghai Dialect. In *Dialect*, vol. 2: 145–155.

———— 1988. *Urban Shanghai Dialect.*Shanghai Educational Publishing House.

Xu, Debao. 1991. *Mandarin Tone Sandhi and Interface Study between Phonology and Syntax*. Ph.D. dissertation, University of Illinois at Urbana-Champaign.

Ye, Jun. 2001. *The Grammatical Function of Chinese Sentence of Prosodic Structure*. Shanghai, China: East China Normal University Press.

Yin, Yuxia. 2012. *A Comparative Study of Rule-based Phonology and Optimality Theory: Argumentation from Chinese Tone Sandhi.* Ph.D. dissertation, Nankai University, Tianjin, China.

Yip, M. 1980. *The Tonal Phonology of Chinese*. Ph.D. dissertation, MIT.

———— 1989. Contour Tones. *Phonology Yearbook*, vol. 6.

———— 2002. *Tone: Cambridge Textbooks in Linguistics*. Cambridge University Press.

You, Shuxiang. 2015. *Prosodic Phonology of the Fuzhou Dialect*. MS. University of Wisconsin-Madison.

Yu, Hui. 2014. *Chinese Loanword Phonology: A Phonetic and Phonological Analysis of English Loanword Adaptation in Chinese*. Tianjin, China: Nankai University Press.

Zec, D. 1988. *Sonority Constraints on Prosodic Structure*. Ph.D. dissertation, Stanford University.

———— 1993. Rule domains and phonological change. In S. Hargus and Ellen Kaisse (eds.), *Studies in Lexical Phonology*. New York: Academic Press, 365–405.

———— 1999. Footed Tones and Tonal Feet: Rhythmic Constituency in a Pitch Accent Language, *Phonology*, vol. 16: 225–264.

Zee, E. 1988. Autosegmental Approach to Shanghai Tone Sandhi, *Studies of the Chinese Language*, vol. 5: 331–350.

Zee, E. & I. Maddieson. 1980. Tones and Tone Sandhi in Shanghai: Phonetic Evidence and Phonological analysis, *Glossa*, vol. 14: 45–88.

Zhang, H.-M. 1989. Syntactic Domain or Prosodic Domain? To appear in *Proceedings of Mid-America Linguistics Conference*, vol. 25. Kansas.

———— 1990. Chongming Phrasal Phonology. To appear in *Proceedings of Western Conference on Linguistics*, vol. 20. Texas.

———— 1991. The Grammaticalization of *bei* in Chinese. To appear in *Proceedings of International Symposium on Chinese Languages & Linguistics*, vol. 2. Taiwan.

———— 1992. *Topics in Chinese Phrasal Tonology*. Ph.D. dissertation, UCSD.

———— 1996. On Directions and Tiers of Tone-Spreading: Case Study of Danyang, *Studies in the Linguistic Sciences*, vol. 26.1/2: 399–408. Urbana.

———— 1997. The C-command Approach to Morphosyntax, *Chinese Language and Linguistics*, vol. 3: 495–524. Academia Sinica, Taipei.

———— 2008a. On Language Change: A Case Study of Morphosyntactic Diffusion. In *Language and Linguistics*, Monograph Series Number W-8, pp. 243–260. Taipei: Academia Sinica.

———— 2008b. Phrasal phonology and Chinese Tone Sandhi. In *Linguistics Theory and Chinese Studies*. Beijing: Commercial Press, 521–535.

Bibliography 227

―――― 2008c. Labial-labial Co-occurrence Constraint in Cantonese, *Revista da Ciencia Linguistica de Macau*, 31/32: 46–56. Macao.

―――― 2014. Some Issues on Prosodic Phonology and Chinese Prosodic Studies, *Contemporary Linguistics*, vol. 16.3: 303–327. Beijing, China.

Zhang, H.-M. & M. Y. Chen. 1995. Morphosyntactic diffusion hypothesis. In *New Asia Academic Bulletin, vol. XI: Studies of the Wu Dialects*. Chinese University of Hong Kong Press, 69–89.

Zhang, H.-M. & X.-J. Jin. 2011. Tonal Representation of Chinese Wenzhou Dialect, *The Bulletin of Chinese Linguistics*, vol. 5.2: 137–160.

Zhang, H.-M. & C.-Q. Song. 2013. Some issues in the study of Chinese poetic prosody. In *Breaking down the Barriers: Interdisciplinary Studies in Chinese Linguistics and Beyond*. Special issue of *Language and Linguistics*. Taipei: Academia Sinica, 1149–1171.

Zhang, H.-M. & Y.-X. Yin. 2012. Pros and Cons of Optimality Theory: Some Thoughts on Phonological Issues, *Studies of the Chinese Language*, vol. 6: 483–499.

Zhang, H.-M., Y.-X. Yin & C.-Q. Song. 2011. Pingyao Tone Sandhi. Paper presented at *The 19th Annual Conference of International Association of Chinese Linguistics*. Tianjin, China.

Zhang, H.-M. & H. Yu. 2009. Study of Chinese Reduplications in Lexical Phonology, *Journal of Linguistics Studies*, vol. 39: 506–521.

Zhang, H.-Y. 1979. Tone Sandhi in Chongming, *Dialect*, vol. 4: 284–302.

―――― 1980. Trisyllabic Tone Sandhi in Chongming, *Dialect*, vol. 1: 15–34.

Zhang, J. 1999. Duration in the tonal phonology of Pingyao Chinese. In Matthew K. Gordon (ed.), *UCLA Working Papers in Linguistics*, vol. 3. 147–206.

Zhang, Y.-S. 1983. Tone sandhi and syntax in Zhuang. In *Study of Minority Languages in China*. China: Chengdu.

Zhang, Z.-S. 1988. *Tone and Tone Sandhi in Chinese*. Ph.D. dissertation, OSU.

Zhengzhang, S.-F. 1964. Tone Sandhi in Wenzhou, *Studies of the Chinese Language*, vol. 2: 106–152.

Zhou, Ren. 2011. *Interactions between Prosody and Grammar in Chinese*. Beijing: The Commercial Press.

Zhu, D.-X. 1956. On Adjectives in Contemporary Chinese, *Yuyan Yanjiu*, vol. 1: 83–112.

―――― 1982. *Lecture Notes on Chinese Grammar*. Beijing: The Commercial Press.

Zwicky, A. 1982. Stranded to and Phonlogical Phrasing in English, *Linguistics*, vol. 20: 3–57.

―――― 1990. *Syntactic Representation and Phonological Shapes*. To appear in Inkelas-Zec (1990).

Zwicky, A. & E. Kaisse, eds. 1987. Syntactic Conditions on Phonological Rules, *Phonology Yearbook*, vol. 4.

Author index

Baker, M. C. 4
Bao, Z.-M. 60
Booij, G. 13, 171

Cao, J. 105
Cao, W. 105
Chan, K.-M. 34, 60, 68, 69
Chen, M. 10, 11, 12, 13, 15, 19, 20, 21, 22, 24, 25, 26, 27, 31, 33, 38, 49, 51, 57, 60, 82, 84, 87, 105, 106, 109, 114, 115, 116, 117, 142, 143, 163, 164, 165, 171, 172, 177, 182, 186
Chen, Z.-M. 49
Cheng, C.-C. 106, 107
Cheng, L. 106, 109, 112, 113, 114
Chomsky, N. 1, 4, 5, 21, 22, 59, 63, 181
Chung, R.-F. 19, 22, 23, 24
Cowper, E. 112

Deng, D. 105
Dong, X. 105
Duanmu, S. 10, 11, 12, 44, 45, 46, 49, 60, 64, 69, 70, 90, 92, 96, 98, 100, 101, 102, 105, 139, 140

Feng, S. 105, 127, 129, 130, 131, 132, 204, 206, 207

Ghini, M. 17
Gravetter, F. 127

Haegeman, L. 4
Halle, M. 1, 10, 96
Hayes, B. 4, 10, 13, 14, 96, 135, 141, 150, 151, 192
Hou, J.-Y. 76
Hsiao, Y.-C. 10, 19, 142, 143, 164, 169
Hsu, H.-C. 19, 143, 164
Huang, C.-T. James 19, 26, 30

Hung, T. 34, 39, 40, 44, 45, 57, 106, 109, 169
Hyman, L. 9, 14, 181, 182, 192

Inkelas, S. 14, 171, 182, 192, 201
Ito, J. 13, 87, 186, 192, 196, 199, 201

Jin, S.-D. 90

Kaisse, E. M. 4, 6, 7 8, 9, 20, 22, 24, 59, 63, 74, 106, 108, 181, 188, 190
Kiparsky, P. 6

Ladd, D. R. 14, 192
Li, A. 105
Li, Z. 34
Liberman, M. 10, 12
Lin, J.-w. 19
Lin, T. 68
Lü, S.-X. 63
Lukoff, F. 1

Ma, Z. 68
McCarthy, J. 14, 15, 183, 201
Maddieson, I. 90
Mair, V. 204
Mei, T.-L. 204
Mester, A. 87, 186, 192, 196, 199
Mishra, S. 199
Mohanan, K. 6

Napoli, D. J. 13
Neijt, A. 13
Nespor, M. 4, 13, 14, 135, 141, 150, 151, 181, 182, 192, 202, 207

Odden, D. 14, 192

Pan, W.-Y. 55
Poser, W. 26

Author index 229

Prieto, P. 17
Prince, A. 10, 12, 14, 15, 183, 201
Pulleyblank, D. 6

Reinhart, T. 21, 36, 40, 59, 70, 71,
   75, 103
Rice, K. 112

Sandalo, F. 17
Sapir, E. 210
Selkirk, E. 4, 8, 9, 12, 13, 14, 15, 16,
   17, 18, 19, 20, 33, 56, 57, 63, 90, 92,
   93, 94, 95, 96, 98, 100, 101, 102, 112,
   113, 135, 137, 139, 140, 150, 151,
   171, 181, 182, 183, 184, 188, 190,
   192, 202
Shen, T. 90
Sherard, M. 90
Shih, C. 12, 34, 106, 109, 110, 111, 112,
   114, 142, 169, 171
Smolensky, P. 14, 183
Steriade, D. 26

Tang, J. 19, 26
Thompson, S. 172
Ting, P.-H. 60
Truckenbrodt, H. 15, 17, 31, 184, 192

Vergnaud, J. R. 10, 96
Vogel, I. 4, 13, 14, 135, 141, 150, 151,
   181, 182, 192, 196, 199, 200, 202, 207

Wallnau, L. 127
Wang, H. 105
Wang, L. 171
Wang, W. S.-Y. 177
Wee, L-H. 106
Wright, M. 10, 34, 90
Wu, W. 105

Xu, B. 163
Xu, D. 106

Ye, J. 105
Yip, M. 60, 90

Zec, D. 13, 14, 171, 182, 202
Zee, E. 90
Zhang, H.-M. 19, 27, 34, 49, 50, 53, 60,
   68, 105, 112, 142, 163, 177, 193, 194
Zhang, H.-Y. 180n1
Zhang, J. 84, 86
Zhang, Z.-S. 106, 171
Zhou, R. 105
Zhu, D.-X. 209

Language index

Chichewa 184
Chimwiini 13, 182
Chinese dialects: Chengdu dialect
45–6; Chongming dialect 3, 49, 50,
151–63, 188, 189, 191, 193, 194, 203;
Danyang dialect 3, 18, 60–71, 72, 74,
75, 76, 103, 189, 202, 212; Fuzhou
dialect 3, 10, 19, 34–43, 45, 57, 189,
202, 212; Hakka dialect 22; Huinan
dialect 3, 49, 51; Jin dialect
76; Mandarin 3, 8, 10, 11, 12, 60,
105–33, 168–71, 187, 202, 203–11,
214; Min dialect 19, 34, 46; Pingyao
dialect 3, 18, 19, 64, 76–90, 103,
186, 187, 189, 194–8, 202, 203, 212;
Ruicheng dialect 3, 18, 72–6, 103, 189,
202, 212; Shanghai dialect 3, 13, 18, 45,
46–9, 90–103, 134–41, 151, 152, 163,
166–8, 182, 189, 190, 191, 202, 212;
Taiwanese dialect 10; Wenzhou dialect
3, 13, 49, 55; Wu dialect 46,
49, 56, 60, 152; Xiamen dialect 3, 13,
18, 19–34, 57, 141–51, 163–6, 173,
180, 182, 185, 186, 188, 189, 190, 191,
202, 212; Xinzhuang dialect 3, 49, 53

English 3, 7, 19, 183
Ewe 8, 13

French 8, 13, 182, 210

Hausa 183

Japanese 7, 196, 198, 200

Kimatuumbi 8

Papago 13

Subject index

Alignment theory 15, 31, 183, 185
Align-Wrap theory 17, 18
arboreal mapping 182, 183
Argument/Adjunct Dichotomy
    Hypothesis 36
Auxiliary Reduction 7

base melody 61
base tone 46, 90, 91, 92, 95, 137, 148, 153,
    157, 158
The Branch Condition 108
branchingness 112, 182, 191, 202

Category-Based Approach 14
c-command 3, 40, 59, 60, 70, 72, 74, 75,
    76, 83, 103, 140, 185, 189
citation tone 20, 33, 34, 35, 60, 62, 69,
    76, 77, 79, 90, 91, 105, 106, 119, 121,
    126, 144, 145, 146, 152, 153, 156, 168,
    188, 191
clash deletion 10
clitic group 13, 114, 116, 121, 124, 135,
    141, 150, 152, 153, 154, 156, 158, 161,
    162, 164, 170, 171, 174, 179, 182, 188,
    193, 203, 207, 208, 210
clitic groupTS 153
cliticization 7, 124
clitics 116
column lowering rule 65

default tone 90, 95
degenerate foot 96
directionality 82, 87, 186, 188, 189
direct mapping 46, 92, 126, 157, 161,
    162, 188
Direct Reference Approach 9, 59, 63, 90,
    103, 181
Direct Reference Theory 18
discourse/focus-based Hierarchy 203

domain 1, 3, 8, 9, 10, 12, 13, 14, 16, 17,
    18, 19, 21, 22, 31, 32, 33, 34, 35, 36,
    38, 39, 40, 43, 46, 59, 60, 61, 63, 64,
    65, 68, 69, 70, 71, 72, 74, 75, 76, 82,
    86, 87, 89, 90, 91, 92, 93, 94, 95, 96,
    98, 100, 101, 103, 105, 106, 107, 108,
    109, 112, 113, 116, 117, 121, 124, 125,
    126, 127, 132, 133, 135, 136, 137, 139,
    140, 141, 142, 143, 144, 145, 146, 151,
    153, 162, 164, 166, 167, 168, 171, 172,
    181, 182, 185, 186, 187, 188, 189, 190,
    191, 192, 193, 194, 195, 196, 199, 201,
    202, 203, 206, 207, 208, 209, 211, 212,
    213, 214
domain c-command 8, 22, 181
D-structure 4, 5, 7
dual trochee 11
duple meter 109

edge c-command Principle 82, 191, 194
edge Principle 93
Edge-based theory 15, 18, 33, 34
empty category 30, 32, 33, 186
end-based approach 14
end-based hypothesis 182
end-based mapping 182
even tone 105, 210
external sandhi rule 9, 181

fast speech rule 9
flapping 7
foot 3, 11, 12, 36, 39, 43, 50, 84, 96, 109,
    110, 111, 112, 114, 127, 133, 145, 171,
    173, 183, 199, 200, 201, 203, 205, 206,
    207, 210, 211
foot formation rule 39, 109, 114, 169
functional category 24, 27, 31, 120
functional relation 1, 3, 19, 20, 22, 24, 30,
    34, 36, 38, 39, 43, 49, 56, 57, 76, 79, 80,

232   *Subject index*

82, 83, 100, 101, 102, 103, 135, 146, 150, 188, 190, 194, 202, 212
function word 3, 93, 95, 100, 104, 113, 135, 136, 137, 139, 140, 141, 142, 144, 145, 146, 147, 148, 150, 151, 164, 174, 188, 212

Government and Binding 4
The grid-only approach 12

head dominance condition 43, 44
high vowel devoicing 7

immediate constituent 35, 93, 109, 114
indirect reference approach 9, 63, 89, 133, 182
indirect reference theory 18
The Information-Stress Principle 11
inner category 199, 200
intonational phrase 12, 112, 113, 116, 121, 124, 125, 126, 182, 185, 187, 201, 203, 208, 209
IP-bound 114, 116, 117

K-condition 22, 24

left-branching structure 36, 39, 40, 62, 72, 81, 157, 159, 161, 162
lexical category condition 31
Lexical Diffusion Hypothesis 177
Lexical Integrity Principle 39, 40, 111
Lexical Phonology 6, 7
lexical rule 6, 7
lexical word 3, 15, 30, 34, 93, 95, 112, 135, 137, 150, 182, 186, 189, 190, 212
liaison 13, 125, 209
The Locality Condition 26
logical form 4, 7

major prosodic category 196, 199
Match Theory 15–17, 18, 32, 33 103, 121, 183, 184, 185, 186
m-command 1, 18, 22, 23, 27, 28, 185, 186,
metrical grid 12, 13, 210, 211
metrical hierarchy 201
metricalization 124, 171, 172, 173, 174, 175, 176, 177, 178, 179, 180
Metrical Phonology 133, 210, 211
Minimalist Program 5
minimal prosodic domain 82
minor prosodic category 196, 199
MiP/MaP theory 197–9

mora 13, 183, 192, 200
morphosyntactic structure 13, 15, 109, 115, 117, 118, 154, 155, 156, 158, 172, 180

neutralization 162, 163, 172
neutral tone 121, 144, 146, 148, 153, 160, 189
neutral TS 121, 124
non-empty categories 30, 34, 186
Non-head Stress Hypothesis 45, 46, 48, 49
Non-head stress rule 11, 44

oblique tone 152, 163
Optimality Theory 2, 3, 14, 92
outer category 199, 200

P1 rule 7, 8, 9, 181
P2 rule 7, 9, 10, 181
parameter 9, 10, 13, 33, 45, 112, 124, 125, 182, 188, 189, 190, 191, 207, 213
phonetic form 4
phonological phrase 8, 13, 15, 17, 31, 32, 33, 34, 87, 88, 89, 90, 112, 113, 114, 119, 120, 121, 124, 126, 170, 171, 182, 183, 184, 185, 186, 187, 188, 196, 201, 202, 203, 207, 208, 209
phonological word 13, 87, 193, 201
phonosyntactic rule 8, 9
Phrasal Phonology 4, 7, 19, 212
phrasal TS 40, 49, 188
ping 76, 152, 210
poetic prosody 203, 210, 211
Post-lexical Phonology 4, 7
post-lexical rule 1
post-P-structure rule 9
pre-P-structure rule 9
principles of directional cyclicity 82
prosodically syntax-sensitive approach 190
prosodic domain formation principle 82
prosodic hierarchy 2, 3, 9, 12, 13, 14, 16, 17, 87, 89, 112, 121, 124, 125, 133, 183, 186, 187, 190, 191, 192, 196, 199, 200, 201, 202, 203, 206, 207, 208, 209, 210, 211, 212, 213, 214
Prosodic Lexical Phonology 201
Prosodic Morphology 201, 207
Prosodic Phonology 2, 3, 4, 12, 13, 14, 121, 126, 133, 181, 182, 187, 188, 192, 201, 203, 206, 210, 211, 212
prosodic structure 1, 2, 6, 9, 12, 13, 14, 15, 16, 17, 32, 33, 89, 90, 93, 109, 119, 120, 121, 171, 182, 183, 185, 186, 187, 188, 190, 192, 197, 200, 212, 213, 214

Subject index 233

prosodic-syntax model 213
prosodic unit 2, 11, 12, 14, 17, 89, 90, 93, 109, 112, 114, 121, 124, 127, 133, 135, 169, 170, 171, 182, 183, 184, 186, 187, 192, 196, 197, 198, 199, 200, 201, 203, 205, 206, 207, 208, 210, 211, 212
prosodic word 3, 15, 17, 87, 88, 89, 90, 93, 94, 95, 96, 112, 114, 121, 124, 126, 135, 137, 171, 182, 183, 185, 186, 187, 188, 196, 197, 199, 200, 203, 206, 207, 208, *209*, 211
P-structure 8

qu 76, 105, 152, 210

recursivity 6, 17, 32, 119, 133, 192, 193, 194, 195, 197, 198, 199, 200, 203, 214
regulated style verse 210
relation-based mapping 182
Rhythm-based Hierarchy 201, 203
rhythmic effect 3, 135, 143, 163, 164, 165, 166, 167, 168, 169, 170, 171, 172, 173, 212
right-branching structure 36, 126, 133
ru 152

sandhi tone 34, 35, 41, 42, 43, 46, 77, 79, 95, 137, 142, 144, 145, 153, 157
shang 76, 128, 131, 152
śloka 203, 204
S-structure 4, 5, 7
stipulation of prosodic recursivity 203
stress 3, 9, 10, 11, 12, 19, 34, 44, 45, 46, 49, 64, 65, 68, 69, 70, 96, 100, 129, 133, 139, 205, 206, 210
Stress Clash Rule 65, 139
Stress Equalization Convention 10, 64, 96
Stress Erasure Convention 10
Stress Reduction Rule 65
Strict Layer Hypothesis 2, 3, 14, 16, 90, 133, 192, 213

super-foot 109, 110, 112
syllable 10, 11, 12, 20, 22, 34, 35, 36, 38, 39, 40, 41, 42, 43, 46, 61, 65, 69, 70, 77, 81, 82, 84, 85, 86, 88, 89, 90, 92, 96, 106, 107, 109, 111, 112, 114, 118, 121, 125, 127, 129, 132, 133, 140, 141, 143, 144, 148, 153, 154, 155, 156, 158, 159, 160, 161, 162, 163, 164, 165, 168, 170, 171, 172, 183, 186, 189, 200, 201, 203, 204, 205, 206, 207, 209, 210
syllable-tone-sensitive 104n15
syntactic unit 15, 181, 183, 185, 187, 188, 189, 190, 202, 208
Syntax-based Prosodic Hierarchy 2
Syntax-insensitive Approach 182

T-model 4
Tonal Domain Formation 65
tonal phrasing 13
tone bearing unit 104n12
tone sandhi 1, 108
Tone-Stress Principle 11

utterance 121, 125, 182, 188, 203, 208, 209

vowel harmony 10
vowel shortening 8, 13, 126
VP-shell 30

The Weight-to-Stress Principle 11
word final rise 85
word length preferences 105
word-tone-sensitive 100
Wrap-Align Theory 32, 33, 34, 184, 186
Wrapping Theory 15, 31

X-bar 14, 124, 182, 192, 207, 212

ze 210